100 YEARS
1882
1982

CAL
BLVE
AND
GOLD

Rich Campbell drops back to pass against San Jose State in 1979. Cal's most prolific passer, Campbell threw for 305 yards in the 13-10 victory.

The Wonder Team of 1920 is arguably Cal's greatest ever. The starters are: (left to right) Brick Muller, Bob Berkey, Duke Morrison, Charley Erb, Pesky Sprott, Crip Toomey, Dan McMillan, Stan Barnes, Lee Cranmer, Fat Latham and Cort Majors.

"Dan" McMillan "Stan" Barnes
"Lee" Cranmer
"Fat" Latham
"Capt." Cort Majors

Before Start of Stanford Game Nov 19 1920

100 YEARS OF BLVE & GOLD

A PICTORIAL HISTORY OF CALIFORNIA FOOTBALL

BY NICK PETERS

JCP CORP. OF VIRGINIA

The inspirational Joe Roth is the only Cal quarterback to throw for more than 375 yards in two games with 380 against Washington in 1975 and 379 against Georgia in 1976.

Library of Congress Catalog Number 82-80432
ISBN 0-938694-10-3

JCP Corp. of Virginia
P.O. Box 814
Virginia Beach, Virginia 23451

Book design by W. Bradley Miller

*Jack Swaner leads the way for Jackie Jensen. Swaner
and Jensen formed one of the greatest rushing
combinations in Cal history. Their most productive
season was 1948, when Jensen rushed for more than
100 yards five times and Swaner four.*

CONTENTS

Vic Bottari takes off on a 30-yard gallop in the first quarter of the 1938 Rose Bowl with Alabama's Perron Shoemaker and an official in hot pursuit.

All-American Chuck Muncie (42) searches for a hole during his 143-yard eruption against Southern Cal in 1975. Muncie powered the Bears to a 28-14 upset.

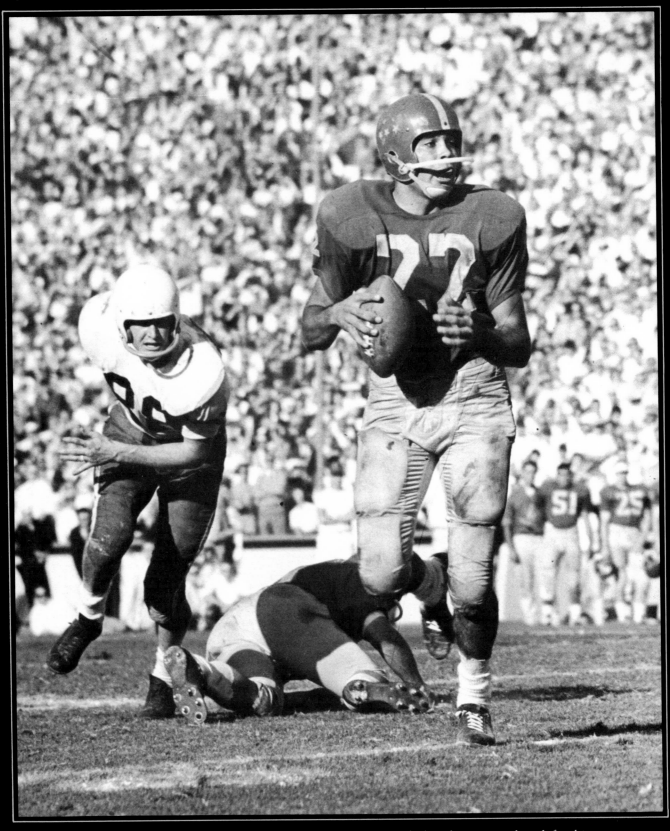

Joe Kapp (22) is best remembered for his courage and determination. Not a picture quarterback by any means, Kapp endured losing seasons in 1956-57, but he blossomed as a senior to lead the Golden Bears to the Rose Bowl. He was Cal's last great running quarterback, doing as much damage with his legs as with his arm, including a 92-yard touchdown run against Oregon in 1958. Nobody has made a longer run from scrimmage for Cal since.

INTRODUCTION

It's true enough that I haven't been around for all of the hundred years of California football; it just seems that way to me sometimes. As a youngster growing up in the East Bay and later as an undergraduate at Berkeley, I've been fairly awash in the UC football tradition for as long as I can recall. It is a tradition, I might add, that, despite some woeful seasons of late, still is extraordinarily rich.

Long before I'd ever seen a game at Memorial Stadium, I was made keenly aware that there were few human endeavors more important that Cal football. My Uncle Bob, a prototypical Old Blue, felt as strongly about his alma mater as Churchill felt about the British Empire — and he was every bit as protective. Bob had me waving blue and gold pennants before I had mastered the pacifier. Jelly Belly Johnny Meek, Sam Chapman and Vic Bottari were as real to me as any of my own relatives in those formative years.

Still, it was not until 1941 that I actually saw a game in the stadium. I sat — or rather squirmed — with the other kids in the section set aside at the south end for grammer school traffic boys. Seeing the games for free was our reward for good works during the school week, and it was the only conceivable reason I ever wanted to be a traffic boy in the first place. My biggest thrill that year was to have been at the Big Game in Palo Alto against Clark Shaughnessy's last team at Stanford, which I was to have attended with my father and Uncle Bob. It turned out to be a banner day for the Bears — a 16-0 upset win — but a miserable one for me. On the Friday before the game, I was sent to bed with the mumps. I was obliged to listen to the game on the radio, with tears streaming down my swollen cheeks, as Al Derian, my hero of the time, did Stanford in with a 46-yard touchdown run on Cal's first offensive play. I still was in bed two weeks later when the Japanese bombed Pearl Harbor. I heard that one on the radio, too.

When I was 15, I broke my collarbone playing junior varsity football at Berkeley High School and was sent to see a Berkeley physician named Muller. Despite my extensive background in things UC, I failed at the time to make any connection between this Muller and Cal football. Then, as I was led into the good doctor's office, it hit me. This wasn't just any Dr. Muller. The great shoulders and flat face were instantly recognizable. This was Brick Muller,

star of the Wonder Teams, the man considered at that time to have been the university's greatest player ever. Brick examined my injury and expressed concern that a piece of broken bone was dangerously close to a nerve. He pressed his giant thumbs against that bone and pushed it up and away from the danger point. I fainted dead away in his arms — not from the excruciating pain, I told my friends later, but from the thrill of it all.

For awhile, it seemed as if Cal football history had begun with Muller's Wonder Teams of the twenties and ended with the Thunder Teams of Bottari et al in the late thirties. Oh, what a dismal array the university fielded through the war years and immediately afterward. And then came Pappy Waldorf. He arrived on campus just a year or so before I did, and he gave us teams of matchless brilliance. Those were great names — Rod Franz, Johnny Graves, Jack Swaner, Jim Monachino, Pete Schabarum, Johnny Olszewski and the single player who, in my opinion, stood highest above them all — Jackie Jensen, the Golden Boy. Jensen was a marvel of versatility and one of the most exciting broken field runners in football history. God rest his soul.

There have been some lean times since Pappy, but, as this fine book will show, there also have been some brilliant individual performers. And maybe now that Joe Kapp is back, we'll have some winners once again. I'm an Old Blue myself now, and I'd like that. And so, heaven only knows, would my Uncle Bob.

Ron Fimrite
Sports Illustrated
California '52

CHAPTER
1

100 YEARS
1882
1982

CAL
BLVE
AND
GOLD

Andy Smith, Cal's greatest coach ever, stands on the sideline observing a Wonder Team workout. Note the megaphone at his side in the event instructions had to be barked. Smith guided the Bears to a 74-16-7 record in 1916-25.

Chapter One
SUCCESS ON THE SIDELINES

IN THE BEGINNING
NO COMPETITION

When Princeton and Rutgers clashed in the first intercollegiate football game in New Brunswick, New Jersey, on November 6, 1869, the grid sport wasn't feasible at the University of California. Only 35 students were enrolled at the time at Cal, which had been chartered in 1868 after opening its doors as Contra Costa Academy in 1853 in Oakland.

By 1877, however, there was enough interest in the sport on campus to warrant a clash between the freshmen and the sophomores for the class championship. It was the first organized football game on the West Coast, and it took place on November 3. The historic contest was underway at 11 a.m. and concluded at 1:30 p.m., with the sophomores kicking two goals to none for the frosh.

One of the freshmen, not content with defeat, grabbed the ball and dashed around campus with the sophomores in pursuit. He stumbled and finally was downed 90 minutes later, bringing an end to the proceedings. Five years later, California was ready to field an all-university team, but there were no other Bay Area colleges with which to engage in battle.

Finally, a game was arranged with the Phoenix and Wanderers Clubs of San Francisco, and it was scheduled to be played on December 2, 1882, at the city's Recreation Grounds. Cal's first game ever attracted 150 fans. It was a rugby-type affair with haphazard scoring rules. The Berkeleyans scored two tries (touchdowns), but the opposition was declared the winner, 7-4, with one goal kick (field goal).

On February 24, 1883, Cal posted its first gridiron victory. It toppled the Phoenix Club, 7-6, before 250 fans. The first game on campus, with 450 in attendance, wasn't played until 1885. One year later, the Bears began playing American football, and Oscar Howard was named their first official coach. That squad went 6-2-1, including two forfeits over Hastings Law School, which declined because of "academic pressure."

The Bears were successful against local club teams, but heavy rains washed out the entire 1889 schedule. In the spring of 1892, Stanford provided the first intercollegiate competition. Cal really got serious about its football in 1893,

An unidentified player appears set to punt from his own end zone during Cal's 0-0 tie with Reliance Athletic Club in 1894. Notice the carriages parked just beyond the end zone.

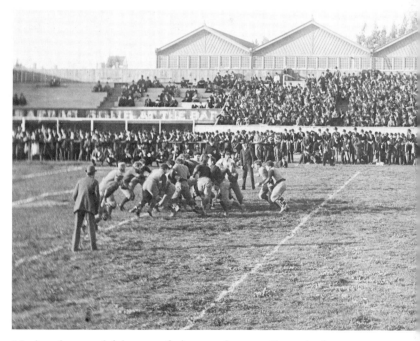

Under the watchful eyes of three rather nattily attired officials, Cal and the Reliance Athletic Club battle it out at midfield during their 0-0 tie in 1894. A sizable crowd turned out to view the action at the field at Haight Street in San Francisco.

when all-time All-American Pudge Heffelfinger of Yale came west to coach the team.

In 1896, with Frank Butterworth coaching, Cal made its first trip out of the Bay Area. A 6-2-2 season was capped with a Christmas-New Year's holiday trip to Los Angeles. The Bears won four games in one week, downing the L.A. Athletic Club, Redlands High, San Diego High and Whittier High. By 1898, Cal went big time, hiring Garrett Cochran to coach the team at a salary of $1,500.

The 1898-99 Bears were the school's first powerhouse. They were 15-1-3 those two years, once gaining 882 yards in a 22-0 Big Game romp, outscoring the opposition 363-7 and losing only to the famous Carlisle Indians of Pop Warner, 2-0, in the first intersectional played by Cal.

Under coaches Frank Simpson and James Whipple, the Bears stitched together a string of 25 games without defeat in 1901-03, winning 23 and tying two others. Following the 1905 season, however, the school abandoned the rough American game and switched to rugby. Coach Jimmy Schaeffer fielded crack rugby squads, frequently traveling to Canada for games.

Cal returned in 1915 to the American brand of football which was growing ever more popular in the East, and Schaeffer, though ignorant of that style of play, agreed to stay on and coach. He accepted the job secure in the knowledge the Bears would have a new football boss in 1916, and he set out to select that man in the spring of 1915. His decision ultimately changed the face of West Coast football, especially at California.

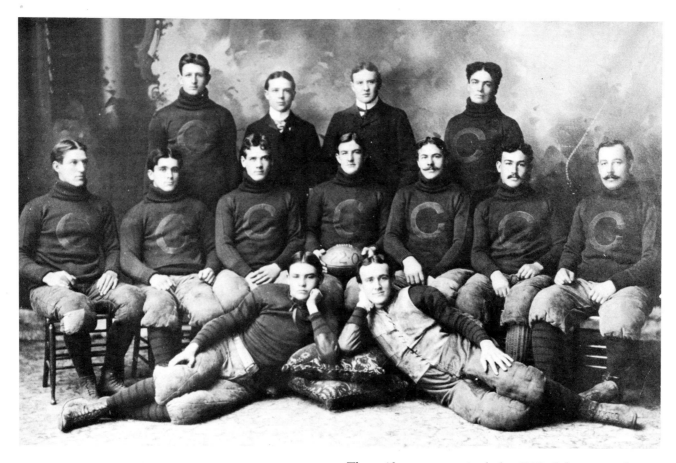

These 13 men comprised the 1898 Cal varsity, the first great team fielded by the school. The Bears, who went 8-0-2 and outscored opponents 221-5, posed following a 22-0 Big Game triumph. The group included: (top row, left to right) Pete "Kangaroo" Kaarsberg, assistant coach Addison Kelly, head coach Garrett Cochran and Volney Craig; (middle row) James Whipple, Bart Thane, Lol Pringle, Percy Hall, Fred Greisberg, Harry Cornish and Fred Athearn; and (front row) Lloyd "Wrec" Womble and Warren "Locomotive" Smith. Womble and Smith are regarded as two of the greatest players in the first 50 years of Cal football.

Early 1900s football action on the Berkeley campus finds Cal taking on an unidentified opponent. Note that the players did not have much shoulder padding, but they were well-protected by leather facial masks. Also note the lack of grass on the field.

The 1895 Bears display a typical formation. Observing the size and shape of the ball, there is little doubt why the forward pass was not an important part of the game during that period.

Cal president Benjamin Ide Wheeler addresses the students in 1905, informing them that the game of football would be abolished at the conclusion of that season.

Rugby replaced American football as Cal's prime gridiron sport from 1906 to 1914. Players pursue the bouncing ball during one of the Big Games of that era.

ANDY SMITH
OF WONDROUS DREAMS
AND WONDER TEAMS

Schaeffer hit the road prior to the 1915 season with a twofold mission: to find a competent coach for Cal, and to learn about the American game for his own sake that fall. His travels first took him to Seattle, where the great Gil Dobie provided a fountain of information. Then he headed for the Midwest, where he ran into a reluctant Bob Zuppke at Illinois.

But it was a fortuitous stopover, nonetheless, for a Champaign bartender tipped Schaeffer on Andrew Latham Smith, who was coaching Purdue at nearby Lafayette, Indiana. Smith, a former Philadelphia prep, was a fullback at Penn State in 1901-02. He transferred to Pennsylvania and was an All-American as a senior in 1904 on a 12-0 squad.

Andy Smith became a head coach in 1909, guiding Penn's fortunes the next four years before switching to Purdue. He was 9-3-2 as the Boilermakers boss in 1913-14 and met with Schaeffer prior to the 1915 campaign. Jimmy did a good selling job on Cal's potential, and Smith agreed to take the Berkeley offer in 1916. Cal graduate manager John Stroud worked out the details with Smith following the 1915 season (Cal was 8-5 and Purdue was 3-3-1 that year), and Andy joined the Bears for spring practice in 1916.

Smith, a rawboned taskmaster, fielded a 6-4-1 squad in 1916 and was a so-so 5-5-1 in 1917, a season which brought two significant victories. The Bears posted their first major Pacific Coast Conference (it was formed December 2, 1915) win by downing the Oregon Aggies, 14-3, and one week later snapped Washington's unbeaten string, 27-0.

The coach's key move occurred between seasons, however, when Clarence "Nibs" Price (Cal '14) was coaxed to leave his position as head coach of San Diego High and join the Bears as an assistant in 1918. It was a recruiting coup, because San Diego stars Brick Muller, Cort Majors, Pesky Sprott and Stan Barnes followed their coach north.

Muller didn't arrive until 1920, but the other three played in 1918 and laid the foundation for the famed Wonder Teams. But that majestic era of Cal football may never have developed were it not for Smith's consenting to relax his rugged training regimen. During the 1919 season, for instance, Smith held what he called an Elimination Day.

The object was to scrimmage his players until they dropped — the best way to separate the men from the boys. But the Bears, who were coming off a 61-0 whipping of Occidental, couldn't understand the logic of such a tortuous session. After the season, which included the first radio broadcast of a Cal game, some of the star freshmen from the 1919 squad considered transferring away from those tyrannical tactics.

Charley Erb, the leader of the freshmen, was in Bakersfield during the summer of 1920, when Smith and Price paid him a visit. Erb made it clear that Elimination Day was distasteful, not to mention unbearably exhausting, to the Bears. Smith was understanding and Erb agreed to talk with the players about returning to Cal. On the trip home, Price convinced Smith to abandon Elimination Day. The rest is history.

With team captain Majors, Erb and the three other San Diegans playing prominent roles, Cal fielded in 1920 what is regarded as the finest Golden Bear aggregation of all time. It truly was a Wonder Team, scoring 510 points, surrendering but 14 and posting seven shutouts in a 9-0 swath. After Ohio State was crushed, 28-0, in the forerunner of the Rose Bowl, Cal was crowned No. 1 in the nation.

Smith's teams did not lose another game until the third week of the 1925 season, when the powerful Olympic Club posted a 15-0 victory. That ended a streak of 50 games without defeat, a 46-0-4 record. In those 50 games, Cal averaged 32.9 points per game and relinquished 2.8 while registering 33 shutouts. Among the blankings was an incredible 127-0 whipping of St. Mary's. The Bears outgained the Gaels by a staggering 670-16, and, following the defeat, St. Mary's dropped football the remainder of the 1920 season.

The streak began after a 7-0 loss to Washington in the final game of the 1919 schedule.

The ties were against Washington & Jefferson (0-0) in the 1922 Rose Bowl, Nevada (0-0) in 1923, and Washington (7-7) and Stanford (20-20) in 1924. The Indians 20 points were the most scored on the Wonder Teams.

The 1920 squad, voted the greatest of all-time in the twenties, was comprised of ends Muller and Bob Berkey, tackles Dan McMillan and Barnes, guards Lee Cranmer and Majors, center Fat Latham, quarterback Erb, halfbacks Sprott and Crip Toomey and fullback Duke Morrison.

It was a tribute to Smith's coaching that the tradition of excellence continued when those men were replaced by a new wave of standouts. By 1923, players like Jimmy Dixon, Snook Mell, Bill Blewett and Jack Witter were in starring roles. The 1923 squad, in fact, was the finest Cal ever has produced defensively. They posted nine shutouts in a 9-0-1 season, outscoring opponents 182-7.

Cranmer, recalling the Wonder Teams in an

The Wonder Team of 1920, which was an unblemished 9-0, is shown on the defense (dark jerseys) in this action shot. Cort Majors (second from right) is identifiable. The Bears gave up only 14 points that season, scoring 510!

interview with Portland sports columnist L.H. Gregory, claimed that the 1920 squad was by far the best. "As good as the other teams were," Cranmer said, "none of them quite came up to the 1920 eleven. What made the 1920 team so great was the fire and inspiration of youth, plus fine material and the most wonderful collective team spirit I believe ever existed on a football eleven.

"The difference between that team and the one of 1921 was that in 1920 we knew we were good, that we had the stuff, but we were out to demonstrate it. In 1921, we knew we were good, so good that we sometimes felt we didn't have to prove it. The 1921 team felt its oats at times and was hard to handle. In 1920, we listened to everything Andy told us. In 1921, he had his troubles."

According to Cranmer, Smith was ahead of his time as a coach. "Andy knew football so thoroughly and his rival coaches so completely that, in his blackboard talks and lectures before any specific game, he would tell us exactly what to expect," Cranmer explained. "He never missed. Andy sized up everything that was ever sprung on us by another team and warned us about it in advance. He seemed to have analyzed the character of the other coach and to know exactly what kind of football he would use."

The sycophantic Brick Morse, a former Cal

Football teams like those produced by Andy Smith deserved a suitable arena. Strawberry Canyon was selected as the site of Memorial Stadium, still one of the most beautiful settings for college football in America.

The Andrew Latham Smith Bench was dedicated in 1927 in memory of the great coach who brought Cal football to national prominence.

In a typical display of power football, the Bears steamroll for a touchdown in 1921 action.

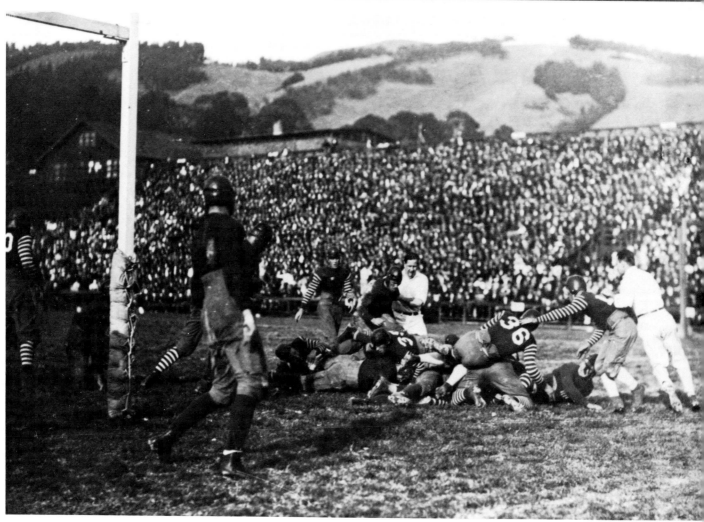

star athlete, coined the Wonder team moniker in a San Francisco newspaper, and it seemed appropriate. Morse also called Smith "Big Swede," but in truth Andy was overworked and on the frail side following the 1925 season. He went back to Philadelphia to see Penn play, contracted pneumonia and died suddenly on January 8, 1926.

He had willed his personal estate to Cal and to his fraternity, Sigma Alpha Epsilon, and requested that his ashes be scattered over Memorial Stadium. At memorial services on January 15, members of the Wonder Teams led the student body to the stadium while the funeral peal sounded from the campanile. An Army plane flew overhead and dropped Smith's ashes on the turf.

On December 31, 1927, the Andy Smith Bench was dedicated prior to Cal's 27-13 triumph over Pennsylvania. Penn coach Lou Young had played under Smith, so it was fitting that the ceremonies would take place at a game between the beloved coach's favorite schools. Two of Smith's best sayings are engraved on the plaque attached to the bench:

"We do not want men who will lie down bravely to die, but men who will fight valiantly to live ... winning is not everything, and it is far better to play the game squarely and lose than to win at the sacrifice of an ideal." Those words are repeated annually at the Axe Rally preceding the Big Game, to insure that Andy

Smith's legacy forever will be a part of the California spirit.

And why not? After all, Memorial Stadium was The House That Smith Built. He and the Wonder Teams never will be forgotten.

STUB ALLISON
A LULL BEFORE THE THUNDER

Smith had let it be known that if he were to leave California, Price should be his successor. So it was a mere formality when Nibs took over for the 1926 season. Price had difficulty filling those big shoes, but he survived a 3-6 record in 1926 because of his tremendous popularity. There was an improvement to 7-3 in 1927, and he seemed headed for better times. But they were short-lived.

The 1928 varsity tied mighty USC and finished 6-2-2, earning the Rose Bowl bid while the unbeaten Trojans were snubbed for political reasons. In 1929, Cal went 7-1-1, was the PCC co-champion and had the distinction of being the first band of Bears to play in the East. The Bears defeated Penn, 12-7, before 70,000 at Philadelphia.

That was the year of the Great Depression, and it was Price's stock that took a sharp drop one year later. The 1930 Bears were 3-3 when a trip to Los Angeles found vengeful USC humiliating them, 74-0, accumulating 734 yards to Cal's 123. There was one positive aspect of

All-American guard Ted Beckett closes in on a St. Mary's ball carrier during Cal's 7-6 win in 1930.

Cal's Sam Chapman (second from left) is smothered by USC's Gil Kuhn (59) and Homer Beatty, but only after Chapman's key interception in the Bears 21-7 triumph in 1935.

The national-champion 1937 Cal Thunder Team lines up for photographers prior to the season opener with St. Mary's. The Bears, who went 10-0-1, presented a lineup with a backfield (back row, left to right) of quarterback Johnny Meek, fullback Ken Cotton, left half Vic Bottari and right half Sam Chapman. The line (front row, left to right) featured end Perry Schwartz, tackle Milt Pollack, guard Vard Stockton, center Bob Herwig, guard Ray Hanford, tackle Dave de Varona and end Henry Sparks.

that trip, however. The Southern Seas Support Group was formed by Stan Barnes among others. The large alumni group was greatly to benefit future Cal coaches.

The Bears rallied from their worst defeat ever, but they were flat in an 8-0 victory over Nevada. The following week, Price's doom was sealed. Stanford crushed Cal, 41-0, gaining 470 yards to 166. Price resigned, and graduate manager Bill Monahan went east in search of a replacement. Nibs, meanwhile, concentrated on basketball coaching duties, winning several PCC titles in his 30-year career.

The new football coach was Navy Bill Ingram, who took over a demoralized program and, like Price, was on a roller-coaster ride for a few years. Ingram's first move was significant. He hired Leonard "Stub" Allison and Frank Wickhorst as assistants. The pair contributed to Cal football for more than one dozen years, each becoming a head coach of the Bears.

Unlike his predecessor, Ingram enjoyed immediate success, guiding the 1931 squad to an 8-2 record, including a 19-6 decision over Georgia Tech at Atlanta on the day after Christmas. The Bears were 13-6-4 the next two years before Ingram's ship ran aground. The

1934 team was 4-3 following a 20-0 loss to Santa Clara — Cal's first loss ever to the Broncos — and Allison had to handle the team the following week against USC when Ingram went east to be with his ailing mother.

Ingram's mother died, and to make matters worse, Allison coached the Bears to a stunning, 7-2 victory over the Trojans, which raised eyebrows among the growing legion of Ingram's critics. Navy Bill returned for a 45-13 rout of Idaho, but when Stanford edged the Bears, 9-7, he resigned to enter private business. Electing to sever connections with the University, Ingram declined to accompany the team on its holiday trip to Hawaii.

There were rumors that Temple's Pop Warner was interested in the Cal job, but it took Cal officials only 24 hours to promote Allison. His baptism was a pair of losses in the Islands. Ingram was credited with a 27-14-4 record in four years, but subtracting the USC win and the two Hawaii losses, he actually was 26-12-4. That's not bad, but it wasn't good enough for the demanding Cal standards of the time.

Allison, a former three-sport star at Minnesota's Carleton College and a flyer in World War I, joined Ingram following coaching

stints at Washington, South Dakota and Wisconsin. At Cal, he came closest to reaching the perfection attained by Smith when his 1935-38 Thunder Teams rolled to a 35-7-1 record, including 24 shutouts.

Stub's 1935 squad was a big hit, winning its first nine before succumbing to Stanford, 13-0. That team outscored its foes 163-22, drawing strength from the unbeaten frosh of 1934 which formed the nucleus of Thunder Team success. The Bears slipped to 6-5 in 1936, but they bounced back in 1937 to be crowned national champions with a 10-0-1 record.

That was the best of Thunder Team years. Seniors Johnny Meek, Sam Chapman and Dave Anderson joined junior Vic Bottari to form what many consider the finest Cal backfield of all time. It surely was the best of its era. Sparkling on offense and defense, it swept past all opponents except Washington (a 0-0 tie) and blanked Alabama, 13-0, at the Rose Bowl.

With All-American Bottari leading the charge, Cal was 10-1 in 1938, losing only to PCC co-champion USC, 13-7. But the war years sapped the Bears of much of their strength, and Allison fell on hard times in 1939-44, never posting a winning season and going 23-35-1 those six scarred years. The fizzle drew criticism, but Old Sarge already had proven himself as an outstanding coach. Nonetheless, he was fired following the 1944 season, ending another era of Cal football.

Cal fullback Dave Anderson, with ball, powers through the Stanford line during the 1937 Big Game, a 13-0 victory that capped an unbeaten regular season for the Bears. All-American end Perry Schwartz (99) watches the proceedings.

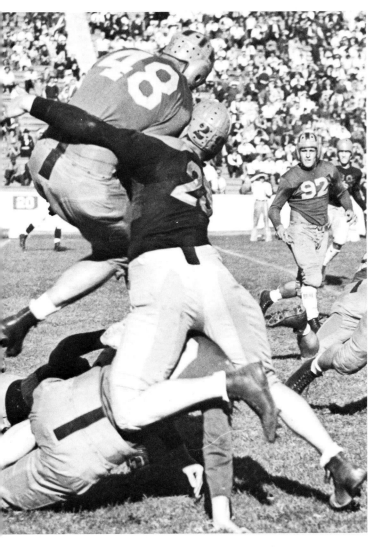

Sam Chapman (48) crashes into Pacific's Clem Swagerty during the opening kickoff in Cal's 20-0 rout in 1937. The Bears Vic Bottari (92) checks out the play.

Vic Bottari (with ball) follows Thunder Team blocking into a wide hole against Southern Cal in 1937. Helping to lead the way is Vard Stockton (88). The Bears were known for their fierce blocking and line play during a 10-0-1 campaign, one which included a 20-6 trampling of the Trojans.

TWO FOR THE PRICE OF ONE

Navy Bill Ingram, who coached the Bears from 1931 to 1934, came up with a unique innovation for the Cal fans — annual double-headers. The idea was to give the Bears a sterner test by having them play two teams the same day. It started in 1932, when Cal opened the season by downing the Cal Aggies, 20-6, and following with a 13-0 blanking of West Coast Navy.

The historic twin-bill marked the 50th anniversary of Cal football on September 17, 1932, and gave the Bears their first game with another school in the U.C. system. Crip Toomey, a Wonder Team star, coached the Aggies, and Tom Hamilton, later the commissioner of the Pac-8, coached and played for West Coast Navy.

As it turned out, the double-headers did little more than flex the Bears muscles. They were an annual event until 1940, but through the 1938 twin-bill, the hosts were 14-0 and outscored the opposition 420 to 6. The final double-header was staged in 1939, Cal defeating the Aggies, 32-14, before losing to Pacific, 6-0.

The eight double-headers each included the Aggies, now known as U.C. Davis. COP provided the opposition four times, Nevada twice and Whittier and West Coast Navy once apiece. In the 1936 twin-bill, Cal used a center named Stan McCaffrey against COP. Today, McCaffrey is the president of what is now UOP.

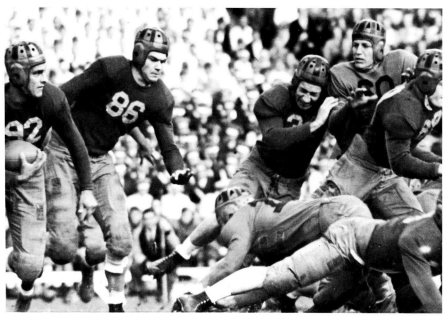

All-American halfback Vic Bottari (92) watches his teammates clear a path against UCLA in 1938. Other Bears identified on this play are Louis Smith (86), Bill Plasch (blocking UCLA's No. 60, Slats Wyrick), Tommy Ray (right) and Dave Anderson (foreground). Cal blasted the Bruins, 20-7.

DERIAN

En route to a 50-yard touchdown run with an intercepted pass, Al Derian, Cal's diminutive halfback, darts past a UCLA tackler. The Bears won the 1941 contest, 27-7.

The masterminds of Cal's 10-1 PCC co-champions of 1938 were head coach Stub Allison (center), line coach Frank Wickhorst (left) and backfield coach Irv Uteritz. Allison guided the Bears to a 58-42-2 record in 1935-44, and Wickhorst had an unsuccessful fling as Cal's head coach in 1946.

Cal's Orv Hatcher (arrow) follows a wall of blockers — including Jack McQuary (53), Jim Jurkovich (44), Charles Donohoe (83), Bill Elmore (49) and Vern Allen (24) — for a gain against Southern Cal in 1940. Circled at right, USC's Jack Banta (33) is illegally holding Ted Staffler (52), a violation which went undetected during the Bears 20-7 victory.

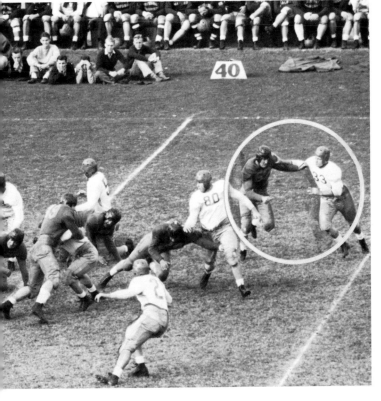

Pappy Waldorf (right) and his first California coaching staff prepared to greet more than 250 aspirants at the start of spring practice in 1947. Pappy's brain trust includes: (front row, left to right) Wes Fry, Eggs Manske, Zeb Chaney and Bob Tessier; (rear row, left to right) Roger Harding, Joe Merlo and Nibs Price.

PAPPY WALDORF
THE REIGN OF THE GENTLE GIANT

Lawrence "Buck" Shaw was hired for the 1945 season, but he made it clear he was interested in coaching the new San Francisco entry in the All-American Football Conference in 1946. So he signed only a one-year contract. At the conclusion of a 4-5-1 campaign in 1945, Shaw became the coach of the first 49ers, and he later led the Philadelphia Eagles to an NFL championship.

When Shaw quit, the search again was on for a successor. The search committee finally decided on Wickhorst, a former Illinois teammate of Red Grange and later an All-American tackle at Navy. Wick was a popular figure in Berkeley because of his years as an assistant under Ingram and Allison. So he was awarded a three-year contract, and success was anticipated because of the large turnout for football following the war.

Wickhorst, instead, experienced one of the most dissension-ridden seasons ever at Cal. He was not hired until the summer, so he didn't have the benefit of spring practice to evaluate talent. There were judgment errors which may have contributed to a disastrous 2-7 season, and there was discontent because many of the Bears were enlisted men during World War II, whereas Wick was a high-ranking Naval officer.

He was not respected by many of his players as an authority figure, and the rest of the student body and Cal fans weren't particularly fond of the string of weekly defeats. So pressure mounted, and Wickhorst was relieved of his duties following a 25-6 Big Game loss, with the University paying off the last two years of his contract.

Athletic director Brutus Hamilton was dispatched to find a successor, and such was the temper of the time that the one he found had to be a great one.

Lynn "Pappy" Waldorf more than filled the bill. A gentle giant at 260 pounds, the fatherly Waldorf was a tremendous organizer, a quality which paid off in coordinating alumni and

This unusual photograph of a short gain by Jackie Jensen (arrow) in the 1947 season opener with Santa Clara shows 21 of the 22 players and two officials in action. Bears identified in the play are Bob Celeri (22), George Fong (10), John Cunningham (89), Bill Main (43), Doug Duncan (53), Frank Van Deren (86) and Jim Turner (79). The Pappy Waldorf Era dawned with a resounding 33-7 triumph.

All eyes are on Pappy Waldorf as Cal's rookie head coach greets his 95-man squad prior to the 1947 opener. Under Waldorf, the Bears were transformed from a 2-7 loser to a 9-1 winner.

Halfback Ted Kenfield takes a handoff from
quarterback Bob Celeri (22) and scoots for yardage in
the 1947 Big Game. The Bears had to come from
behind to jolt upset-minded Stanford, 21-18.

Cal halfback Billy Main avoids Washington State
tacklers while breaking loose for a 21-yard gain in
1948 action. The Bears walloped the Cougars, 44-14.

student support behind a strong coaching staff and gifted athletes.

Not since the days of Andy Smith had Cal been so consistently outstanding in football. Hamilton got much more than he bargained for in Waldorf: a man of high character who in only one year made Golden Bear followers forget the past and anticipate a promising future. Except for the Rose Bowl season of 1958 and a taste of success in 1968 and in the mid-1970s, Cal has not been a constant winner since those marvelous early Waldorf years in the late forties.

Waldorf, the son of a Methodist minister, was reared in the Cleveland area and attended Syracuse University. He didn't command much attention as a student or as a 177-pound sophomore tackle, but he grew to 230 pounds as a senior and was an All-American. He had spurned pro ball for a job with a lumber company in Washington, then accepted the head coaching job at Oklahoma City University instead. He also coached at Oklahoma A&M and Kansas State before taking over at Northwestern in 1935.

The Wildcats were successful, but Pappy had

an eye on the West Coast when he visited for the Shrine Game. Such was his interest in California that it didn't take much coaxing from Hamilton to have Waldorf break a three-year contract with two seasons remaining. And, when he came to Berkeley in 1947, it didn't take him long to sweep the dirt under the rug.

Pappy's immediate success was astounding. On Cal's first play of the 1947 season, George Fong bolted 39 yards for a touchdown. It was a good omen, and an avalanche of touchdowns and victories followed. That 1947 squad staged one of the most amazing turnarounds in college history, going 9-1 for an improvement of six and one-half games! Only USC, a 39-14 winner, kept Cal from the Rose Bowl, but the Bears served notice that they were the ones to be reckoned with. They beat Navy, 14-7, before the largest crowd — 83,000 — in Memorial Stadium history, and they crushed Wisconsin, 48-7.

The 1948 and 1949 squads each went 10-1, losing Rose Bowl heartbreakers. The 1950 team was 9-1-1, not losing until Pasadena. In 1951, Waldorf coached his last great Cal squad, one which went 8-2 and rewrote numerous offensive

Cal's vaunted one-two punch of Jackie Jensen and Jack Swaner, shown here during a touchdown march against Oregon State in 1948. Swaner (with ball) darts into the end zone behind Jensen. Also in on the action are Gene Frasetto (76), Jon Baker (69), Frank Van Deren (86), John Cunningham (89), Rod Franz (67), Bill Main (43) and Dick Erickson (20).

Murray Olderman depicted the Bears domination of West Coast football under Pappy Waldorf with this cartoon in the Sacramento Bee.

Glenn Gulvin (76) helps out as two unidentified Bears smother Pennsylvania's Bagnell for a 4-yard loss in 1950 action at Memorial Stadium. Cal posted a 14-7 victory.

records, including 638 yards against Minnesota. In his first five years as Cal coach, Waldorf was a remarkable 46-6-1, averaging 26.7 points a game and relinquishing 11.3.

Pappy even claimed a distinction that had eluded the legendary Smith. After that loss to USC in 1947, the Golden Bears had 33 consecutive regular-season victories before a 7-7 tie with Stanford in 1950. That mark was extended to 38 regular-season contests without defeat before USC snapped the string with a 21-14 triumph in 1951.

Waldorf, who died near his Berkeley Hills home in 1981, was modest about his accomplishments at what was supposed to be a "coaches' graveyard." He attributed his overwhelming early success to strong support and talent. The assistance included capable assistants like backfield coach Wes Fry, line coach Bob Tessier and end coach Eggs Manske.

The standout players included All-Americans Rod Franz, Jackie Jensen, Jim Turner, Forrest Klein, Les Richter, Jim Monachino, Carl Van Heuit and Johnny Olszewski. Others like Paul Keckley, Frank Brunk, Jack Swaner, Jim Marinos,

Jim Cullom, Bob Celeri and Pete Schabarum perhaps were not of the same star caliber, but they were equally instrumental in the five-year reign of terror marred only by frustrating Rose Bowl defeats.

"We were successful because we had the organization and the numbers," Waldorf recalled during an interview in the seventies. "We had 255 men turn out for football in my first spring practice in 1947. There were no scholarships and tuition was not a factor. A lot of players were on the G.I. Bill and Eggs got most of the athletes jobs.

"I tried to take advantage of the numbers. We had two Ramblers (junior varsity) teams and a freshman squad. There always was a supply of talent and our depth won a lot of games. We also started recruiting vigorously. There were 77 counties in California and I went to all of them. I'd find Cal alums and get support groups going, urging them to send youngsters to the University. Our numbers gave us momentum, but in a few years, the other schools caught up."

Though loved by his players, Pappy began hearing ripples of criticism following the Rose

These Bear bruisers, lining up for photographers prior to a Rose Bowl practice session in 1949, were the offensive mainstays of a 10-1 squad. The backs were (left to right) Jack Swaner, Bob Celeri, Pete Schabarum and Billy Main. The line included (left to right) John Cunningham, Jim Turner, Rod Franz, George Stathakis, Ray DeJong, Jim Cullom and Norm Pressley. All but Stathakis also played on the 10-1 Rose Bowl team of 1948.

Sophomore fullback Johnny Olszewski (36) breaks a tackle en route to a long gain in 1950 action at Memorial Stadium. Teammates Jim Marinos (23) and Jim Monachino (35) watch Johnny O as he adds yardage to his season total of 1,008.

Cal's Pete Schabarum outruns two Stanford defenders for the Bears only touchdown in a 7-7 tie with the Indians in the Big Game. Schabarum's score preserved an undefeated regular season in 1950.

Bowl losses. But he was as much a gentleman in defeat as he was in victory. When things started going wrong in his final five seasons, he retained his composure and accepted the downswing following so many years of success.

The Bears weren't exactly pushovers in the mid-1950s. There were stars like Olszewski, Matt Hazeltine, Paul Larson and Jim Hanifan to insure against a complete collapse. But the fact remained that the magic was gone after that record-smashing campaign of 1951. The record kept slipping, from 7-3 in 1952 to 4-4-2 and 5-5. By 1955, it was 2-7-1, and Cal was getting clobbered on occasion.

Ditto in 1956, when a 14-13 loss one week before the Big Game left the Bears in a 2-7

disarray. Pressure began to mount, but Pappy beat the administration to the punch by resigning and maintaining his record of never being fired on the job. It was an emotional week, ending with a dramatic Big Game: the Bears overcame the odds and stunned Stanford, 20-18, as a going-away present.

Waldorf, who later served the 49ers as a scouting expert, concluded his Cal career with 10 years under his ample belt, equaling the longevity of Smith and Allison. Andy (74-16-7) had a better record than Pappy (67-32-4) and Stub (58-42-2), but the others couldn't match Waldorf's 7-1-2 record in the Big Game — an achievement which always will endear him to Old Blues.

All eyes follow this dramatic field goal attempt by Les Richter, one of the greatest linemen in Cal history, against Washington in 1951. The boot placed the Bears ahead, 30-28, and they went on to a 37-28 victory as darkness descended upon Memorial Stadium.

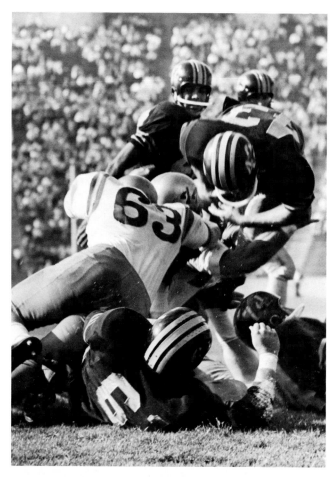

With quarterback Joe Kapp looking on, Cal halfback Jack Hart (43) dives over the Washington line for a touchdown in 1956. The Bears posted a 16-7 victory.

Jubilant students and players mob Pappy Waldorf and carry him off the field following a 20-18 Cal upset in the 1956 Big Game, the popular coach's final contest with the Bears. Waldorf concluded with a 67-32-4 record at Berkeley.

THE BOWL GAME THAT WASN'T

Controversy raged during the 1949 football season on the relative merits of Cal's Bob Celeri and COP's Eddie LeBaron. Each had support as the finest quarterback in the Bay Area, but there was no way to truly settle the issue because the Bears and the Tigers did not meet during the regular season.

But the ingenuity of three collegians, including former Cal halfback Ted Kenfield, saved the day. They concocted a dream game between graduating seniors from Cal and COP — including Celeri and LeBaron of course — and scheduled the much-anticipated contest for Lincoln's Birthday at Lodi's rain-soaked Grape Bowl near Stockton.

Tickets cost $2.50, and a 21,000-plus sellout was assured when demand exceeded the supply. The 49ers provided the uniforms, and each of the 44 players was thinking of a $1,000 payday. But the game transcended monetary considerations. It was Celeri vs. LeBaron, and interest in the showdown was remarkable. In fact, some of the Tigers underclassmen had to be dissuaded from participating, lest they lose their eligibility.

Neither of the diminutive quarterbacks went high in the pro draft, but Celeri distinguished himself by playing on two PCC champions, and LeBaron rewrote the COP record book before earning MVP honors at the East-West Game. Unfortunately, defense ruled the day at the Grape Bowl, and the COP grads squeezed out a 7-6 victory, continuing Cal's pattern of frustrating post-season defeat in the Pappy Waldorf Era.

Waldorf, incidentally, was not on the sidelines during the impromptu Lodi clash. Neither was his COP counterpart. The schools couldn't be officially involved, so it was more of a glorified sandlot affair. But no game of its kind ever commanded more local attention, and the San Joaquin Valley fans still were buzzing long after the final gun.

Senior quarterbacks Bob Celeri (33) of Cal and Eddie LeBaron (right) of College of the Pacific are the focal points in an unofficial football game at Lodi's Grape Bowl in February 1950.

RAY WILLSEY
MILD SUCCESS IN WILD TIMES

It was regarded as a surprise when Pete Elliott was named Waldorf's successor in 1957. Elliott, a former Michigan superstar, at age 30 became the youngest head coach in Cal history, and he brought with him only one year of head coaching experience — at Nebraska in 1956 — after having served as an aide under Bud Wilkinson on the great Oklahoma teams of the early 1950s.

Elliott didn't have great success as a Cal rookie coach. He won only one of 10 games, but the record wasn't indicative of the competitive spirit the Bears exhibited with the fiery leadership of athletes like Joe Kapp and Jack Hart. Of those nine losses, six were by a total of 27 points, including two-point defeats against UCLA, Oregon State and Stanford.

Things were supposed to be much better in 1958, but an 0-2 start against COP and Michigan State left some doubt. The Bears rallied behind Kapp and Hart to win seven out of the next eight and land in the Rose Bowl, but Iowa snapped them back to reality there with a 38-12 runaway. Then, following a 2-8 collapse in 1959, Elliott departed for the greener pastures of Illinois. And the worst was yet to come.

The Bears followed a similar trend in hiring in 1960 when Marv Levy, a coach as young and inexperienced as Elliott, was signed. Levy, a former star athlete at Iowa's Coe College, had been the head coach at New Mexico for two years when Berkeley beckoned. It was not a marriage made in heaven.

Suffering from a lack of talent and recruiting problems, Levy had trouble winning despite a talented staff which included future head coaches Mike White, Bill Walsh and Dick Stanfel. He was 4-24-2 the first three years, and by the grace of Craig Morton, Levy equaled his victory total with a 4-5-1 campaign in 1963. But an 8-29-3 overall record couldn't save his job, and he was fired without much fanfare.

Levy landed on his feet by coaching Montreal to a championship in Canada and then signed with the Kansas City Chiefs, a far cry from those humble beginnings in Berkeley. "Times were tough at Cal," he recalled. "It was difficult to get black students enrolled and a lack of talent hurt me more than inexperience. Morton was my one player. He made us competitive."

If Levy thought he had had it rough, his stay at Cal was mild compared to what Ray Willsey, his successor, had to endure at Berkeley in the mid-1960s. It seemed like constant turmoil. There

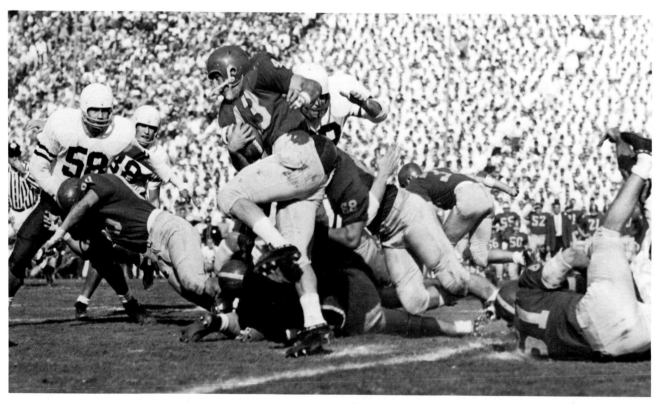

Jack Hart, Cal's best runner of the late fifties, fights for yardage against Stanford in the 1958 Big Game at Memorial Stadium. The Bears edged the Indians, 16-15, and made their last Rose Bowl appearance.

Jack Schraub makes a tumbling catch of a deflected Craig Morton pass to pull Cal to within 20-22 of heavily favored Duke in 1963. The Bears then tied the game with a two-point conversion.

Ray Willsey, a former player under Pappy Waldorf, made an impressive debut as Cal's head coach in 1964, posting a 21-14 victory over Missouri and Dan Devine. Willsey was carried off the field after the game. Passing hero Craig Morton is at lower left.

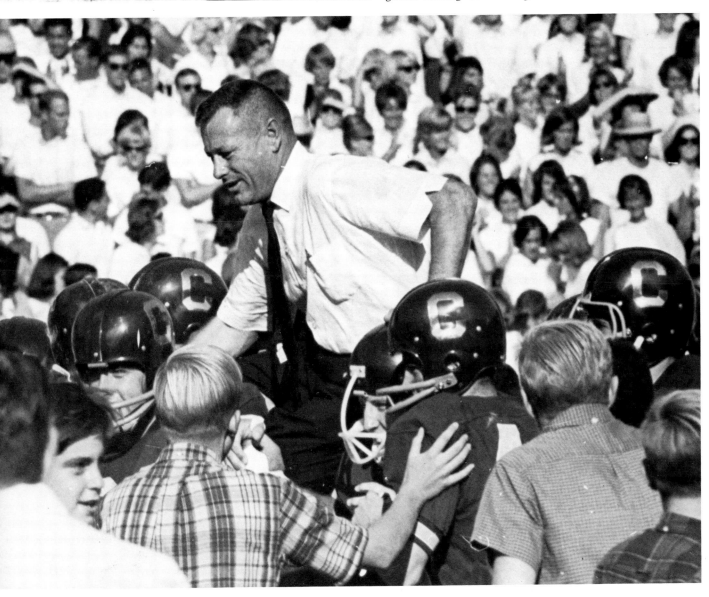

A mud-caked Craig Morton is surrounded by East players in the 1965 Shrine Game at Kezar Stadium. Morton's pass to Cal teammate Jack Schraub gave the West an 11-7 victory.

Cal's Bear Minimum defense of 1968 was anchored by these four down linemen and linebacker Irby Augustine (88). The linemen are (left to right) Larry Reis, Steve Schulz, All-American Ed White and Mark Hultgren. The 1968 Bears contained six opponents to one touchdown or less.

was the famous Free Speech Movement, anti-war protests, a revolt of black athletes, People's Park, tear gas and riot police — a climate not conducive to recruiting and football success.

But Willsey, a former Cal back under Waldorf, was a tough bird who looked adversity in the eye and did something about it. Because he was an Old Blue, alumni support was polarized, and there was a trickle of standout athletes bolstering the program. He also overcame the lack of gifted athletes in the skill positions by emphasizing defense and using that facet of the game as an equalizer.

It was a different approach, one born of necessity. Willsey never said it would be easy, but he made the best of a bad situation without a whimper. Instead, his Cal teams were competitive and registered numerous upsets. The fact that he coached at the .500 level during the stormy sixties was a great achievement — perhaps unappreciated at the time, but

significant in retrospect.

As a rookie coach in 1964, Willsey had the benefit of senior All-American Morton, and that had to be the most exciting 3-7 squad in Cal history. There was an opening, 21-14 upset of Missouri and Dan Devine and a stunning, 27-13 upset of Navy, in which four of Roger Staubach's passes were intercepted. There also were five defeats by a total of 26 points, including a 26-21 heartbreaker won by USC with 50 seconds remaining.

The pattern continued without Morton. Jerry Bradley's catch in the end zone with no time jolted Penn State, 21-17, in a 5-5 season in 1965, and Michigan was upset in 1967. One year later, Willsey's defense was at its best. With Ed White — later an all-pro offensive guard with the Vikings and the Chargers — anchoring the defensive line, the 1968 Bears were off to a 5-1 start, outscoring opponents 166-32.

The only blemish at the time was a 10-7 loss to Army, which occurred when a much taller receiver reached over a diminutive defensive back to grab the winning touchdown. Then, a fumble near the goal line helped Washington salvage a 7-7 tie, and the quick start turned into a 7-3-1 finish. White, safety Ken Wiedemann, linebackers Irby Augustine and Mike McCaffrey and halfback Gary Fowler were the stars of Cal's best team in the sixties.

By 1969, help was on the way. The fog had lifted, and Willsey was beginning to become more offense-minded. His prize recruiting catch was tailback Isaac Curtis of Santa Ana High, a move which ultimately contributed to Willsey's downfall. The 1970 squad went 6-5 with upsets of USC and Stanford, and that record was duplicated in 1971, Willsey's controversial final season with the Bears.

An eligibility conflict stemming from a required test resulted in 1971 in the Curtis Case. Improprieties were discovered by the NCAA, and Cal was stripped of its 1970 national track-and-field championship because Curtis, a sprinter, had scored in the meet. Willsey defied the NCAA and played Curtis in the fall, but the coach didn't get sufficient administrative support, and he became the sacrificial lamb to appease the NCAA.

It was a tough blow to a man who had worked so hard to keep Cal football respectable during trying times. Willsey left with a 40-42-1 record, quite admirable under the circumstances. A few months later, Curtis also gained his freedom from an unfortunate situation. He transferred to San Diego State, was immediately eligible and became a standout wide receiver who continued his success as an all-pro with the Bengals.

Fullback John McGaffie plunges over a pile of bodies for a 1-yard touchdown in Cal's 43-0 romp over Syracuse in 1968. McGaffie was the co-captain of a 7-3-1 squad that was the Bears best of the 1960s.

Tailback Isaac Curtis takes a handoff from quarterback Dave Penhall. Curtis brought excitement to Cal's offense, but irregularities in the handling of his transcript during recruiting led to the dismissal of Coach Ray Willsey following the 1971 season. Despite transferring to San Diego State, Curtis still ranks first in career kickoff returns and second in single-season all-purpose running at Cal.

Leaping linebacker Loren Toews recovers a UCLA fumble at the L.A. Coliseum in 1971. Marv Kendricks of the Bruins fumbled the ball after being hit by Cal's Mark Wendt (75). The Bears posted a last-ditch, 31-24 victory for their only win over prime nemesis UCLA in the 1970s.

MIKE WHITE
OFFENSE RULES THE ROOST

Just as the sixties were rocky, so was the controversial reign of Mike White, who came to Cal in 1972 full of fire. The enthusiastic and youthful White, who had been an end for the Bears under Waldorf and Elliott, was signed after Cal won a recruiting tug-of-war with Stanford, which also wanted him as head coach. He was an Indians assistant at the time, but the lure of his alma mater proved too strong.

There were immediate adjustment problems at Berkeley. Willsey backers — and there were many among Old Blues — resented his firing and would have been reluctant to accept anyone. To them, the brash and aggressive White was unbearable, especially when he didn't go out of his way to embrace alumni support. White also made promises, vowing to bring Cal back to prominence with a pro-style passing attack.

The critics scoffed when White's first two teams were a combined 7-15. The offense was exciting, all right, but the Bears defense was tissue-thin, as evidenced by scores of 49-13 and 61-21 registered by UCLA, a 50-14 romp recorded by USC and a 66-0 disaster administered by Alabama in the 1973 opener.

White, eating crow and munching on humble pie, didn't back down. He had confidence in his system, and it gradually began to pay off. With Steve Bartkowski at the throttle in 1974, the Bears suddenly were respectable. They tied mighty USC and finished 7-3-1. Fans were taking notice of the offensive explosion, and they liked what they saw — an entertaining brand of football that neutralized the physical strength of opponents.

By 1975, White and his Bears were in high gear. Bartkowski had gone to the NFL's Falcons, but junior college transfer Joe Roth stepped in and picked up the slack. He had help from multipurpose back Chuck Muncie and superstar receivers Wesley Walker and Steve Rivera. That explosive collection of talent went 8-3, tied for the Pac-8 title and topped the NCAA in total offense with perfect balance — 2,522 yards on the ground and 2,522 yards through the air.

With Roth suffering from cancer which was to claim his life a few months after the season, the Bears were 5-6 in 1976. They rebounded in 1977 to go 7-4, which later was changed to 8-3 because of a forfeit. White, now at Illinois, was fired a few weeks after the season because of philosophical differences with athletic director Dave Maggard, and Roger Theder, the No. 1 assistant, was promoted.

Theder, like White a former Stanford assistant

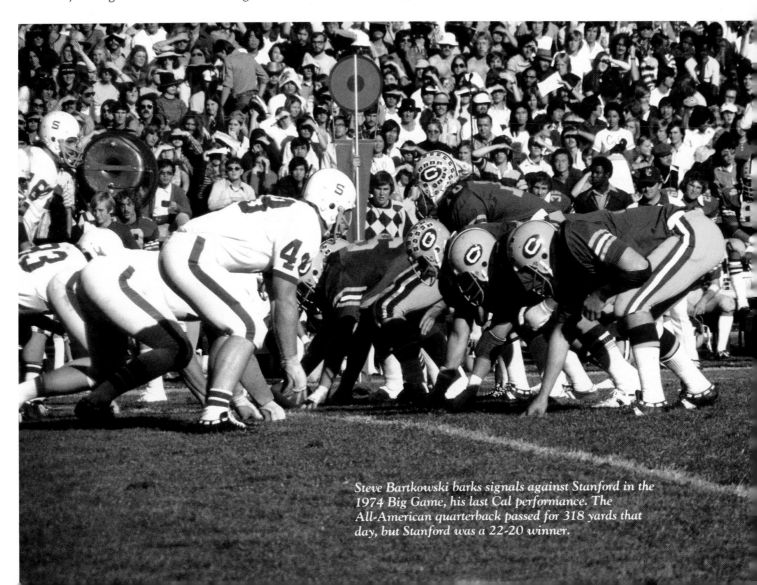

Steve Bartkowski barks signals against Stanford in the 1974 Big Game, his last Cal performance. The All-American quarterback passed for 318 yards that day, but Stanford was a 22-20 winner.

with a penchant for passing the football, was 6-5 as a rookie in 1978, and he took Cal to the Garden State Bowl in 1979. But he slipped to 5-17 in 1980-81 and was dismissed following the 1981 season, unable to come close to White's 35-30-1 career record.

In somewhat of a surprise move, Maggard hired energetic Joe Kapp to become Cal's head coach in 1982. Kapp had no previous coaching experience, but he was able to unite Old Blues alienated by Willsey's departure and White's first impression. Many regarded the selection of Kapp as a unique coaching experiment, but Old Blues who came to love his swashbuckling style as a player firmly believed he would bring success to the sidelines.

Cal defenders Kim Staskus (58) and Karl Crumpacker (18) close down on USC's Anthony Davis while Rob Swenson comes in to help during Cal's stunning, 15-15 tie with USC in the L.A. Coliseum in 1974.

Cal quarterback Joe Roth drops back to pass in 1976 action. Roth, the Bears inspirational leader, played that emotional season with cancer attacking his body, and he died three months after its conclusion.

Chuck Muncie powers for yardage against Stanford in 1975. An electrifying combination of size and speed, he could run with power, was an excellent receiver out of the backfield and often was a devastating threat as a passer on the tailback option play.

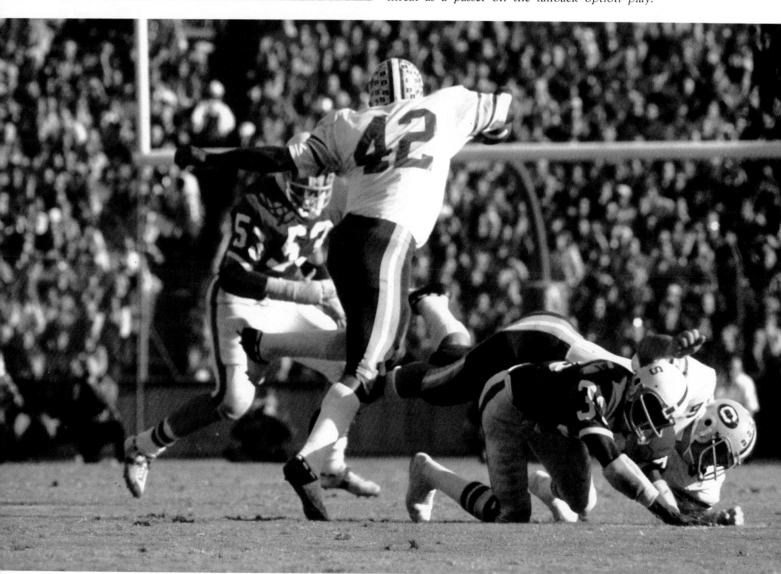

Wesley Walker (99) and Steve Rivera teamed up in the mid-1970s as one of the greatest receiving tandems on any college football team. Rivera specialized in running precise patterns while Walker was the deep threat.

Ralph DeLoach (94), Craig Watkins and Terry Saffold (48) smother USC quarterback Rob Hertel during the Bears 17-14 triumph at Memorial Stadium in 1977.

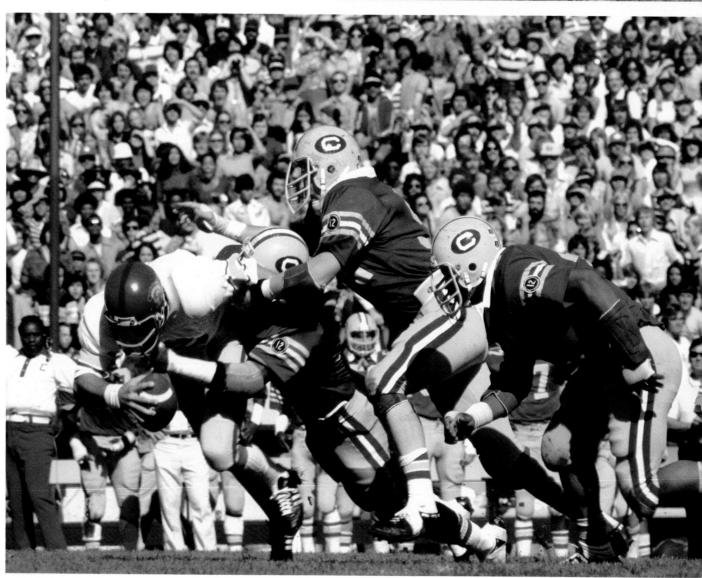

Charlie Young pivots away from center against USC in 1977. Young and Paul Jones led the Bears to a 17-14 upset win in the Joe Roth Memorial Game. Two weeks earlier, Young amassed a school-record 399 yards in total offense against Oregon State.

In this sequence, Joe Rose hauls in what would be the winning touchdown in the 1979 Big Game. He then drops the ball in disgust as the referee rules that he was out of bounds. In a surprising and controversial turn of events, the referee reversed his decision after consulting with another official. In allowing Rose's score, the referee explained that he had been confused by the end-zone decoration and misjudged the end line.

Quarterback Rich Campbell checks things out at the line in 1979 action. The junior standout enjoyed record-smashing success that year, establishing school marks for pass completions, 216, and yardage, 2,618.

Safety Ron Coccimiglio (27) makes one of his four 1980 interceptions on this play against San Jose State. Teammate Kevin Moen (26) looks on.

Jubilant Bears Tim Lucas (48), Reggie Camp (90) and Kirk Karacozoff (50) celebrate after Dupree Marshall (right foreground) recovers a John Elway fumble on the Stanford 3 in the 1980 Big Game. Moments later, Cal scored to break a 21-21 tie and went on to a 28-23 upset victory.

Cal's John Tuggle (31) follows tight end Don Sprague's blocking for a short gain in the 1980 Big Game. Tuggle rushed for 110 yards and two touchdowns in the Bears 28-23 upset.

Rich Dixon (left) and Ron Rivera, two of Cal's finest
linebackers in recent years, combine forces to sack
Georgia quarterback Buck Belue in 1981 action at
Athens. Dixon was injured later in the game and was
sidelined the remainder of the season.

Halfback Carl Montgomery is all alone on this touchdown gallop against Oregon State in 1981. Montgomery tied a modern school record with four touchdowns and gained a season-high 113 yards against the Beavers.

Quarterback J. Torchio ascended from a non-scholarship walk-on to a Cal regular in 1981. Taking over for injured Rich Campbell, Torchio engineered a Big Game upset in 1980 and became the No. 1 quarterback when Gale Gilbert was injured in the 1981 opener.

Joe Kapp, shown helping to coach the Bears in spring practice during the mid-1970s, made his interest in the profession official in 1982 by becoming Cal's head football coach.

All-American candidate Harvey Salem (73) blocks against Washington State. Tim Galas (65) and Brian Bailey (71) also provide protection for the Cal quarterback.

CHAPTER
2

100
YEARS
1882
1982

CAL
BLVE
AND
GOLD

The 1899 Cal varsity, which went 7-1-1 while outscoring its foes 142-2, participated in the first intersectional clash in the Bears history, bowing to the Carlisle Indians, 2-0, on Christmas Day in San Francisco.

Chapter Two
GREAT VICTORIES, MORAL AND REAL

With more than 650 games under its belt, California football has provided its fans with dozens of thrillers and great games. Aside from the Big Game, which has a history of its own, a few games stand out as having contributed significantly to Cal gridiron history. The first of these significant contests was a classic matchup between Cal and the Carlisle Indians, just before the turn of the century.

CARLISLE 2, CAL 0
DECEMBER 25, 1899

When Garrett Cochran came from Princeton to handle Cal's coaching duties in 1898, the Bears were picking up the pieces from a winless campaign of 1897. Cochran guided his first team to an 8-0-2 record and improved to 7-0-1 in 1899. The Bears outscored the opposition 142-0, and they were regarded as perhaps the finest team ever produced in the West. To prove the point, they extended an invitation to Carlisle Indian School to play on Christmas Day.

Carlisle, under rookie coach Pop Warner, was an Eastern powerhouse, and the game was billed as the East-West Championship. The quick and clever Indians had forged a 7-2 record against the best in the East, upsetting Penn, 16-5, and drubbing Columbia, 45-0, in a game where Warner introduced the crouching start for backs. The Indians were in excellent condition, having kept fit on the transcontinental train ride by racing the puffing locomotive up grades in the Rockies.

A lineup that included crack linemen Martin Wheelock, Thaddeus Redwater and Hawley Pierce, plus drop-kicking quarterback Frank Hudson and All-American halfback Isaac Seneca, intrigued the Bay Area fans. A crowd of 15,000 showed up at the 16th and Folson Field in San Francisco for Cal's first intersectional clash. What they saw was not a band of savages, but rather a cohesive, well-disciplined unit.

"We like our boys to win their games," said Dr. Carlos Montezuma, the Carlisle spokesman, "but the chief object is not to demonstrate the Indian's wonderful athletic ability, but to use the sport as one element of having the men meet civilization. We have come to the Pacific Coast not to exhibit our so-called savagery, but for a nobler and higher purpose: to demonstrate what education means to the Indian when given under the same conditions enjoyed by the white boy."

When they arrived at the game site, it didn't take long for the Indians to rediscover some of the white man's ways. Their chief asset was speed, but they found the field sandy, a condition which also hindered the accuracy of Hudson's kicking. Wheelock kicked off, but the Bears punted on first down. Cal, with a string of 10 straight shutouts dating back to 1898, wanted to demonstrate its defensive skill. Crunching tackles by Wrec Womble and Lol Pringle stopped Carlisle cold, and the Indians were forced to punt.

Cal's Pete "Kangaroo" Kaarsberg made 13 yards on a fake kick, but the Bears couldn't get past their own 28 and a punt seemed in order. Kaarsberg, however, reportedly thought that another fake had been called, and he started running toward the end when the center flipped the ball to quarterback Frank Ellis. The quarterback had called a real punt, so when he turned around and pitched the ball, Kaarsberg wasn't there.

The ball bounced within four feet of the goal with Kaarsberg and Carlisle's Pierce in hot pursuit. Kangaroo got there first, preventing a touchdown, but Pierce hit him so hard that the Bear and Pierce landed 10 yards beyond the goal line. It was ruled a safety, and those two points were the only points scored all day. Carlisle came out on top, 2-0, in what was regarded as a moral victory for Cal and a major upset. "The two best teams in the country today are, beyond a doubt, Carlisle and California," declared Warner. The Bears indeed proved they could play against the best of the East, thereby triggering a history of intersectional success.

WASHINGTON 13, CAL 7
NOVEMBER 13, 1915

The 1915 game with Washington was another loss — 13-7 — and another moral victory, but it will go down among the great upsets in Cal history. Why? Because it came exactly one week after Washington hammered the Bears, 72-0, at Berkeley, outgaining Cal by a convincing 642-53 and showing a whopping 34-3 advantage in first downs. Coach Gil Dobie's mighty Huskies figured to whip the Bears even more convincingly in the Seattle rematch.

The 1915 Bears had resumed American football after nine years of rugby, and Jimmy Schaeffer was retained as coach until a successor could be found. The Bears were feeling their way until the 72-0 debacle awakened them. They knew what to expect at Seattle, and it was an inspirational performance that kept the mighty Huskies scoreless for three quarters. Cliff Canfield, Bill Russell, Rudy Gianelli and Roy Sharp were particularly outstanding for Cal.

Washington took a 7-0 lead early in the fourth quarter, but Gianelli made an acrobatic touchdown catch on a pass from Sharp and added the extra point for 7-7. There was one minute to play and the Huskies had the ball at midfield when they finally exposed Cal's inexperience. A fake pass resulted in a 45-yard gain to the 5, and the Huskies punched it over for the victory. They celebrated by carrying Sharp off the field, a tribute to the Bears remarkable achievement that day.

CAL 27, WASHINGTON 0
NOVEMBER 3, 1917

The 1917 season was Andy Smith's second at Cal, and the Golden Bears extended their losing streak to five in a row by dropping the first three games of the year. Then came four straight victories, including a significant 14-3 triumph over the Oregon Aggies. It was a big win because it came against a team with a long history of college football, whereas Cal had been away from rugby for only two years.

One week after the Aggies were downed, the Bears affirmed their gradual rise to prominence under Smith. Like most collegiate powers, Washington's squad was depleted by World War I, but the Huskies came to Berkeley on November 3 with a record of not having tasted defeat since 1907, accumulating an incredible 59-0-4 record, mostly under the leadership of Gil Dobie.

Cal welcomed back football in 1915, but due to a dispute over player-eligibility rules, the Big Game that year was held with Washington rather than Stanford. In the contest at Berkeley, the Huskies clobbered the Bears, 72-0. The debacle roused the Bears, who almost turned the tables against the Huskies the following week in Seattle before losing, 13-7. The tremendous reversal of form was a great moral victory for Cal.

MONTY PUNTING   VARSITY-ORIGINALS, 7 - 0   CALIFORNIA FIELD, OCTOBER 9

"The signals rattle, a pigskin thud — they're down"——

American Football's Back!
"It's Root, Hog, or Die"

All Classes Celebrate
1866 - 1915
On the eve of the Big Game—California versus Washington

Joint Football Banquet
An Old - Time Good Time
Save the Date

Friday Night, November 5

A Great Mob
A Square Meal
Lots of Song and Jubilation
A Battery of Twenty One-minute Speeches

Commercial Club, San Francisco
Top Floor, Merchants Exchange   Two Dollars a Plate

Under the auspices of the Association of Alumni Classes

Cal's Andy Rowe, however, scored on runs of 2, 40 and 15 yards in the second quarter for a 21-0 halftime lead, and Carlton "Dummy" Wells added a 10-yard touchdown run in the third period to complete a 27-0 rout. The Huskies, outgained 381-127, hardly resembled the Dobie juggernaut of years past. But the Bears were affected by the war, too, and hardly were an awesome aggregation. This game, nonetheless, served notice that Cal would replace Washington as the king of the Coast, and by 1922, there was no argument. That year, the Wonder Team prevailed, 45-7, in what was regarded as Smith's greatest victory.

CAL 14, PENNSYLVANIA 0
JANUARY 1, 1925

While Stanford was bowing to Notre Dame's Four Horsemen in the Rose Bowl on New Year's Day in 1925, Cal staged a post-season classic of its own, one arranged between Smith and his

The 1917 Cal squad was Andy Smith's second, but it was the first to indicate that the balance of power in West Coast football was about to shift to the Bears. The pivotal game was against Washington, which had not lost since 1907, compiling a 59-0-4 record. The Bears, led by Andy Rowe's three touchdowns, crushed the Huskies, 27-0.

alma mater, Penn. The 1924 Bears were 7-0-2, including the fabled 20-20 tie with Stanford, while Pennsylvania was 8-0-1, outscoring the opposition 203-16 and posting seven shutouts.

This wasn't an East-West clash of Rose Bowl proportions, yet it attracted 65,000 to Memorial Stadium. It amounted to the last hurrah for Smith, who was to coach only one more year, and the Bears didn't disappoint. Demonstrating a balanced attack, 166 yards rushing and 154 through the air, Cal scored on touchdowns by fullbacks John Young and Robert Griffin and a pair of conversion kicks by Glenn "Scoop" Carlson. Final score: Cal 14, Pennsylvania 0.

CAL 0, USC 0
OCTOBER 20, 1928

A crowd of 74,245 showed up at Memorial Stadium for a mid-season clash of unbeaten Cal and USC on October 20, 1928. Nibs Price's Bears didn't figure to play on even terms with Howard Jones' mighty Trojans, but Cal's defense rose to the occasion and constantly repelled the USC attack. The Trojans finished with a 212-120 yardage edge, but they couldn't cross the goal line against their inspired hosts.

The final 0-0 tie was the only blemish on a 9-0-1 season for the Trojans, who outscored their opponents 267-59 in 1928. Moreover, it marked the only time a Jones-coached USC squad had been blanked. The Bears biggest weapon that memorable day was Benny Lom, who punted for à 38-yard average and discouraged returns with his high, booming boots.

CAL 0, ST. MARY'S 0
OCTOBER 5, 1929

From 1919 through 1923, Cal made a shambles of the annual series with St. Mary's, walloping the Gaels by a combined 257-0. But Slip Madigan was brewing trouble for the Bears, who were played on even terms from 1924 on, in games that were thrillers to the bitter end. Such an occasion attracted 69,917 on October 5, 1929, for the second game of the season, especially since Madigan fielded one of his strongest teams.

As they had done against USC the year before, the Bears overcame their opponent's offensive superiority with an outstanding defensive effort. St. Mary's outgained Cal 218-65, but the Gaels didn't have a good chance to score until the final quarter. They were stopped on the Bears 9, and Cal took over. Lom fumbled moments later and the Gaels recovered on the Bears 25. They eventually reached the 4, but Cal held again and a 0-0 deadlock was in the books.

CAL 15, USC 7
NOVEMBER 2, 1929

Later that season, on November 2, Cal and USC tangled in the Los Angeles Coliseum. Both teams were undefeated, but the Trojans were heavily favored on their home turf. They were 15-0-1 since the 1928 season, the scoreless tie with Cal being the only blemish in that span. Also, the Trojans hadn't dropped a PCC contest since 1926, so 76,120 showed up for the spectacle.

A fumble recovery by Edwin Griffiths got the Bears going in the first quarter. A 13-yard pass from the ubiquitous Lom to Lee Eisan and a 23-yard run by Griffiths did the big damage, and Rusty Gill punched it over from the 1 for the TD. Griffiths' PAT made it 7-0. In the second period, Lom was to record a play that vaulted him to All-American prominence.

Back in punt formation on the Cal 15, Lom faked the kick and completely outfoxed USC end Garrett Arbelbide. Benny dodged two would-be tacklers and bolted 85 yards for a touchdown, actually running 95 yards from punt formation. It ranks among the most stirring runs in Cal history.

Later, Roy Riegels blocked Ernie Pinckert's punt for a safety and a 15-0 halftime lead against the shocked Trojans. USC, which scored in the third period, outgained the Bears 292-254 and made five more first downs, but Cal had the only statistic which really counted — a 15-7 advantage on the scoreboard.

CAL 14, ST. MARY'S 13
OCTOBER 7, 1933

The 1933 Cal-St. Mary's game, played on October 7, 1933, was a classic, and 55,000 saw it on a warm day at Strawberry Canyon. Madigan's Gaels were a 2-1 favorite, and they met those expectations by jumping to a 13-0 lead before the game was five minutes old. George Wilson's 20-yard run set up a 38-yard TD burst by Nick Nichelini. Ed Gilbert kicked the extra point, then later blocked Arleigh Williams' punt. Fred Canrinus recovered the loose ball and dashed 10 yards for a 13-0 lead.

The Bears had been jittery during the week leading up to the game because of published accounts of the Gaels size and strength. When the Cal players arrived at Memorial Stadium on the morning of the game, coach Stub Allison presented each member a half-ticket to the game. "What are these for?" one of the Bears asked.

"Well," replied Allison, "I just got to thinking that when those St. Mary's guys toss you fellows over the stadium, you'd like to have a ticket to

Benny Lom, Cal's all-purpose backfield star of the late twenties, displays his punting form during a Memorial Stadium practice. Lom's kicking played a key role in two big games against USC. In 1928, his high, booming punts were Cal's biggest weapon in holding the heavily favored Trojans to a 0-0 tie. Then, in 1929, with the Trojans perhaps concerned about their inability to get a decent return of his punts the year before, Lom faked a kick and bolted 85 yards for what proved to be the winning score as Cal topped USC, 15-7.

Andy Smith, Cal's most successful football coach, plots strategy with his staff prior to a 1925 New Year's Day victory over Pennsylvania, 14-0, at Memorial Stadium. From left: Brick Muller, Nibs Price, Smith, Dr. Albert Boles and Dan McMillan.

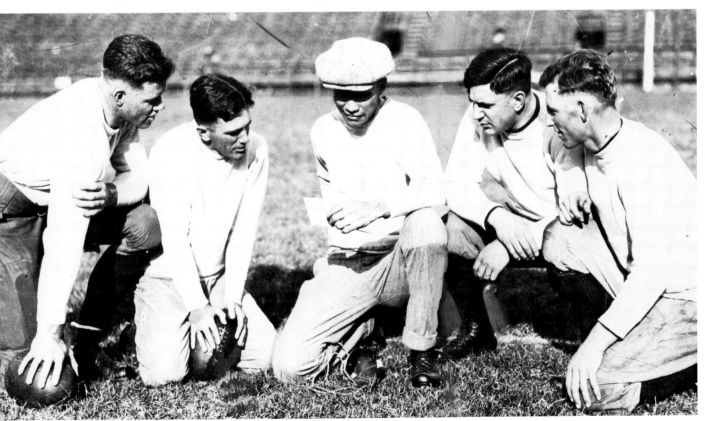

get back in and see the show."

Laughter replaced fear for the moment, but it didn't seem the Bears had gotten the message, judging from the early 13-0 deficit. But with Williams and James Keefer, who had a 26-yard run, doing the bulk of the work, Cal marched 73 yards in the second quarter and Williams went over from the 3. He added the conversion, and it was 13-7 at the half.

After a scoreless third quarter, the Bears needed a break to fulfill their upset hopes. They got it with four minutes remaining, when Chuck Williams blocked a punt, giving Cal possession on the St. Mary's 15. Jack Brittingham made 3 yards on an end around and sophomore Floyd Blower twisted and turned his way to a memorable 12-yard TD for 13-13. The Bears didn't want another tie following a wild, 12-12 affair in 1932, so Blower calmly booted the PAT, and the Gaels were stunned, 14-13. They were outgained 248-147 as well.

CAL 14, UCLA 2
NOVEMBER 2, 1935

UCLA hadn't been playing big-time football very long, but in 1935 Cal's cousins from Westwood assembled their strongest squad ever and went unbeaten through their first seven games, including an upset of Stanford's Vow Boys. Cal was unbeaten, too, so a crowd of 75,000 gathered on November 2 at the Los Angeles Coliseum for the most meaningful contest ever between members of the U.C. system.

Fred Funk's punting gave the Bruins early field position and a 2-0 lead when Don Fowler was trapped behind the goal line for a safety while attempting to handle a punt. Blower's punts then backed UCLA against its goal. Larry Lutz blocked Funk's kick, and Vard Stockton picked it off in the air, racing 12 yards for a touchdown and a 7-2 lead in the second quarter.

Arleigh Williams (60) shakes loose for a gain of 9 yards against St. Mary's in 1933. Cal teammate George Relles (65) blocks for Williams as Bob Carlton (15) looks on. The Bears fell behind, 13-0, but rallied to win, 14-13.

Don Fowler, behind a block from Bob Gilbert, plows through UCLA defenders for a short gain. The Bears won this 1935 battle of unbeatens at Los Angeles, 14-2.

UCLA's Fred Funk eludes the grasp of Cal's John Brittingham (53) at the L.A. Coliseum in 1935. All-American guard Vard Stockton (88) and tackle Bob Carlton (center) rush to help.

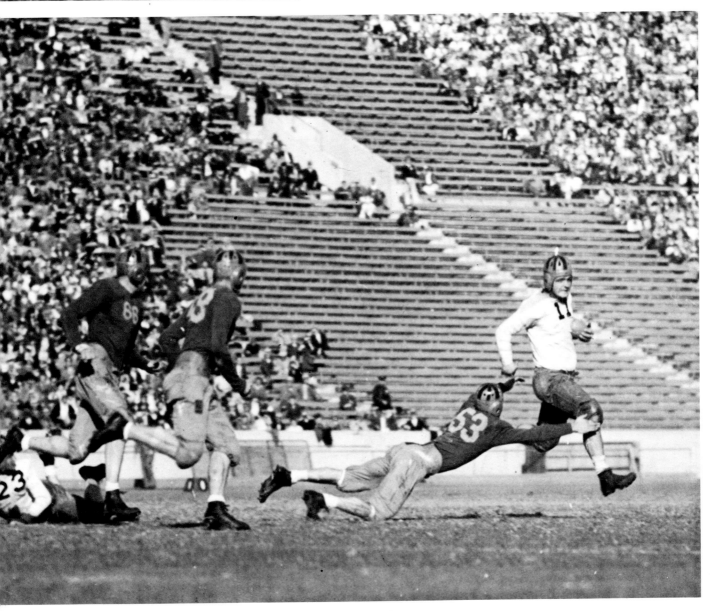

Bob Herwig's interception in the fourth quarter set up Cal's final score. Blower, faking an off-tackle play, dropped back and passed to Brittingham, who caught the ball on the Bruins 14 and completed a 40-yard pass play. Sam Chapman's kick completed the 14-2 victory, slapping down UCLA's first in a series of fine teams. Cal was outgained 88-134, however, winning on defensive superiority.

CAL 12, NAVY PRE-FLIGHT 6
DECEMBER 6, 1942

The 1942 Golden Bears weren't much to rave about, concluding the regular season with a 4-5 record, posting no significant victories and being walloped in the Big Game, 26-7. At nearby Moraga, the U.S. Navy established a pre-flight training school, and its staff and students included such former collegiate standouts as Cal's Vic Bottari, Stanford's Frankie Albert and Bobby Grayson, Northwestern's Eggs Manske and Notre Dame's Joe Ruetz.

A crowd of 25,000 was in attendance on December 6, 1942, expecting the military men to run roughshod over Cal. A 34-yard pass from Bottari to Manske, who later became an assistant under Pappy Waldorf, gave the Navy squad a 6-0 lead. But in the third period, All-American lineman Bob Reinhard grabbed a 16-yard pass from Grover Klemmer for a tie, and the Bears posted a stunning upset when Gene Pickett bolted 44 yards for a fourth-quarter TD and a 12-6 victory.

The game was the first in a series of eight Cal games against military installations during the war years. The Bears concluded the rivalry with a 6-0 victory over Navy Pre-Flight in 1945, but they were winless in between, dropping one-sided decisions to Navy Pre-Flight in 1943 (39-0) and 1944 (33-6) and to Del Monte Pre-Flight in 1943 (47-8), as an example of the military teams' might.

Vic Bottari (68), a former Cal superstar, was on the other side in the Bears 12-6 victory over Navy Pre-Flight in 1942. Here, he looks for a hole before being dropped by the Bears Jim Jurkovich (22).

All-American Bob Reinhard, better known for his line play and punting, scores on a 16-yard pass play from Grover Klemmer as the Bears stun Navy Pre-Flight, 12-6, in 1942. As he crosses the goal line, Reinhard eludes tackle attempts by ex-Cal All-American Vic Bottari (right) and Santa Clara's Nello Falschi (28).

CAL 16, USC 10
OCTOBER 15, 1949

A crowd of 81,499, including Governor Earl Warren, crammed into Memorial Stadium on October 15, 1949, to watch Cal and USC battle for the inside track to the Rose Bowl. It didn't look good for the Bears, who the previous week lost star halfback Charley Sarver to a knee injury. Cal also was without injured Les Richter and Pete Schabarum.

Bootlegs by quarterback Bob Celeri for 17 and 21 yards and his TD pass to Bob Minahan gave the Bears a 7-0 halftime lead following Jim Cullom's PAT. But the Trojans got going and tied it on Bob Martin's 1-yard plunge and Frank Gifford's kick early in the final period. Gifford then sent USC ahead, 10-7, with a field goal.

When Cal athletic director Brutus Hamilton termed the Bears performance as "athletic beyondness," he must have had the ensuing play in mind. Frank Brunk, a 177-pound halfback, took the kickoff 2 yards deep in the end zone and began a heroic dash to sudden fame. Knocked off balance at the 20 and again at the 25, he stayed afoot and raced to the USC 37, where Gifford was poised for the tackle.

Against Southern Cal in 1949, Frank Brunk, a reserve halfback, registers what is regarded as the most dramatic run in Memorial Stadium history. Early in the fourth quarter, with the Trojans ahead, 10-7, Brunk takes the kickoff 2 yards deep in the end zone to begin his march into the Bear record book. Brunk eludes two tacklers and avoids the diving clutches of Frank Gifford en route to a 102-yard touchdown run, spurring a 16-10 victory.

Gifford made contact, but Brunk shook loose and scooted to the end zone, climaxing a breathtaking, 102-yard touchdown. It tied the longest in Cal history at the time and still is regarded as the most dramatic TD witnessed at Memorial Stadium. Cullom's conversion kick and a safety registered by Ed Bartlett completed the stirring, 16-10 upset and made good on the Bears vow to win one for Charley.

CAL 14, WASHINGTON 7
NOVEMBER 4, 1950

Cal was a one-touchdown underdog for the November 4, 1950, showdown in Seattle with Washington which, like the Bears, was unbeaten in conference play. The odds seemed justified when an interception gave the Huskies the ball on Cal's 41, and quarterback Don Heinrich needed only eight plays to make it 7-0 in the second quarter.

But quarterback Jim Marinos wasn't about to make the same mistake again. Instead, he completed seven of his last nine passes to lead a Cal comeback. A 63-yard march ended with Schabarum's 6-yard TD, and Richter's PAT created a halftime tie. Sophomore fullback Johnny Olszewski went to work in the second

half, and 55,000 Husky fans were sent home disappointed.

Johnny O, who rushed for 119 yards in 16 carries, did the bulk of the work on a third-period drive, and Marinos passed to Schabarum for the winning TD. Defense prevailed the rest of the way, Cal pressuring Heinrich and twice stopping the Huskies inside the Bears 10 in the final period. The 14-7 victory forged Cal's third Rose Bowl trip in as many years.

CAL 14, USC 12
OCTOBER 18, 1958

The 1958 clash with USC on October 18 at the Los Angeles Coliseum was the game that enabled the Bears to turn the corner en route to their last Rose Bowl appearance. It wasn't a great team, but it got the job done. A recovered fumble inside the 10 prefaced Bill Patton's 1-yard run for a 6-0 Cal lead in the first quarter. Joe Kapp then accounted for 69 yards on an 80-yard march, Patton going over from the 2 and adding a two-point conversion run for 14-0 in the second period.

But the Trojans never go down easily. A 95-yard drive ended with Angelo Coia's 3-yard

Gifford

TD run and a 14-6 score at the half. Late in the third period, Don Buford's 20-yard punt return set up a 40-yard drive, quarterback Al Prukop rolling out for a 19-yard TD for 14-12. USC tried to pass for the tying two points, but Kapp — who else? — intercepted.

Adding significance to this win is the fact that Cal failed to defeat the Trojans for the next 11 consecutive games. The Bears came close in 1964, losing with 50 seconds to go at the Coliseum, but they didn't snap the hex until they returned to Los Angeles and posted a 13-10 upset behind giant-killer Dave Penhall in 1970.

CAL 21, MICHIGAN 7
SEPTEMBER 21, 1968

Cal traveled to Michigan for an intersectional match early in the 1968 season, and Gary Fowler's three touchdowns and a stellar defensive effort there paved the way for the Bears first winning season since 1958. The veteran Wolverines were heavily favored in the season

opener, played on September 21, but they were stung 5:57 into the game when Fowler's 13-yard TD capped a drive which featured passes by quarterback Randy Humphries to Wayne Stewart and Paul Williams.

The first of three Ron Miller conversions made it 7-0, and it quickly was 14-0 when Fowler scored from the 6 with 1:32 to go in the opening period. Tight end Jim Mandich's 8-yard TD pass from Dennis Brown gave 71,386 Michigan fans hope, making it 14-7 at the half. But Fowler's 6-yard TD and Miller's kick increased Cal's lead to the final 21-7 in the fourth quarter.

Fowler gained 78 yards in 18 carries to outshine Michigan All-American candidate Ron Johnson, who was limited to 48 yards in 21 tries by a Bear Minimum defense. Linebacker Irby Augustine registered 13 tackles, and safety Ken Wiedemann accounted for 11 of the winners' 16 pass deflections. The Bears outrushed Michigan, 240-99, and actually had an easier time with the

Between blocks by Frank Sally (70) and Jeff Snow (74), Billy Patton (with ball) squirms over from the 2 for Cal's final touchdown in a 14-12 squeaker over Southern Cal in 1958. Patton accounted for all the Bears points with two touchdowns and a two-point conversion. Quarterback Joe Kapp (22) watches the action after his handoff.

Wolverines than with the plane ride home. A faulty tail section forced a landing at Denver, where emergency vehicles lined the airport and created a few moments of tension before the pilot performed a smooth landing to much applause.

CAL 28, USC 14
NOVEMBER 1, 1975

Mike White struggled through a shaky beginning as Cal's coach, but it was all worth it because of what happened against USC on a crisp November afternoon in 1975 before 51,871 at Memorial Stadium. After all the years of frustration, the Bears finally were in a Rose Bowl race, and the fact that USC had not tasted defeat in 18 games merely added to the emotion and intensity of this nationally televised game.

Wesley Walker's 16-yard pass from Joe Roth opened the scoring, but Ricky Bell's 12-yard run created a 7-7 halftime tie. Roth passed 4 yards to George Freitas, only to have Vince Evans

dash 30 yards for 14-14 at the end of three quarters. Then Roth's 1-yard run, Tom Newton's 11-yard TD and the last of four Jim Breech conversions capped a magnificent triumph — Cal 28, USC 14 — Cal's finest hour of the exciting seventies.

In the game within a game, Chuck Muncie outplayed Bell in a battle of All-American backs. Muncie rushed for 143 yards in 18 carries and caught five passes for 62 yards, while Bell totaled 121 yards in 27 carries. Roth completed 19 of 31 passes for 244 yards, and Steve Rivera caught nine passes for 131 yards. The Bears rolled up 477 yards, and linebacker Phil Heck was the hero of a dynamic goal-line stand.

By the time the two clubs met again in Berkeley, the courageous Roth had succumbed to cancer. Within nine months, the first Joe Roth Memorial Game was played, and 76,780 jammed Memorial Stadium on October 29, 1977, as Charlie Young and Paul Jones powered a 17-14 Cal upset.

Tom Newton (33) breaks loose for an 11-yard touchdown, the final tally in Cal's 28-14 upset of Southern Cal in 1975. Quarterback Joe Roth (background) thrusts his hands upward anticipating the referee's signal.

CHAPTER
3

100
YEARS
1882
1982

CAL
BLVE
AND
GOLD

All-American center-linebacker Bob Herwig, recovering
fumble, was the defensive standout of the 1938 Rose
Bowl victory over Alabama. Herwig thwarted the
Crimson Tide with an interception on the Cal 6
early in the game and later pounced on this fumble
by Alabama's Herschel Mosely on the Bears 2. The
recovery prevented a 'Bama score in Cal's 13-0 shutout.

Chapter Three
ROSES AND THORNS

Mention bowl games and Cal fans probably would just as soon change the subject. The Golden Bears, you see, have appeared in nine bowls and have a 2-6-1 record to show for them. In fact, they haven't tasted post-season victory for more than 40 years — not since the Thunder Team blanked Alabama at the Rose Bowl in 1938.

CAL 28, OHIO STATE 0
1921 ROSE BOWL

Its record notwithstanding, Cal has contributed greatly to bowl lore. You name it, the Bears probably have done it, while applying Murphy's Law to post-season play. If something can go wrong in a bowl game, the Bears have shown that it probably will — against them!

How else can one explain the stunning scoreless tie in 1922, when Washington & Jefferson stumped the Wonder Team? Or Roy Riegels' infamous wrong-way run in 1929 against Georgia Tech? Or Pappy Waldorf's three consecutive losses by a total of 17 points? Or Temple's 1979 upset in the Garden State Bowl, the only time Cal appeared in a bowl game other than the Rose?

Indeed, the Bears have had their share of bad luck in such games, but there have been numerous highlights, too.

Going back through history to the 1921 Rose Bowl, then still called the East-West Game (not to be confused with the unborn charity Shrine Game), undefeated powerhouses from Cal and Ohio State clashed in what ranks among the most historically significant post-season contests. Although the Golden Bears had trampled their opposition by a collective 482-14 while fashioning an 8-0 record, the Buckeyes came west with a 7-0 record and a 150-20 scoring bulge and were made an 8-5 betting favorite.

The preposterous odds underscored the fact that West Coast football wasn't respected in the East, despite recent bowl triumphs by Washington State and Oregon. The prevailing attitude was that the Western style of play was inferior, which undoubtedly accounted for the fact that Walter Camp didn't see fit to name a West Coast athlete to his All-America squad until the 1920 Wonder Team embarrassed him into doing so.

Interest in the game was so rabid, 100,000 tickets could have been sold. But Tournament Park, or Exhibition Park as it also was called, had only a 42,000 capacity. So some phony

An unidentified Cal player punches toward the goal line in this action from the 1921 Rose Bowl against Ohio State.

tickets were printed, creating a furor, and by the time the anxious crowd was seated, the Golden Bears already had begun asserting themselves against the best the East had to offer.

Cal received the kickoff, but the Bears were forced to punt. Archie Nisbet's boot sailed high and far to Ohio State All-American Pete Stinchcomb. Brick Muller and Brodie Stephens rushed downfield and reached Stinchcomb before the ball did. Instead of signaling for a fair catch, Stinchcomb elected to test the Bears defensive might.

It was a mistake. Muller hit him high and Stephens went downstairs. The resulting contact jarred the ball loose from the startled Stinchcomb, and Cal's Fat Latham recovered on the Ohio State 28. Muller's 13-yard reception of a Pesky Sprott pass was the key gain, and Sprott scored three plays later. Crip Toomey's kick made it 7-0.

Ohio State drove to Cal's 8 on the next series, but Hoge Workman's fumble was retrieved by Muller, ending the threat. The Bears couldn't move, so Nisbet sent a punt soaring 62 yards from scrimmage to the Buckeyes 32. Early in the second quarter, the most memorable play of the game unfolded, bringing Muller instant national fame and completely demoralizing Ohio State.

Cal earned a first down on the Buckeyes 39, and Nisbet bulled for 2 yards to the 37 and feigned an injury to set off some Wonder Team trickery that had been well-rehearsed. While Nisbet was on the ground, his teammates casually strolled into formation. Suddenly, Nisbet was on his feet, stooping to flip the ball back to Sprott.

He faked a run and pitched back to Muller, coming around from left end. Muller moved laterally and backwards to his right until he reached the Cal 47. Stephens, meanwhile, raced downfield, deep into Ohio State territory. As he passed Stinchcomb, the Buckeyes safety supposedly asked, "Just where do you think you're going?"

Seconds later, Stephens caught Muller's line-drive, diagonal pass on the goal line and took it over for an unprecedented touchdown. "I simply didn't believe anybody could throw the ball that far," said a disbelieving Stinchcomb. Press-box exaggeration turned it into a record-shattering 70-yard play.

"It's my recollection the play started on Ohio State's 38," Sprott later said, "I handled the ball some 10 yards back of the line of scrimmage before flipping it to Muller, who dropped back another 15 yards before throwing it to Stephens on the goal line." Simple math makes it a 63-yard pass by that account, but exhaustive research by Los Angeles sportswriter Maxwell

Stiles 20 years later officially established it as a 53-yard gain.

Sprott's touchdown and Toomey's third conversion made it 21-0 at the half. Karl Deeds' TD and Charley Erb's PAT concluded the scoring in the fourth quarter at 28-0, but it was the amazing Muller strike that commanded all the attention. Ironically, it took a forward pass to make people take notice of Muller, who is recognized as one of the greatest ends of all time.

Muller also completed a 55-yard pass in the game, but it was disallowed because Cal was ruled to have had only six men at the line of scrimmage. Muller completed three passes and caught three others. Defensively, he terrorized Stinchcomb with sure tackling. The Bears rushed for 244 yards and outgained the Buckeyes, 346-238.

The Western Conference, which later became the Big Ten, didn't take the stinging defeat lightly. It refused to play in the Rose Bowl until the Big Ten signed its pact with the PCC in 1947. Historically speaking, the 1921 East-West Game earned new respect for West Coast football. What Cal achieved that day opened new avenues for the region, which continued to produce great teams and its share, at last, of All-Americans.

CAL 0, WASHINGTON & JEFFERSON 0 1922 ROSE BOWL

Ohio State had underestimated the Bears the year before, but the West Coast obviously hadn't learned a lesson from that experience. Perhaps influenced by the battering of the Buckeyes and a whopping Wonder Team 312-33 scoring advantage during the 1921 campaign, the West generally ridiculed the selection of Washington & Jefferson as Cal's opponent in 1922. Western writers didn't know the difference between Washington & Jefferson and William & Mary, and that ignorance was to prove embarrassing.

"All I know about Washington & Jefferson is that they're both dead," wrote a columnist. The Presidents disparagingly were referred to as Willie & Jake, and much criticism was directed at their coach, Greasy Neale, who was relatively new at coaching football while concentrating on his major league baseball career. But W & J came to Pasadena with a 10-0 record, outscoring its opponents 222-33 and posting six shutouts.

Andy Smith didn't take the Presidents lightly. The field was reduced to a quagmire by steady rain, and on the eve of the game, the Cal coach predicted the 0-0 outcome. In fact, his Bears were fortunate to get a tie. They gained only 49 yards and two first downs, and a 36-yard touchdown run by W & J's Wayne Brenkert was nullified because of holding by All-American Russ Stein away from the ball.

Neale and his squad applied psychological warfare to add to the Bears frustration. It may not have affected the results, but it showed Cal's players that two could play that game. The crafty Berkeleyans, remember, had resorted to some trickery to set up the famous Muller-to-Stephens pass in 1921. The W & J mind-games definitely left an impression on Cal halfback Don Nichols.

"I'll never forget them," he said years later. "They were a bunch of tough monkeys and they were mighty cute at getting us off our guard. Stein fixed me up beautifully. We were lining up on offense when he looked my way and said, 'Say, Nichols, don't you have an uncle in Pittsburgh?' I told him no, but he persisted, saying the man was a dead ringer for me. I was paying no attention to the game because a fictitious Pittsburgh uncle was on my mind."

Muller, however, was the object of most of the shenanigans. The All-American end suffered all season from an assortment of ailments and injuries, so he didn't start. But he wanted to play and was inserted in the second period, conspicuous with a clean uniform while the other players were caked with mud. The W & J

Cal defenders pursue a Washington & Jefferson running back in action from the 1922 Rose Bowl, nearly drowning a blocker in the process. On a field flooded by heavy rains, the best the Bears could manage was a 0-0 tie against the Presidents.

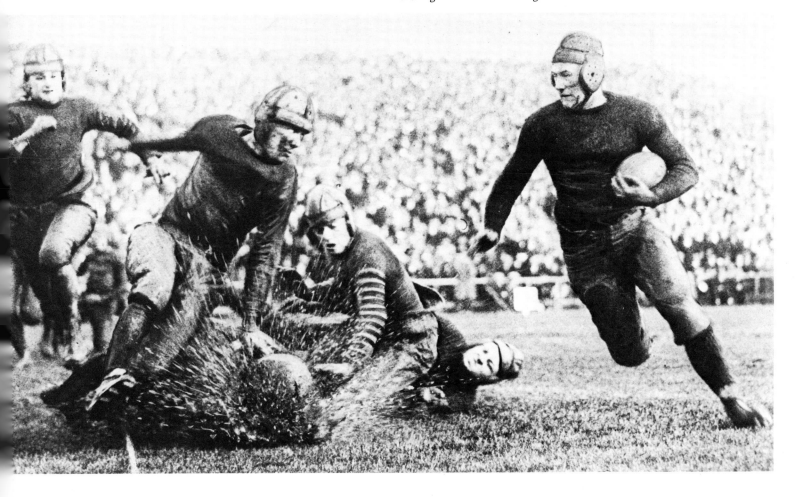

players immediately surrounded the Bears superstar and mocked awe.

"So this is the great Brick Muller — we are deeply impressed," said Presidents end Herb Kopf. "We are humble in the presence of the great Muller. May I introduce myself?" The diminutive Kopf then walked up to Brick and wiped his muddy hands on Muller's jersey. The other W & J players followed suit, one of the cracking, "Now we can go home and tell Mother we've touched an All-American."

Brick's face was as red as his hair, but the big Bear showed remarkable restraint, perhaps being cooled by the steady drizzle. The verbal jabs continued, however. Later in the game, Kopf asked Muller if he thought it was going to continue raining. "How should I know?" Brick snapped. "I thought you would," Kopf said, "because you've been on your back all afternoon."

To be sure, little went right for Cal that afternoon. The Bears salvaged a tie only because of an official's call and the booming punts of Nisbet, who averaged 39.7 yards on 13 kicks. It was the last East-West Game played at Tournament Park, and W & J halfback Swede Erickson earned the distinction of playing in the post-season classic for two different teams, previously appearing with Great Lakes against Mare Island during World War I.

GEORGIA TECH 8, CAL 7
1929 ROSE BOWL

If Muller thought he had it rough in 1922, his treatment was mild compared to the humiliation suffered by Roy Riegels against Georgia Tech in 1929. His misdirected dash gave him ignominious distinction and the nickname, "Wrong Way Riegels," overshadowing his accomplishments as an All-American player. Muller seldom was reminded of his experience, but Riegels lived with the memory of his for more than 50 years after it happened.

Cal, which had been snubbed by the Rose Bowl Committee when it won the conference championship in 1922, discovered that justice was served following the 1928 campaign. Undefeated USC was the champion, but the Trojans were at odds with the Rose Bowl brass, and the Bears were selected after going 6-1-2 and posting six shutouts. Tech was 9-0, outscoring foes 213-40, including four blankings.

The most famous Rose Bowl play of all occurred in the second quarter of a scoreless tie. Tech had a first down on its own 25. Halfback Stumpy Thomason took a handoff and burst through the left side of the line to the 30, where he was hit hard by Benny Lom, the Cal safety. The ball squirted from Thomason's grasp

and bounced in front of Riegels, who was pursuing the play.

Riegels scooped up the ball and started running to his right, but two Tech tacklers were in his path. He turned sharply to avoid being hit and suddenly saw daylight. Thoughts of a touchdown raced through his mind, so Riegels started streaking toward the end zone. Unfortunately, it was the wrong end zone.

"What's the matter with me? Am I crazy?" blurted famous radio announcer Graham McNamee, one of the few people who immediately realized something was screwy. Many of the 66,404 spectators didn't. Nor did some of the Golden Bears. Tackle Steve Bancroft yelled to guard Bert Schwarz, "Boy, am I glad I didn't pick up that fumble!" Schwarz asked why. "If I had the ball," Bancroft replied, "I'd have run the other way!"

So confused were some of the Bears, they instinctively began blocking for Riegels. Lom, however, realized what was happening and took off after his turned-around teammate, pleading for him to stop. "You're going the wrong way!"

The infamous, 66-yard Wrong Way run by Roy Riegels commanded the most attention following Georgia Tech's 8-7 decision over Cal in the 1929 Rose Bowl. Riegels (with arrow) approaches the loose ball, gets twisted around and takes off in the wrong direction while being pursued by teammate Benny Lom (28), whose hit on Tech's Stumpy Thomason had caused the fateful fumble. The freak play resulted in a Georgia Tech safety, providing the winning points for the Yellow Jackets.

Lom shouted while gaining ground on Riegels. But the din of the crowd and earflaps made it impossible for Riegels to hear.

"I didn't use my head," Lom said as he recalled those frantic moments. "I tried to shout to Roy instead of tackling him. I was much faster than he was, but I wasted my breath hollering at him. I found I couldn't run and shout at the same time. If I hadn't tried to yell, I could have nailed him on the 20."

Instead, Lom finally reached Riegels at the 10. But Roy shook him off, shouting, "Get away from me — this is my touchdown!" Lom lunged at his irrational teammate again, got a hand on him at the 3, and finally stopped him at the 1. A Tech tackler bowled over the Bears and sent them into the end zone, but the official ruled the ball dead at the Cal 1. Riegels had completed a 66-yard run — the wrong way.

The Bears immediately went into punt formation, and Lom took the snap deep in the end zone. Tech tackle Vance Maree blocked the kick, and the ball shot straight up. Cal's Stan

Barr gained control long enough before the ball rolled out of the end zone, and Georgia Tech was awarded a safety and a 2-0 lead.

Late in the same period, with the ball on Cal's 35, Lom grabbed a Tech fumble in the air and bolted 65 yards to a touchdown. But referee Herb Dana ruled that the ball was dead before the fumble, nullifying the run and leaving Tech ahead, 2-0, at the half. Riegels, who had been on the bench in tears, was being consoled by his teammates as they ran off the field.

"Roy was a great kid," assistant coach Clint Evans recalled. "He could have alibied, but he didn't. I asked him if he had gotten a bump on the head and he shook his head. He just said he'd made one helluva mistake. Nibs (Price) put him back in the game for the second half and Roy was brilliant."

Tech center Peter Pund, who outweighted Riegels by 20 pounds, agreed. "That was a tough break for Riegels, but don't ever get the idea he isn't a wonderful center," the Engineers All-American said. "He's the best I've played

against all season. He's a battler and he never quit. Some boys might have folded up after that situation, but Riegels didn't. I admire him for it."

On the series following a heroic goal-line stand by Cal in the third quarter, Thomason's 14-yard run increased Tech's lead to 8-0. With 1:15 remaining in the bizarre contest, Lom passed to All-American end Irv Phillips for a 10-yard touchdown, and Barr booted the extra point for a final 8-7 verdict in the zaniest and most discussed Rose Bowl game ever played.

Wrote Warren Brown, a Bay Area native working in Chicago: "In a game that must take its place among the comical football classics of all time, Georgia Tech, champion of all the South, cuffed down some of the claims of Pacific Coast supremacy with a 8 to 7 victory over California in the annual intersectional uprising today. No game that was ever played before in the long series of Tournament of Roses spectacles ever offered the wild and woolly aspect of this contest."

Amen. For on that particular day, everything seemed to work against the Bears, as usually has been their custom in bowl games. In addition to Riegels' regrettable dash, there was a misplacement of the ball costing Cal 10 yards

and a Lom kick blocked by Maree whereby the ball deflated. But at least most of the Bears could forget about the game and go about their business. Riegels couldn't.

He received offers for all sorts of wrong-way promotions, ranging from backward walkathons to upside-down cakes. Constantly the brunt of jokes, Riegels cut short a coaching career and went into private business. "I was sensitive about it for a long time," Riegels said, "But everyone else thought it was funny, so I finally decided all I could do was laugh with them."

CAL 13, ALABAMA 0
1938 ROSE BOWL

Alabama came to Pasadena in 1938 with an enviable Rose Bowl record, never tasting defeat and outscoring opponents 80-39 in four games, including a 7-7 tie with Stanford in 1927. The Thunder Team was 9-0-1, and the Crimson Tide was 9-0, clobbering foes 225-20 and registering six shutouts. A crowd of 90,000 assembled to watch this clash of titans.

Unlike Cal's previous post-season games — and its next three — there was no controversy, just plain hard football. The mechanical precision of the Thunder Team wasn't spectacular, but it was effective, and Alabama

Vic Bottari (92) reels off a 14-yard run in the 1938 Rose Bowl. He gets his initial block from quarterback Johnny Meek (left), who hurled his body toward 'Bama end Tut Erwin (15). Up ahead, fullback Dave Anderson (56) is ready to clear the way, along with All-American end Perry Schwartz (under Anderson's arm). Bottari scored both touchdowns in Cal's 13-0 victory.

really never had a chance. The Bears scored twice, and their stout defense took over from there for Cal's third shutout in four Rose Bowl appearances.

All-American center-linebacker Bob Herwig got the Bears going with an interception on the Cal 6. Taking no chances, Sam Chapman punted on first down, sending one high and long. Perry Schwartz bulled downfield under a head of steam and knocked a blocker into the ball carrier causing him to fumble. Schwartz recovered at the Cal 39.

The ensuing 61-yard march featured the powerful running of Chapman and Vic Bottari. A 13-yard run by Bottari was the big gainer, and Chapman darted 7 yards to the 4, where it was third-and-goal. Bottari cut over tackle and scored. Chapman's PAT made it 7-0 at the half.

Alabama took the second-half kickoff, but a fumble on the second play gave Cal the ball on the 'Bama 45. The Bears drove to the 12, but a 15-yard penalty pushed them back to the 27. Bottari then was thrown for a 14-yard loss to the 41, and Cal was forced to punt. But the Bears held and got the ball back on the Tide 47. Chapman's 12-yard reverse made the most thunder, and Bottari again scored from the 4 for the final 13-0.

Vic Bottari, who was the rushing standout for Cal's 1937 Thunder Team, scores his first of two touchdowns in the 13-0 Rose Bowl rout of Alabama in 1938. Bottari's TDs each covered 4 yards.

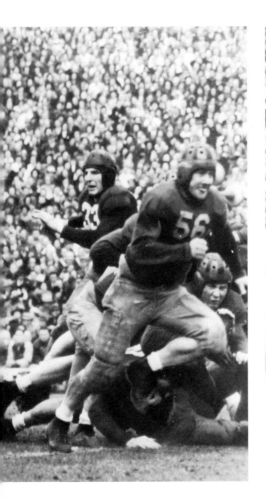

NORTHWESTERN 20, CAL 14
1949 ROSE BOWL

Northwestern came into the 1949 Rose Bowl a six and one-half point favorite, and a crowd of 93,000 showed up to witness one of the most exciting Rose Bowl games in history — one which had a little of everything, from great plays to controversy to a classic student-pupil coaching clash. The Wildcats Bob Voights, at 31 the youngest man to coach a team at the Rose Bowl, played under Lynn Waldorf at Northwestern before Pappy headed west.

It was billed as a match of wits between the two men and a clash of vaunted running attacks featuring the Bears Jackie Jensen and Jack Swaner against the Wildcats trio of Frank Aschenbrenner, Ed Tunnicliff and Art Murakowski. They didn't disappoint. Northwestern rushed for 273 yards, Cal added 173, and the spectators were treated to the two longest runs in Rose Bowl history.

The annual event never had seen such sustained action. Midway through the opening period, Aschenbrenner sliced through left tackle, bolted through a converging Cal secondary and dashed a record 73 yards for the first touchdown. Jim Farrar's PAT made it 7-0. Swaner returned the kickoff from the end zone to the 33, where Jensen circled left end, cut inside and smashed through a swarm of tacklers for a 67-yard scoring burst. Jim Cullom's conversion kick made it 7-7.

Despite those long gallops, the game probably was decided on a controversial 1-yard TD in the second quarter. The Wildcats drove to the Cal 1, and Murakowski crashed through the left side, fumbling when hit by Norm Pressley. Referee Jimmy Cain, however, ruled Murakowski had crossed the goal line before losing the football, thereby giving Northwestern a 13-7 lead (the kick was missed) over the loud howls of the Bears and their supporters.

There apparently was some justification for the complaints. Movies and still pictures supported Cal's claim as the controversy raged for weeks following the game. One of the loudest protests was registered by Cal's Will Lotter, who recovered the fumble in the end zone. But field judge Jay Berwanger, the first Heisman Trophy

This photograph portrays the Rose parade — 1949 style.

Cal's one-two punch of Jack Swaner and Jackie Jensen went to work quickly in the 1949 Rose Bowl against Northwestern. Swaner (13) returns a kickoff from the Bears end zone to the Cal 33 while Jensen (36) keeps his eyes on the play. On first down, Jensen circled left end and cut back across the field for a 67-yard TD run, helping to tie the game at 7-7. Jensen later was injured and didn't return to action as Northwestern posted a 20-14 triumph.

winner, was standing on the goal line and instantly signaled a touchdown.

"I'll bet my life Murakowski was over the goal line by two feet," insisted Northwestern's George Maddock. "What's more, I recovered the fumble in the end zone, Lotter didn't." Murakowski insisted he was over the goal line with the football and fumbled while being pushed back.

"I was across the goal line with the ball," he recalled, "then someone grabbed me from behind and pulled me back. That's when I fumbled and that's the action the still pictures show."

The possible bad break notwithstanding, Cal had its chances to win the game. It didn't seem that way when Jensen suffered a cramp on his first carry of the third quarter, but the Bears played like men possessed without their Golden Boy. Frank Brunk, Jensen's substitute, made some great runs on an 83-yard march late in the period, and Swaner scored from the 4 for 13-13. Cullom's kick gave the Bears a one-point lead.

Cal's momentum continued in the early stages of the fourth quarter, with a pass from Dick Erickson to John Cunningham just missing near the Northwestern goal line. The Wildcats took

In one of the most controversial plays in Rose Bowl history, referee Jimmy Cain ruled that Northwestern's Art Murakowski fumbled the ball after crossing the goal line, thereby giving the Wildcats a touchdown in their 20-14 victory over Cal in 1949. The two sequences show Murakowski losing the ball after being tackled by Norm Pressley. Murakowski's feet clearly hadn't reached the goal line, but Cain judged that the ball crossed the goal line while still in the Wildcat's possession.

over on their 12 with time running out and 88 yards to go. Tunnicliff was hit hard by Stormy Hileman on first down, and he fumbled — but, again, it was ruled too late.

Given another chance moments later, Tunnicliff became the game's hero. The Wildcats worked the ball to Cal's 43. Tunnicliff took the long snap from center and raced down the left sideline for the touchdown that shocked the Bears and lifted the Wildcats to a 19-14 lead with 2:59 remaining. Farrar's conversion made it a final 20-14 as Bob Celeri's desperation passes failed, and the valiant losers left the field muttering about Murakowski, Aschenbrenner and Tunnicliff, who helped the winners rush for 273 yards.

OHIO STATE 17, CAL 14
1950 ROSE BOWL

Going into the 1950 Rose Bowl, Cal was regarded as the finest postwar PCC team. With a 10-0 record, the Bears figured to end the Big Ten's dominance of the game. The Buckeyes came west with a 6-1-2 mark and were the underdogs, but Celeri's luckless afternoon

extended Waldorf's Pasadena jinx. Instead of losing with 2:59 to go, as they had the previous year, the Bears were edged out on Jim Hague's 17-yard field goal with 1:57 remaining.

There was no major controversy in this one, but the 100,963 spectators saw their share of Cal mistakes. Celeri was off to a good start, connecting with Brunk for a 54-yard, second-period pass that set up Jim Monachino's 7-yard TD. Cullom's toe gave the Bears a 7-0 halftime lead.

Then, Vic Janowicz, a Heisman Trophy winner, intercepted a Celeri pass and returned 36 yards to Cal's 30. Fred "Curly" Morrison eventually bulled over from the 2, and Hague's kick created a 7-7 tie. Three minutes later, Celeri was back to punt on Cal's 26. Bill Trautwein blocked the kick, and teammate Jack Lininger recovered the ball and carried it to the 6. On fourth-and-goal from the 2, Jerry Krall scored, Hague's PAT kick sailed through the goal posts, and Ohio State took the lead, 14-7.

Monachino then stunned the Buckeyes with a 44-yard touchdown run, and Cullom's kick made it 14-all. Early in the final period, Brunk's

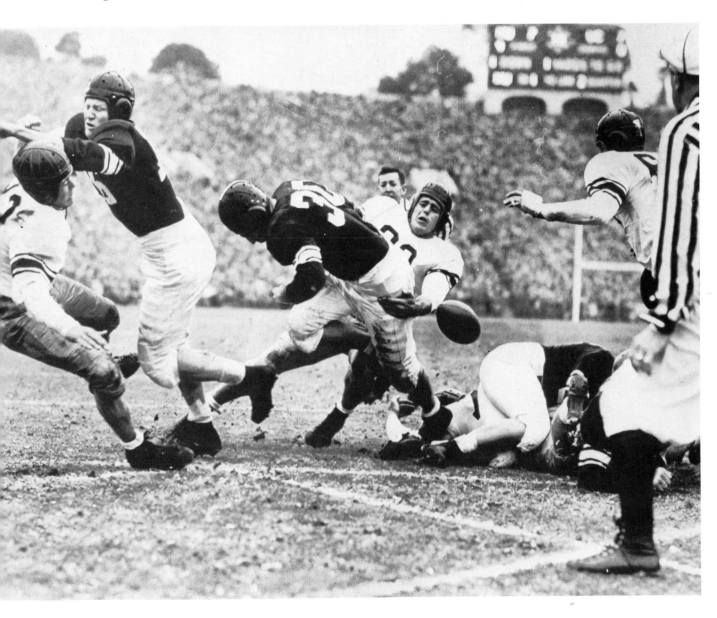

running carried Cal to the Ohio State 26, but the drive bogged down. Just as they were sure of victory, as they had been the year before, the luckless Bears suddenly had things go wrong.

This time it happened when Celeri was on his 16, prepared to punt. A low snap from center and a hard-charging Buckeyes line changed the complexion of the game. Celeri, trapped, ran desperately to his left and tried to get a kick off left-footed. It didn't work. The ball glanced off his foot and bounced out of bounds on the 13. Cal relinquished only 1 yard in three downs, but Hague's boot on fourth down broke the tie and, for the second straight year, the hearts of Old Blues. Final score: Ohio State 17, California 14.

MICHIGAN 14, CAL 6
1951 ROSE BOWL

The Big Ten had a four-game winning streak at Pasadena, but the experts seemed to think it was time for Cal finally to end the nonsense in 1951. After all, the Bears entered the game 9-0-1, outscoring opponents 218-76. Michigan, on the other hand, didn't field one of its better teams. The Wolverines were 2-3-1 at one point of the season before rallying to win their last three.

Most of the controversy in this one centered around the luckless Waldorf and his strategy, because the Bears once again went down to narrow defeat, and critics around the nation demanded the Big Ten pull out of its Rose Bowl contract and find a more representative rival. Poor Pappy. If things had broken right, Cal would have enjoyed at least an 18-0 halftime

lead, and the outcome might have been different.

As it were, Cal broke out of the gate emotionally charged. The Wolverines didn't touch the ball for 10 minutes. On the third play of the game, the Bears Pete Schabarum went all the way on a 73-yard run, but the play was nullified by a man-in-motion penalty. Cal eventually marched to the Michigan 15, but a fumble turned the ball over.

On their next possession, the Bears went ahead, 6-0, in the second quarter on a 39-yard pass from Jim Marinos to Bob Cummings. Cal continued to dominate the half, penetrating the Michigan 10 in the final minute. It was third-and-two on the 3 when Monachino, with good blocking and a clear field, slipped and lost a yard. On fourth down, Schabarum was stopped cold, and the Wolverines left the half trailing only 6-0.

"Had Monachino kept his footing, he'd have been a cinch to score," claimed field judge Lloyd Larson. "He had clear sailing through a big, open hole." Instead, he fell, and Pappy was chastized by the press for sending Schabarum through the line on fourth down instead of going for the chip-shot field goal and a possible 9-0 lead.

Michigan, which was outgained 192-65 and trailed in first downs 10-2 in the first half, completely turned the tables after the intermission. Down the stretch, the Wolverines showed a 226-52 yardage advantage and made 15 first downs to Cal's two. Quarterback Chuck Ortmann and fullback Don Dufek proved the

Carl Van Heuit was named All-America at defensive back in 1950. Twice honored as Cal's outstanding defensive player in the Rose Bowl, he also was a dangerous punt-returner, ranking third in career and season average return.

Cal's Jim Monachino (35) bolts for a 7-yard touchdown run against Ohio State in the 1950 Rose Bowl. Monachino takes the pitch from quarterback Bob Celeri (22) and gets key blocks from halfback Pete Schabarum (32) and guard Ray DeJong to break loose. The second-quarter TD gave Cal a 7-0 lead, but despite another Monachino score, the Bears lost on a late field goal, 17-14.

difference against a bunch of Bears possibly emotionally spent following their first-half frustration.

The third quarter was scoreless, but Michigan had established ball control with runs and screen passes. An 80-yard march in the final period ended when Dufek plunged over the goal line from one foot away. Harry Allis' conversion earned a 7-6 lead with 5:37 left to play. A fourth-down gamble by the Bears failed on their 13, and within three plays, Dufek had scored from the 7. Allis' kick concluded the scoring at 14-6.

Ortmann's short passes baffled the Bears, and the Michigan leader clicked on 15 of 19 for 146 yards. As Morrison had done the year before (113 yards in 25 carries), fullback Dufek pounded the Bears for 113 yards in 23 tries. Coach Bennie Oosterbaan's boys rolled up 291 yards after a sluggish start, and he called it "our best game of the season" — a small consolation to the jinxed Bears.

IOWA 38, CAL 12
1959 ROSE BOWL

Moving on to the 1959 Rose Bowl, at least the Bears were true to form for a change. They were expected to crumble before the powerful Big Ten champs, and they did, giving the Midwesterners their 12th triumph in 13 Rose Bowl games. Hawkeyes coach Forrest Evashevski was flu-ridden with a 101-degree temperature on the eve of the game, but there was nothing the matter with an Iowa squad which set four Rose Bowl records in the gross mismatch.

The Hawkeyes shattered marks for rushing yardage — 429 — and total offense — 516. Halfback Bob Jeter erased Aschenbrenner's record with an 81-yard touchdown run, and his total of 194 yards in nine carries — 21.6 — wiped out Bobby Grayson's 1934 record of 151 yards for Stanford against Columbia.

"I never saw so many players go by me so fast in my life," admitted Cal quarterback Joe

Cal's Bob Cummings (white jersey) grabs a 39-yard scoring pass from Jim Marinos to give the Bears a 6-0 lead over Michigan in the 1951 Rose Bowl. The defender is Don Dufek, whose two second-half touchdowns powered the Wolverines 14-6 victory.

Halfback Grover Garvin (15) shoots through a
hole with the help of a block by Frank Sally (70) at
the 1959 Rose Bowl. The Bears Terry Jones (right) is
the downfield blocker.

Kapp, whose fiery temper erupted prior to the game when it had been suggested that the 7-3 Bears didn't have a chance. Cal coach Pete Elliott, probably aware that his smallish line couldn't handle the Iowa forward wall, understated, "Iowa could move the ball ... if they're not great, they're close to it."

With 298-pound Mac Lewis tearing apart the Cal line, Iowa marched to a 20-0 halftime lead on quarterback Randy Duncan's 1-yard sneak, Duncan's 7-yard TD toss to Jeff Langston and Don Horn's 4-yard run. Jeter's 81-yard burst and Willie Fleming's runs of 37 and 7 yards for the Hawkeyes added three TDs in the second half. Jack Hart scored both of the Bears touchdowns, on a 1-yard run and on a 17-yard pass from Kapp, but those 12 points didn't even come close to Iowa's total of 38.

TEMPLE 28, CAL 17
1979 GARDEN STATE BOWL

The 6-5 Golden Bears (later changed to 7-4 because of a forfeit) hadn't been to a bowl game in more than 20 years. So they quickly accepted an invitation to play in the Garden State Bowl at the Meadowlands, home of the New York Giants, on December 15, 1979. Favored Cal didn't seem to take Temple seriously, but Owls coach Wayne Hardin, a former UOP player, came up with some wrinkles to forge a 21-0 first-quarter lead and hold off the Bears.

Temple scored on its first three possessions, using inside traps and misdirection plays to stump a Cal defense which had been stingy in the opening period all year. The sleeping Bears finally awakened in the second quarter, and All-American quarterback Rich Campbell threw TD passes of 12 yards to Matt Bouza and 14 yards to Joe Rose, chalking up 14 for the Bears and making it 21-14 at the half.

A Campbell-to-Bouza pass on the first play of the final period netted 47 yards to the Temple 25, but the Bears had to settle for a 34-yard Mick Luckhurst field goal, cutting the Owls edge to 21-17 with 9:30 to go. Temple came back, however, with a strong ground game and scored the clinching touchdown with 6:47 remaining. Cal outgained Temple 381-264, and Campbell completed 25 passes for 241 yards, eight to Rose and seven to Bouza. But the final outcome, 28-17, kept Cal winless in post-season competition since 1938.

Halfback Jack Hart, Cal's bright spot in a 38-12 loss to Iowa at the 1959 Rose Bowl, makes this catch inside the 5 as teammate Tom Bates looks on from the end zone. Hart scored on a 1-yard run and on a 17-yard pass from Joe Kapp.

Rich Campbell tried to rally Cal with 25 completions for 241 yards, but the 21-0 lead that Temple built in the first quarter was too much to overcome as the Owls prevailed, 28-17, in the 1979 Garden State Bowl.

CHAPTER
4

100 YEARS
1882
1982

CAL
BLVE
AND
GOLD

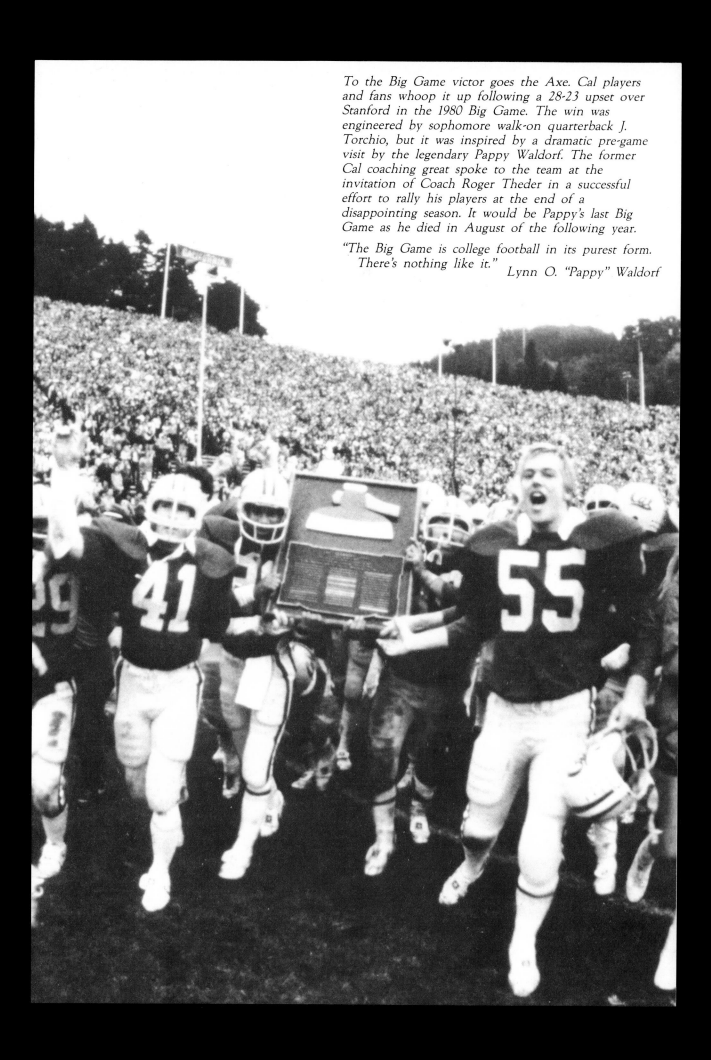

To the Big Game victor goes the Axe. Cal players and fans whoop it up following a 28-23 upset over Stanford in the 1980 Big Game. The win was engineered by sophomore walk-on quarterback J. Torchio, but it was inspired by a dramatic pre-game visit by the legendary Pappy Waldorf. The former Cal coaching great spoke to the team at the invitation of Coach Roger Theder in a successful effort to rally his players at the end of a disappointing season. It would be Pappy's last Big Game as he died in August of the following year.

"The Big Game is college football in its purest form. There's nothing like it."
Lynn O. "Pappy" Waldorf

Chapter Four
THE BIG GAME

When Stanford opened its doors at Palo Alto in September of 1891, a small faction at Berkeley greeted the news with as much enthusiasm as the Peninsula school. The Golden Bears, you see, already were serious about their football, but they had no worthy opponent with which to establish a traditional rivalry, as was the custom in the Ivy League.

Roy Gallagher, who was to be the Bears manager in 1892, immediately issued a challenge to Stanford, requesting a game on Thanksgiving Day of 1891. Stanford sensibly elected to wait until it formed a football team and agreed to stage the historic first meeting between the schools at the field on Haight and Stanyan streets in San Francisco on March 18, 1892.

Each team brushed up by beating local high schools and losing to the Olympic Club. One of the prep teams, Berkeley Gymnasium, was routed 30-0 by the Bears. When Stanford played the same school, a few Cal players managed to don Berkeley Gymnasium uniforms, hoping for a first-hand scouting report. Stanford was wise to the ploy and stayed with basic plays.

When the big day arrived, nobody had imagined the interest created by the historic first match. The field had a 15,000 capacity, but only 10,000 tickets were printed, and they went fast. Herbert C. Hoover, later to become the 31st President of the United States, handled business affairs that day and diligently watched for gate-crashers.

The two teams were transported from plush San Francisco hotels in tallyhos, and high enthusiasm was generated as they marched onto the field. But when referee Jack Sherrard called captains George Foulks of Cal and John Whittemore of Stanford together for the coin toss, an oversight was detected: in all the pre-game excitement, no one had thought to bring a football!

As luck would have it, a sporting goods dealer was in attendance. He hopped on his horse and rode downtown to fetch a football. He returned with what was described as a pudgy cross between a punching bag and a football, and following a delay of more than one hour, the kickoff was on at approximately 4 p.m.

Long after Stanford posted a stunning, 14-10 victory, Hoover and his Cal counterpart burned the midnight oil, counting the gold and silver coins. To their amazement, there was $30,000. It

Early Big Game action finds Cal dropping a 6-0 decision to Stanford on Thanksgiving Day in 1894 before a standing-room-only crowd. A group of undaunted spectators watches the action from the rooftop in the background.

readily was apparent that the Big Game would become the premier sporting event on the West Coast and a rivalry to match Yale-Harvard, Princeton-Rutgers and Army-Navy.

The embarrassed Bears couldn't wait a year to gain revenge, so they invited Stanford for a rematch in the fall. On December 17, 1892, a crowd of 18,753 mobbed the Haight & Stanyan Field to watch the two teams tie at 10-10. Stanford imported the legendary Walter Camp to coach its team, and Cal countered with Yale's Lee McClung. The two men also handled the officiating. The Big Game already was big time.

Stanford held the edge in the early games of the series, but it was difficult to determine why. Following a 20-0 drubbing suffered by the Bears in 1896, Cal professor M.E. Jaffa figured he had the answer after scrutinizing the dietary habits of the Cal players.

"The study, as a whole, seems to warrant the conclusion that the team was over-fed," Professor Jaffa wrote. "Not only was the amount of food actually consumed excessive, but the amount of food wasted was very large. The average daily cost per man, 97 cents, greatly exceeds the amount paid by the majority of housekeepers. The cost of meat alone was 35 cents per man per day. Another large item of expense is ale, which costs nearly 20 cents per man per day."

Whatever the reason, the Bears got the burps out of their system and crushed Stanford 22-0 in 1898 and 30-0 in 1899 to somewhat balance the scales. In fact, Cal was beginning to get the upper hand. The Bears had not won a game against Stanford until 1898, but a 6-6 tie on November 14, 1903, left the Peninsula school leading by a narrow 5-4 with four ties.

That game marked the final meeting between the two arch-rivals in San Francisco. It was played on Richmond Field at Sixth and Lake. Others were staged at Haight and Stanyan, Central Park (Eighth and Market), Recreation Park (Eighth and Harrison) and 16th and Folsom. The 1904 Big Game dedicated the $40,000 California Field in Berkeley, and the traditional contest thereafter was played either in Palo Alto or Berkeley, and not on Thanksgiving Day as in the past.

By that time, capacity crowds virtually were assured whenever the teams met. When Stanford was overwhelmed in 1898-99, enthusiasm was running so high in Berkeley that the William Douglas Tilden football statue was dedicated on campus. But that exuberance was curbed in 1905 when Benjamin Ide Wheeler, president of the University of California, decreed an end to American football on campus following the season.

Wheeler was disturbed over the bone-crushing aspects of the game and feared for the safety of the players. It was a time of the flying wedge, where a team would concentrate its attack on one player and leave the defender battered and bruised. It also was an era of small squads — only 22 men played in the first Big Game — and little rest. There was non-stop action, for instance, and it was not until 1905 that the game was divided into halves.

An alternative to American football, according to Wheeler, was rugby. Cal and Stanford adopted the game, but the fans had to be sold. Ralph Merritt, the Bears business manager in 1906, convinced 23,000 people to pay $2 apiece for the opportunity to watch Stanford edge Cal, 6-3, in the first rugby Big Game. The two schools continued the rugby series through 1914, Stanford showing a 5-3 edge with one tie.

By 1909, Cal had a powerhouse under coach Jimmy Schaeffer. The Bears were unbeaten in 1910, and they were winning international competition by 1911. With only seven varsity players returning in 1912, more than 200 men turned out for rugby. That was the year of the famous mud game with Stanford, when days of steady rain left the field resembling a swamp. The two teams sloshed to a 3-3 tie.

California Field was turfed in 1914, and the Bears won 13 straight games before Stanford snapped the streak, 26-8. The Big Game that year was classified among the great American exhibitions of rugby, yet it was to be the final big-time rugby clash between the schools. The Bears were ready to return to American football, but a strange set of circumstances had Washington replacing Stanford as the Big Game foe in 1915-17.

In the early days of football, any student was eligible for the team, some engaging in the sport as graduate students for long collegiate careers. Cal and Stanford decided that only undergraduates in good academic standing were eligible. Most of the leading universities agreed but went one step further, eliminating freshmen from varsity competition. Cal adhered to that regulation, Stanford didn't. As a result, the Bears turned to American football in 1915, and Stanford kept playing rugby, using neighboring Santa Clara as its Big Game foe.

It took World War I to renew the traditional rivalry. Each university was a Student Army Training Corps camp, with all male students subject to military orders. The SATC officers at Cal and Stanford virtually ordered a game, and 19,000 spectators showed up at California Field on November 30, 1918. Bryan "Pesky" Sprott scored seven touchdowns to power a 67-0 Golden Bear romp. Stanford, with obvious justification, refused to call its team

This rare action shot from the 1894 Big Game illustrates the rough-and-tumble style of play prevalent during this era.

In 1899, strutting Cal students march in the first Axe Parade on campus.

representative, so Sprott's record is not considered official. Cal, however, counted the victory in a 7-2 season.

Thanks to the coaching of men like Pop Warner and ex-Bear John Ralston, Stanford held a 40-34 advantage in the series, which includes 10 ties through 1981.

STANFORD 14, CAL 10
MARCH 19, 1892

Such a great rivalry, of course, has had its share of memorable games beginning with the first on March 19, 1892. This game gave a new meaning to spring football, for it marked the beginning of an 84-game series (through 1981) which ranks among the grandest traditional rivalries in the nation. The historic inaugural found the bigger, stronger Bears a heavy favorite. After all, they had been playing for 10

years, whereas Senator Leland Stanford had opened his university only six months before.

Whittemore, Stanford student-body president and a former star at St. Louis' Washington University, was the only Stanford student who had played college football, so he was asked to form a team. He and fullback-manager Carl Clemans quickly realized that they would have to resort to deceptiveness to overcome Cal's weight and experience edge.

The two Stanford stars used clever ballhandling and end runs to gain a 14-0 halftime lead on three touchdowns (four points each) and a goal kick (two points). Clemans is credited with scoring the first TD in the series, using a tricky handoff from halfback Paul Downing on a reverse that resulted in a 45-yard scoring run. Loren Hunt and Ray Sherman scored TDs for Cal in the second half, but the

Members of the 1906 freshman class collecting wood for the Big Game Rally. A few years later, the 1910 Cal rooting section was credited with originating card stunts at college football games. On this historic occasion, the famed Axe was depicted by the students during the Big Game.

104

Bears were playing catch-up ball, and they were still four points short when the game ended at 14-10.

CAL 16, STANFORD 0
NOVEMBER 8, 1902

On November 8, 1902, each team entered the 12th Big Game undefeated, but the Bears were without Warren "Locomotive" Smith, regarded as the finest back ever to play in the West. Stanford accused Smith of professionalism when it was discovered that he had stayed out of school one year and did a little moonlighting as a coach. The Indians insisted they would not play if he was in uniform.

The Bears reluctantly consented and substituted Bobby Sherman for Smith. To be sure, Sherman was no slouch. In a prior game with the Alumni Club, he had scored on a 65-yard run from scrimmage and on an 85-yard punt return, but that was just a tuneup for what was to come against Stanford, which was to regret its decision to protest Smith's eligibility.

The game also featured the punting and kicking of Ovie Overall, whose field goal gave Cal a 5-0 lead. In the final half, Stanford punted to Sherman, who bobbled the ball, recovered it and dodged several would-be tacklers for a 105-yard punt return — the longest in Cal history to this day. Overall's second field goal (they were worth five points then) concluded the scoring for a 16-0 shutout in what was to become known as the "Remember Smith Game."

CAL 9, STANFORD 0
NOVEMBER 24, 1923

More than 73,000 showed up on November 24, 1923, for a day that had been long awaited

In 1912, during the era when Cal and Stanford were playing rugby, days of steady rain turned the Big Game into the "Mud Bowl" as the teams sloshed to a 3-3 tie.

The scoreboard in 1910 is a far cry from today's electronic marvels. It also served as a vantage point for photographers (left).

structure was well underway at Strawberry Canyon. More than one million feet of lumber was used for the stadium, and another 800,000 feet was used for the seats. The construction crew used 600 tons of steel and 12,000 barrels of cement. Landscapers planted 2,500 pine trees on Big C Hill, later to become known as Tightwad Hill.

When the stadium was completed — at a cost of slightly more than $1.4 million — there officially were 72,609 seats, but more than 73,000 spectators showed up for the dedication game on November 24, 1923, against Stanford. The Bears crowned the joyous occasion with a 9-0 victory, and those present were secure in the knowledge that Cal would proudly display one of the finest stadiums in the land for years to come.

The capacity soon was increased to more than

Sparked by the success of Andy Smith's Wonder Team, Memorial Stadium was constructed in what had been known as Strawberry Canyon. A crowd of 73,000 witnessed the Bears 9-0 victory over Stanford in the dedication game, November 24, 1923.

MEMORIAL STADIUM AMONG THE NATION'S FINEST

Cal's 28-0 crushing of Ohio State in the 1921 Rose Bowl Game and the Golden Bears No. 1 national status in 1920 made it apparent that Andy Smith's Wonder Teams needed a football stadium befitting their newfound success. California Field, their home grounds at the time, was woefully inadequate considering the popularity the game enjoyed in the early twenties.

California Field, which had been the Bears home since 1904 following years of playing key games in San Francisco, had a capacity of 27,700. Cal's rise to prominence under Smith made a larger facility imperative, and a committee was launched to erect an 80,000-seat structure in the memory of Californians who died in World War I.

Frank Probert, dean of the school of mining engineering, headed the project, and Robert Gordon Sproul, who later was to head the University, was the treasurer. Sproul pointed out that in 1920 there were 60,000 applications for Big Game tickets — more than twice as many requests as California Field had seats.

A general committee was appointed to add clout to the fund drive for Memorial Stadium. The list read like a who's who of prominent Bay Areans, names like Crocker, Fleishacker, Mills, Wheeler, Durant, Hearst, Johnson, Rolph and Sutro. San Francisco's financial district was combed for contributions, and the fund drive was on.

Within 10 days, 10,000 stadium subscriptions had been sold at $100 each for 10-year double tickets. These ostensibly called for a lifetime of preferential seating with each subscriber's name carved on the seat. The promises weren't kept, but there was so much enthusiasm generated by the imposing project that it didn't seem to matter.

By the summer of 1923, work on the beautiful

ORNIA-STANFORD FOOTBALL GAME
ALIFORNIA MEMORIAL STADIUM
NOV. 24, 1923
PHOTO © 1923 BY MORTON & CO.

— the dedication of magnificent Memorial Stadium. The crowd was almost four times larger than any that previously had witnessed a Big Game, and the banter was especially lively. Stanford fans floated a rumor suggesting that home teams christening stadiums always lost, citing six examples.

"Why, of course they did," agreed Andy Smith. "It was always California they invited to help dedicate their stadiums."

Bill Blewett missed two field goals as Cal failed to take advantage of early opporunties, but the big break came in the second period. Stanford's Ernie Nevers was known for getting his booming punts off slowly, so a hard rush by Babe Horrell blocked the kick and he followed it into the end zone for a touchdown. Blewett's conversion made it 7-0 at halftime, but only because Don Newmayer's interception thwarted the Indians after they reached Cal's 8.

Blewett missed three field goal attempts in the second half, but one of them was fielded by Stanford's Scotchy Campbell, who was swarmed in the end zone for a safety and the final 9-0 score. Horrell, who later was to coach UCLA, was credited with the safety, thereby scoring eight of the nine points.

CALIFORNIA
vs.
STANFORD
FOOTBALL GAME
CALIFORNIA MEMORIAL STADIUM
NOV. 22, 1924 • PRICE 25¢

CAL 20, STANFORD 20
NOVEMBER 22, 1924

The 30th Big Game, which was played on November 22, 1924, is regarded by many as the finest of them all. A crowd of 77,000, plus an estimated 20,000 more on Tightwad Hill, watched Pop Warner's debut in the series, and the old master didn't disappoint while ending the Wonder Team's dominance of the rivalry. Spice was added when Indians halfback Norm Cleaveland was declared ineligible by Stanford following a controversial protest by the Bears.

Each team was undefeated, and interest was so high that scalpers were getting $100 for a pair of tickets. Cal partisans figured their team would win easily with Cleaveland out of action, but the early stages of the game suggested that they had underestimated the might of the Nevers-led Indians.

Murray Cuddeback, who upstaged Nevers that day, booted a second-period field goal for a 3-0 Stanford lead. Cuddeback added a field goal of nearly 50 yards, and Stanford had a surprising 6-0 lead at halftime. With Tut Imlay, James Dixon and Bert Griffin doing the bulk of the carrying, Cal drove 81 yards in the third quarter, Griffin dashing the final 5 for the TD. Glenn "Scoop" Carlson's PAT made it 7-6.

Early in the fourth period, however, offensive fireworks created an explosive finish to a fantastic game. A 16-yard pass play from Dixon to Imlay and Carlson's extra point upped the lead to 14-6. Then John Sargent's fumble recovery gave Cal possession at the Indians 29, and Griffin pounded the Stanford line in a series of short bursts before scoring. Carlson missed the PAT, but there was little concern by the Bears, who enjoyed a "comfortable" 20-6 lead with six minutes to go.

At the time, two key substitutions seemed insignificant, but they along with Carlson's miss proved decisive. Physically battered, Imlay and Dixon were removed from the game by Andy Smith, whereas Warner inserted a big, clumsy halfback named Ed Walker. Walker played only the final 10 and one-half minutes, but what a stretch run!

Stanford took over on its own 35 following the kickoff, and the strong-armed Walker began winging desperation passes. He connected with Fred Solomon for 26 yards to the Cal 39. Then he uncorked a bomb that landed in Ted Shipkey's arms in the end zone. Cuddeback, who had an interception earlier in the game, added the conversion drop-kick, and it was 20-13 with four minutes remaining.

Cal got nowhere and Stanford took over on its 19. Walker and Shipkey hooked up on a

43-yard completion on third down, placing the ball on the Bears 38. Again it was third down, this time from the 36. With the seconds ticking away, Walker calmly faded back and fired a strike to Cuddeback, who darted over the goal line. After catching his breath, Cuddeback booted the extra point, and it ended at 20-all, with Cal gaining 271 yards and Stanford 262.

Walter Camp had briefly coached Stanford in the fall of 1892. He returned at the invitation of the Bears and was congratulating them on the sidelines when the score reached 20-6. Camp, who later placed Horrell on his All-America squad, said it was the greatest game he'd ever seen. Recalling the game following his retirement, Pop Warner said he was so moved by what the Indians accomplished that day against such great odds, he called it the greatest game he ever was involved in.

CAL 6, STANFORD 0
NOVEMBER 21, 1931

Going into the 1931 Big Game, the Bears had been without a Big Game victory for seven years, but they were rated a slight favorite before 87,500 at Stanford Stadium on November 21. Brittle Hank Schaldach did enough damage before leaving with an injury in the fourth

Captains Harry Hillman (left) of Stanford and Ed Griffiths of Cal, flank famed referee Herb Dana in pre-game ceremonies for the 1931 Big Game.

quarter to carry the day for Cal by rushing for 134 of his team's 142 yards on the ground.

Sam Gill recovered a Stanford fumble on the Indians 24 early in the game, and Schaldach carried it to the 11. But Schaldach was thrown back to the 28 when he attempted to pass, and the first quarter was scoreless.

A short punt enabled the Bears to get the ball 35 yards from the end zone. Schaldach carried to a first down on the 25, then hit Joe Smith with a pass for another first down on the 11. On his fourth carry, Hammering Hank bulled over from the 1, but he missed the kick and it was 6-0 at the half.

Schaldach went out of the game after a dazzling 45-yard run, but the superb defensive play of Rusty Gill preserved the shutout. No points were scored in the second half, so the game ended with the halftime score of 6-0.

STANFORD 9, CAL 7
NOVEMBER 24, 1934

Stanford's Vow Boys were only sophomores in 1933 when they escaped with a 7-3 victory at Palo Alto. So when they were juniors in 1934, they were expected to win convincingly over the Bears, who were 4-1 underdogs in a mediocre 6-6 season. A crowd of 65,000 showed up on November 24 at Memorial Stadium to watch the expected carnage.

Instead, it watched a scoreless first half with both teams blowing scoring opportunities. In the third quarter, third-string Stanford end Carl Schott partially blocked Arleigh Williams' punt, giving the Indians possession deep in Cal territory. Bones Hamilton scored on a double reverse for a 6-0 lead.

Schott, who missed the PAT, added a field goal in the final period for 9-0. But the Bears clawed back and scored with two minutes to go on a 33-yard pass from Williams to Jack Brittingham, and Williams' conversion made it a final 9-7. The game was the last for Navy Bill Ingram, who resigned under pressure. His Bears at least proved they were a more formidable foe for Stanford than was USC.

CAL 16, STANFORD 0
NOVEMBER 29, 1941

In 1940, the turnabout Indians were the rage of the nation, carving a 10-0 season out of Frankie Albert's sorcery and coach Clark Shaughnessy's T-formation. But the Big Game served notice that Stub Allison could stump Stanford's offensive machine. In fact, the Tribe was held scoreless the second half and barely survived with a 13-7 victory en route to the Rose Bowl.

The following year proved Allison's strategy was no fluke. Cal entered the Stanford Stadium struggle on November 29, 1941, with a 3-5 record, and the Indians were a solid 6-2, but it didn't matter. On the Bears first possession, halfback Al Derian took off on first down and

Paced by the superb defensive play of All-American halfback Rusty Gill, Cal shut out Stanford to squeeze out a 6-0 victory in the 1931 Big Game.

Arleigh Williams, with ball, concludes a brilliant Cal career in the 1934 Big Game. This play was good for a 5-yard gain with the help of blocks from Bert Welch (53) and Ken Cotton (63).

Stanford, in its revolutionary T formation, threatens to score during the 1940 Big Game. Although Stanford scored twice in the first half, the Bears began to solve the new offense in the second half, and they shut it out completely the following year in a 16-0 Cal victory.

Halfback Al Derian scores on a 46-yard run on the first play of Cal's 16-0 upset in the 1941 Big Game. Derian, who took 96 seconds to reach paydirt, starts the gallop by running to his left behind the blocking of Jack McQuary. He then cuts to his right, eludes Stanford's Crane and is protected by teammates Bob Reinhard (45), Brunel Christensen (68) and Stan Cox (94) en route to the touchdown.

used Jack McQuary's blocking to spring a 46-yard TD run. Joe Merlo's PAT made it 7-0 a mere 1:35 into the game, and 70,000 fans were buzzing.

Nothing changed until the final period, when the 3-1 underdog Bears put the Indians away with an inspired defensive effort. Bob Reinhard, who missed the 1940 game with the flu, placed Stanford in a hole with a 50-yard punt, and the hosts took over on their 11. Brothers George and John Herrero knocked the Indians back for 6 yards in losses on two plays, and Jean Witter blocked Albert's punt for a safety.

Moments later, Reinhard uncorked a 45-yard punt, and the process was repeated. Stanford started on its 20, but Reinhard's savage rush sent Albert reeling for a 9-yard loss. Then John Herrero registered a sack, and Albert was smothered on the 4. Jack Herrero blocked the punt, and the ball dropped into the arms of Reinhard, who scored the final TD, completing the rout at 16-0. The T had been tamed six straight quarters, and exuberant Cal fans reportedly took only 14 seconds to tear down the goal posts.

CAL 21, STANFORD 18
NOVEMBER 22, 1947

Another classic — the 50th Big Game, on November 22, 1947 — is regarded along with the 1924 affair as the finest in the series. Why not? Who could have imagined what would happen when the once-beaten Bears took on winless Stanford before 88,000 at Palo Alto? Cal, in fact, was favored by a whopping 10-1 under rookie coach Pappy Waldorf.

The Bears didn't disappoint at the start, scoring on their first drive when Ted Kenfield raced 29 yards for a touchdown. Jim "Truck" Cullom added the PAT for 7-0. But the Indians rebounded with a 65-yard march and a touchdown pass from Ainslee Bell to Wayne Erickson for 7-6 after one quarter.

With less than 10 seconds remaining in the opening half, George Fong's 1-yard run and Cullom's PAT made it 14-6. Erickson's 2-yard TD cut the lead to two points entering the final period. Then Don Campbell fired a touchdown pass to Bob Anderson, and the Indians silenced the Cal rooting section by taking an 18-14 lead. But the best was yet to come, including a Hollywood-scriptlike ending of which legends are made and memories rekindled.

Cal had the ball on its own 20 with three minutes left, and injured halfback Paul Keckley was on the sidelines, pleading with Pappy for a chance to play. Waldorf was reluctant, but he finally agreed. The rest is a precious moment etched in the hearts and minds of Old Blues. Jackie Jensen took a lateral from quarterback Dick Erickson and intended to run.

Instead, Jensen spotted Keckley 15 yards downfield and fired a horrible pass. But Keckley wasn't going to let his only opportunity or the wobbly pigskin slip away. He latched onto the ball, eluded what seemed like 11 would-be

FERGUSON

COX

TAYLOR

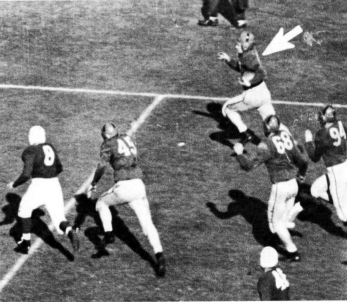

All-American tackle Bob Reinhard jolts Stanford quarterback Frankie Albert (13) for a loss during the Bears 16-0 upset in 1941.

The closing minutes of the 50th Big Game in 1947 produced one of the most stirring plays in the annals of Cal football. With the ball on the 20, Jackie Jensen starts to run, then sees Keckley, who had just re-entered the game after sitting out with an injury. Keckley takes Jensen's pass 15 yards downfield, eludes Stanford's Don Fix and goes all the way, completing an 80-yard touchdown play and giving Cal a 21-18 victory.

tacklers and bolted 65 yards for an electrifying touchdown. The 80-yard play and Cullom's kick made it 21-18 with scant seconds remaining.

CAL 20, STANFORD 7
NOVEMBER 24, 1951

In 1951, Rose Bowl-bound Stanford was 9-0 and favored when 90,000 fans filled Stanford Stadium on November 24 for another Big Game shocker. Cal quickly went 86 yards in 10 plays, Don Robison scoring on a 34-yard touchdown run and Les Richter adding the PAT for 7-0. Then, John Pappa went 21 yards for a TD, and Richter's 40th conversion kick of the season established a school record and created a 14-0 halftime lead.

Pappa, enjoying his finest day as a Bear, made it 20-0 on a 4-yard blast off tackle in the fourth quarter before the embarrassed Indians averted a shutout on a pass from Gary Kerkorian to Sam Morley. The game ended, 20-7. Cal's ground game completely outclassed Stanford's vaunted air attack, the Bears rolling up 316 yards on the ground and outgaining the PCC champs 366-197.

CAL 20, STANFORD 18
NOVEMBER 24, 1956

Cal brought a mere 2-7 record to Memorial Stadium on November 24, 1956, to do battle against the Indians All-American senior quarterback from Oakland, John Brodie. But the Golden Bears were especially emotionally charged

Halfback Ted Kenfield averts a Stanford tackler while dashing 30 yards for Cal's first touchdown in the 1947 Big Game. Teammate Ron Sockolov (74) moves in, along with Stanford's Don Fix.

before a crowd of 81,000 because Waldorf had announced his retirement the previous week.

The Bears were so fired up that they scored on their first three possessions. Herb Jackson dove over the goal line from the 3, and Darrell Roberts added the PAT for 7-0, capping a 67-yard march. Stanford then fumbled on the Cal 37, triggering a 63-yard drive that resulted in a 1-yard TD for Roberts, who also kicked the PAT for 14-0.

With fullback Lou Valli contributing three substantial runs and Jeri McMillan circling left end for a 12-yard TD, the Indians were on the scoreboard in the second period. Jack Hart's 1-yard buck increased the Cal lead, but Brodie's

5-yard TD toss to Ben Robinson enabled the determined Indians to close within 20-12 at the half. Two second-half Stanford drives bogged down before Valli took a pitch and scored on a 14-yard run 2:10 into the final period, concluding the scoring at 20-18.

The victory made Waldorf a winner in his farewell to coaching, and it was regarded as one of his most pleasant memories. Mike White, later to coach the Bears, said it was his most meaningful victory as a player. Sophomore quarterback Joe Kapp rushed for 106 yards in getting the best of the heralded Brodie. Valli set a Big Game record with 209 yards in 23 carries, a 9.1 average, but the Indians ended their disappointing season a 4-6 loser.

All-American Les Richter (67) leads interference for Don Robison during the 1951 Big Game. Robison scored Cal's first TD on a 34-yard run.

Airborne Herb Jackson dives over the goal from the 3 for the first touchdown in Cal's stunning, 20-18 victory over Stanford in the 1956 Big Game.

Les Richter successfully kicked this extra point in a 20-7 Big Game victory in 1951. The conversion, his 40th of the season, established a school record that still stands.

A happy Pappy Waldorf is flanked by Joe Kapp (left) and Herb Jackson, two stars of the Bears 20-18 Big Game victory in 1956. The win capped the brilliant coaching career of Waldorf, who retired following the game.

Sophomore quarterback Joe Kapp, hero of the 1956 Big Game upset, makes a few yards on a keeper up the middle before he's brought down by Ben Robinson (87).

CAL 16, STANFORD 15
NOVEMBER 22, 1958

Two years later, the Bears needed a victory to clinch the PCC's Rose Bowl berth, but it didn't come easy. At the Big Game, played on November 22, Cal scored first as Kapp and Hart powered a 62-yard drive, and Grover Garvin ran for the two-point conversion. Stanford retaliated with a 39-yard pass from John Bond to Irv Nikolai on a double-reverse to the Cal 2, from where Skip Face ran it in for 8-6.

Controversy raged on the two-point conversion attempt because the back judge ruled Nikolai didn't have possession inbounds on a pass from Dick Norman that glanced off Chris Burford's hands. Face's field goal in the second quarter gave the Indians a 9-8 halftime edge.

The Bears roared back in the third period, however, with Hart punching across his second TD and Kapp firing to Wayne Crow for the two-point conversion and a 16-9 lead. Tension mounted late in the game when Norman hit Joel Freis with a 21-yard scoring strike for 16-15. Coach Jack Curtice elected to go for a win instead of a tie, but Face, circling end, was stopped shy of the goal by Billy Patton.

CAL 20, STANFORD 17
NOVEMBER 21, 1959

Two losing teams had nothing but pride at stake the following year, but the 62nd Big Game, played on November 21, 1959, proved to be among the most exciting and entertaining in history for the 90,000 at Stanford Stadium. Crow fired 48 yards to Gael Barsotti for one score and 12 yards to Patton for another, and Patton's PATs gave the Bears a 14-0 halftime lead.

At that juncture, it seemed apparent that this game would be something special statistically. Crow had completed all eight of his passes at the half for 151 yards and two TDs. But Norman was just warming up, connecting on 16 of 18 for 182 yards. His 45-yard pass to

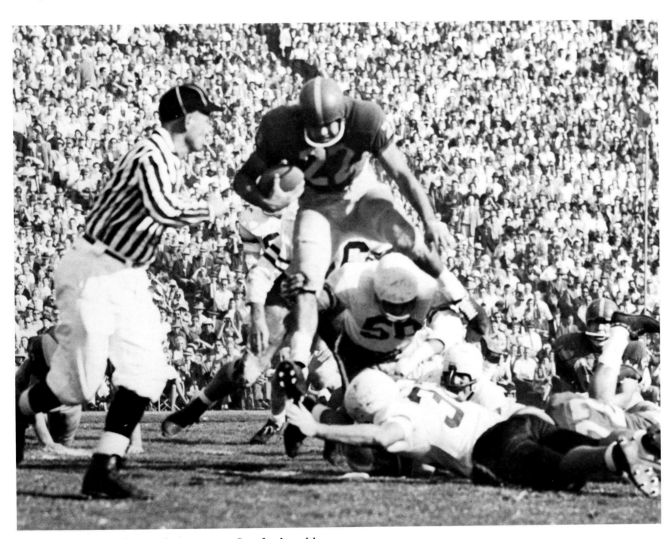

Joe Kapp strains for yardage against Stanford tacklers in the 1958 Big Game. The senior quarterback powered the Bears to victory and a trip to the Rose Bowl.

Robinson prefaced Face's 3-yard TD, and his 9-yard pass to Burford followed by Face's second PAT made it 14-all after three quarters.

Face's field goal gave the Indians the edge with 7:53 to go, but Jerry Scattini's 2-yard run for Cal capped a 64-yard march for 20-17. Patton's two-point try failed, and Norman took over on his own 45 following a penalty with 3:30 remaining. Norman almost gunned down the Bears again, passing the Indians to Cal's 24. On the last play of the game, Norman's receivers were smothered, so he ran and was kept inbounds by Andy Segale, aborting a last-ditch field goal attempt. The game went to Cal, 20-17.

Crow finished 9 for 13, passing for 158 of the Bears 360 yards. But the stats, if little else, belonged to Norman, who shattered the NCAA single-game record with 34 completions in 39 attempts for 401 yards. Burford grabbed 12 of those passes and finished the season with 61, equaling the NCAA record.

CAL 22, STANFORD 14
NOVEMBER 21, 1970

Dave Penhall completed 23 passes against Stanford in 1969, almost pulling off an upset before the Bears bowed, 29-28. But the Cal quarterback wasn't going to be denied in his second chance. Stanford entered the 1970 Big Game on November 21 with the Rose Bowl bid locked and following a loss to the Air Force. The Indians supposedly had suffered a letdown, but the win-hungry Bears weren't fussy.

A Memorial Stadium crowd of 76,800 watched Cal take a 13-7 halftime lead on a pair of long Randy Wersching field goals and a 10-yard pass

Halfback Wayne Crow (10) rambles for a 15-yard gain to the Stanford 49 in the 1958 Big Game. Later in the game, his pass reception for a two-point conversion proved to be the winning margin in Cal's 16-15 win.

A wall of blockers develops for Cal's Grover Garvin (15) in 1959 Big Game action. The trio eager to open some holes is Wayne Crow (22), Walt Arnold (30) and Doug Graham (64).

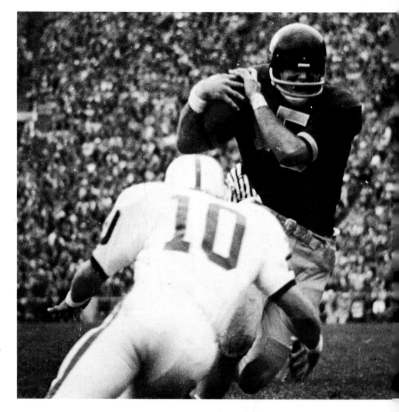

Dave Penhall dodges a Stanford tackler for the winning touchdown in the stirring 22-14 victory over the bowl-bound Indians. Penhall was the hero of the 1970 Big Game, overshadowing rival quarterback Jim Plunkett.

from Penhall to Bob Darby. But Jim Plunkett stormed back with a 74-yard bomb to Jackie Brown, and the Indians pulled ahead, 14-13, on Steve Horowitz' PAT in the third quarter.

A pass interference call which incensed the Indians gave Cal a first down on the Stanford 1, from where Penhall nudged across on third down. The two-point conversion attempt failed with 13:59 to go, and Cal turned to defense to stop the Indians in a major upset, 22-14, Ray Youngblood making a big fumble recovery down the stretch.

Heisman Trophy winner Plunkett clicked on 20 of 37 passes for 280 yards, padding his single-season NCAA record. Penhall completed 18 of 26 passes for 231 yards to continue his sparkling Big Game play. Glue-fingered Steve Sweeney caught five passes for 65 yards, giving a preview of what was to come two years later.

CAL 24, STANFORD 21
NOVEMBER 18, 1972

The memorable, November 18, 1972, Big Game found Sweeney concluding his career with a flurry. The remarkably consistent senior broke virtually every Cal receiving record in 1972, but none of his circus catches matched the splendor of his final collegiate grab for sheer drama and excitement.

Memorial Stadium's field resembled a quagmire, affecting the play of each team, but 68,000 nonetheless showed up to watch the 2-8 Bears shoot for an upset behind freshman quarterback Vince Ferragamo. Eric Cross' 24-yard TD run and Gordon Reigel's 71-yard return with an interception gave the Indians a 14-3 halftime lead, Cal's only points coming on Ray Wersching's 29-yard field goal.

A gang of Cal tacklers smothered a mud-caked Stanford ball carrier just after the handoff from Mike Boryla in the gooey going of the 1972 Big Game.

125

One of the greatest catches in Cal football history was made by Steve Sweeney (88) to punctuate the 1972 Big Game. Cal was trailing and only three seconds remained when quarterback Vince Ferragamo fired desperately toward the end zone. Sweeney made this leaping grab for a 24-21 victory at muddy Memorial Stadium.

With just seconds remaining and trailing, 18-21, Coach Mike White and Vince Ferragamo make their final play selection in the 1972 Big Game.

In the third quarter, Syl Youngblood's 4-yard TD and a two-point conversion pass from Ferragamo to Steve Kemnitzer made it 14-11. Then Youngblood scored again, this time from the 6, and Wersching's PAT gave the Bears an 18-14 lead with 13:31 left to play. Mike Boryla's passes got Stanford moving, and Reggie Sanderson's 4-yard run followed by Rod Garcia's third PAT pushed the Indians ahead, 21-18, with only 3:42 remaining.

Things looked grim for the Bears when Steve Murray picked off a Ferragamo pass, the quarterback's fourth interception of the day. But Cal's defense held, and Ferragamo had a chance for redemption. A pair of pass interference calls paved the way, and the Bears were on the Stanford 7 with 0:03 showing. Time for one play. Sweeney was in the end zone when the scrambling quarterback connected for the winning points. Thousands of delirious Cal fans poured onto the field, making the PAT attempt impossible. Nobody seemed to care, though, and the 24-21 score stood.

CAL 48, STANFORD 15
NOVEMBER 22, 1975

In what undeniably was Cal's finest performance ever at Stanford Stadium, the

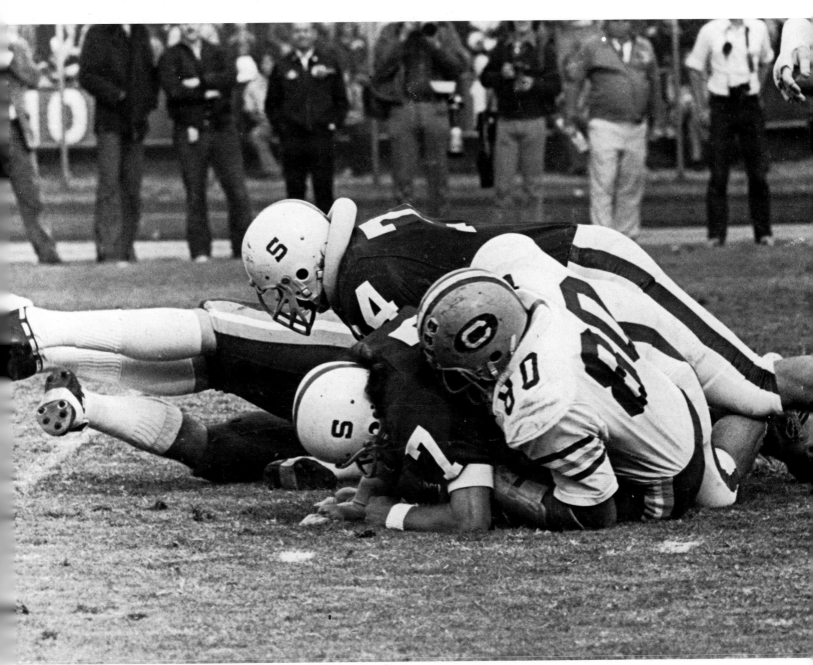

Jeff Barnes (80) and two unidentified Bears overwhelm Stanford blocker Bill Hubbard (74) to sack Guy Benjamin in Cal's crushing, 48-15 Big Game victory in 1975.

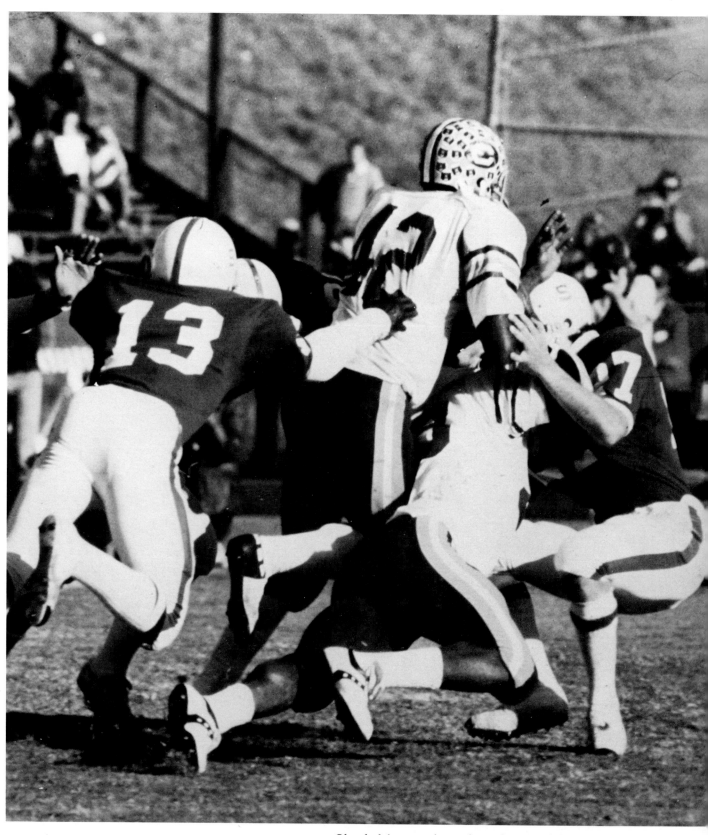

Chuck Muncie plows through several Stanford defenders during his one-man show at the 1975 Big Game. Muncie gained 166 yards rushing and contributed to five touchdowns in a 48-15 runaway.

Chuck Muncie rolls out on the tailback option in the 1975 Big Game. Muncie not only scored four touchdowns in the game, but he also threw a 46-yard scoring strike to Wesley Walker.

Golden Bears clinched the 1975 Pac-8 championship tie before 88,000 well-entertained spectators. The day, November 22, belonged to Chuck Muncie, Cal's record-smashing All-American, who scored four touchdowns, passed for another score and rushed for 166 yards.

Muncie scored on a 7-yard pass from Joe Roth and added a 16-yard scoring run in the opening period. Jim Breech's two PATs made it a quick 14-0. Guy Benjamin threw a TD pass to Tony Hill, but field goals of 48 and 38 yards by Breech and Muncie's 1-yard run made it a 27-6 Cal runaway by halftime.

A safety and a touchdown enabled Stanford to close within 27-15 early in the final period, but this time the Bears wouldn't be denied. In the final 8:19, Muncie scored from the 3, Wesley Walker tallied on a 46-yard pass from Muncie and Paul Jones added a 6-yard scoring run to cap the romp, 48-15. Cal accumulated 488 yards and 27 first downs as the nation's most offensive team.

That one-sided rout, however, was the exception in Big Games. The norm has been that they're hotly contested and tight at the finish. There definitely is something special about the traditional rivalry between the Bay Area schools. Why else would stadiums fill to the brim to watch teams with losing records? Why else would alumni in distant lands and across our nation gather on Big Game day, listening to radio broadcasts of the contest over telephone wires?

Indeed, the Big Game is exactly that.

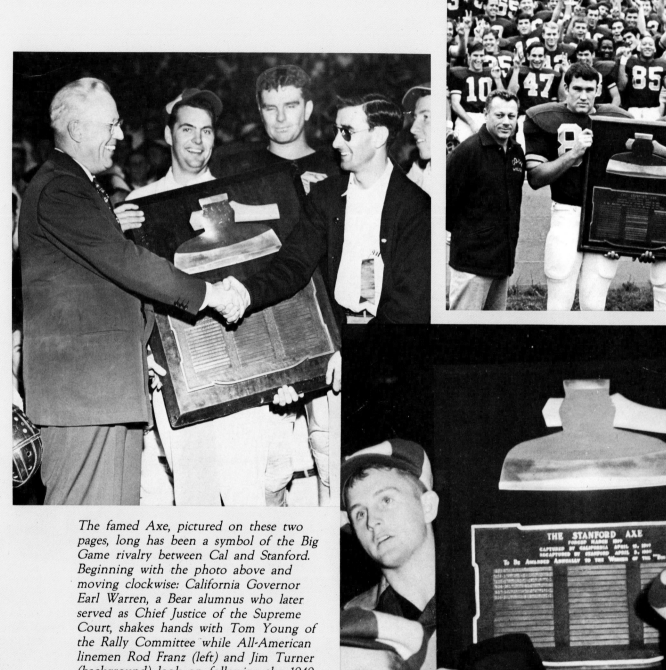

The famed Axe, pictured on these two pages, long has been a symbol of the Big Game rivalry between Cal and Stanford. Beginning with the photo above and moving clockwise: California Governor Earl Warren, a Bear alumnus who later served as Chief Justice of the Supreme Court, shakes hands with Tom Young of the Rally Committee while All-American linemen Rod Franz (left) and Jim Turner (background) look on following the 1949 Big Game; coach Ray Willsey, Mike McCaffrey (center) and John McGaffie pose with the Axe and their 1968 teammates; the prestigious trophy, which had been mounted on a plaque in 1933, is shown following Cal's 1980 triumph; Lol Pringle, a turn of the century Bear standout, proudly displays the Axe in 1899; and a group of students carry the trophy after Cal's victory in 1939.

THE AXE

No Big Game history would be complete without mention of the Axe, which was forged by Stanford way back in 1899. The occasion was a key baseball game between the Bears and the Indians at 16th and Folsom in San Francisco. At a rally on April 13, the eve of the game, the Axe was introduced to the Stanford students, who watched the sharp, heavy instrument decapitate a strawman adorned with blue and gold.

That was just a warm-up. The next day, Stanford rooters taunted their Cal counterparts by cutting pieces of blue and gold ribbon with the Axe and by using it to chop at a designated piece of wood whenever the powerful Stanford nine made a good play. There was a lot of chopping as the Indians jumped to a 6-0 lead, but Pete "Kangaroo" Kaarsberg, also a grid star, belted a bases-loaded triple in the ninth to give the Bears a 9-7 upset.

Overcome with emotion and disgusted by the brandishing of the Axe, a group of Cal men decided to wrest it from Stanford. A scuffle erupted, and the Axe forcibly was taken by Cal students, who raced through the streets of San Francisco. The Axe inadvertently was given to Stanford followers, but it quickly was recovered when the mistake was realized.

Since Stanford students and the police were looking for the stolen instrument, the Cal men had to disguise it for safe transport across the Bay. The handle was sawed off, and the metal head was wrapped in brown paper. The Axe was smuggled across by ferry and eventually was placed in the safe of a Berkeley bank, to be removed only once a year for the Axe Rally.

There were several unsuccessful attempts by Stanford men to regain possession over the years, but they finally pulled it off April 3, 1930, when a committee of 21 executed the perfect crime. While the Axe was being returned to the bank, the group posed as newspaper reporters. Instead of flash bulbs in the cameras, there was tear gas, so those protecting the Axe were overcome. It was taken back to Palo Alto after a brief fight.

By 1933, each side decided the Axe would make an ideal Big Game trophy. It is mounted on a plaque with all the scores listed since 1933. The Axe changes hands only at the Big Game, going to the winning school. Possession seldom lasts more than a year or two, quite a change from the days when it was safely guarded in Berkeley for 31 years.

CHAPTER
5

100
YEARS
1882
1982

CAL
BLVE
AND
GOLD

Hall of Famer Brick Muller was the brightest star on a team of stars, the Wonder Teams of 1920-22. Sixty years later, he is still considered one of the greatest players in Cal grid history.

Chapter Five
HEROES IN BLVE & GOLD

Brick Muller generally is acknowledged as the athlete who placed Cal football on the map. The gifted end was the Bears initial first-team All-American, being so honored in 1921. That suggests there were no great athletes playing for the Blue & Gold during the first 40 years of football at the school, and that simply is not true.

Cal gridders, and those from other West Coast schools, were snubbed by the All-American selectors simply because they were not seen in action. Those were the days when Easterners believed Indians circled the wagons everywhere west of the Mississippi, so they ignored football players who played in the so-called boondocks.

As early as the 1890s, Berkeley was blessed with some outstanding athletes. Arthur "Wolf" Ransome is the first who comes to mind. He was a gifted runner and an extremely accurate punter who starred for the Bears in the 6-6 Big Game ties of 1893 and 1895. But his most impressive achievement was playing in every minute of the 25 Cal games in which he participated. Ransome's son John played for the Bears in the early thirties.

The line standout of the early 1890s was tackle Loren Hunt, but the first great congregation of Cal athletes didn't surface until a few years later when "Kangaroo" Pete Kaarsberg, Percy Hall and Warren "Locomotive" Smith formed an explosive backfield in 1898-99. Those two squads were a combined 15-1-3 under Garrett Cochran, outscoring the opposition 363-7.

Brick Morse, the famed Cal historian, in the mid-thirties named that group the greatest backfield in Cal history. The selection was made before the Thunder Team standouts went unbeaten in 1937, but suffice to say that Kaarsberg, Hall and Smith were at least the best in the first 50 years.

Statistical accomplishments weren't well-documented in the olden days, but in a 22-0 blanking of Stanford in 1898, the Bears accumulated 882 yards in 122 plays. Hall was credited with 183 yards rushing, and Smith added 131. The next year, Stanford was crushed, 30-0, with Smith scoring three TDs and Kaarsberg and Hall adding one apiece. Kaarsberg also had five conversion kicks.

The turn of the century also featured record-breaking runs by Heinie Heitmuller and Bobby Sherman, but the best players of the time were end Lloyd "Wrec" Womble and lineman Orval "Ovie" Overall, who became a star major league pitcher. Overall is best remembered at Cal

Percy Hall was a member of Cal's first great backfield in 1898-99, starring on squads which went 15-1-3.

Dan McMillan played two seasons at Southern Cal, but he transferred to Cal after the war. As a tackle on the Wonder Team, he earned second-team All-America honors in 1920 and, later, a spot in the College Football Hall of Fame.

Walter Gordon, one of Andy Smith's early stars, was named third-team All-American by Walter Camp in 1918. Cal's first prominent black athlete, Gordon went on to a distinguished career serving as Governor of the Virgin Islands. Like a number of early Bears, his son also played for Cal, in 1941-42.

for starring in three Big Games. He blocked a kick for a safety in a 2-0 victory in 1901, booted two field goals in a 16-0 decision in 1902 and kicked the Bears into a 6-6 tie in 1903.

Rugby dominated the scene until 1915, so Cal didn't produce any great football players until Andy Smith took over in 1916. His early stars were halfback Carlton "Dummy" Wells and tackle Walter Gordon. The latter became Cal's first All-American, landing a third-team berth on Walter Camp's team in 1918 and also carving a niche as the Bears first prominent black athlete.

Wells began his college career in 1916, but he served in World War I before returning to campus and starring during the 1919 season. That year, the Bears were trailing USC, 7-13, when he scored a touchdown and kicked the extra point for a 14-13 victory. Later, he scored both TDs in a 14-10 Big Game conquest. Other stars in 1919 were linemen Stan Barnes and Cort Majors and halfback Albert "Pesky" Sprott, who gained more fame with the Wonder Team of 1920.

THE WONDER TEAM
A GALAXY OF STARS

Muller is acknowledged as the star of the Wonder Teams, but he had to share the billing with some illustrious teammates until his sensational, 53-yard pass in the 1921 Rose Bowl vaulted him to national fame. As outstanding as Muller was in 1920, he didn't make a big impression on Walt Camp until that Rose Bowl outing, and he wasn't accorded All-American honors until 1921-22.

At 6 feet, 185 pounds, Muller was fast, agile and powerful, with large hands perfectly suited to grip the rounder football of that era. He possessed springy legs, honed by his experience as an Olympic high jumper, and he was equally adept on defense or offense, throwing the ball or catching it. Brick was the star athlete on a 1919 frosh squad that went 10-1, losing only to the Nevada varsity, 13-12.

When he joined the varsity in 1920, the talent on that squad was awesome. Quarterback Charley Erb and fullback Jesse "Duke" Morrison were sophomores, like Brick, but there also was plenty of veteran support. Another newcomer was tackle Dan McMillan. McMillan had starred at USC in 1916-17, but he transferred to Cal after the war and became a second-team All-American in 1920. The other tackle was Stan Barnes, who later became a judge in California's circuit court.

Barnes and Muller played at San Diego High under Nibs Price, and Wonder Teamers Cort Majors and Pesky Sprott also were on that prep squad. Majors, a guard, actually earned

All-American distinction before Muller, landing third-team honors in 1920, his senior year. Sprott and Morrison weren't as fortunate, but they were the warheads of the potent Wonder Team offense, a one-two punch that flattened many foes.

Sprott, a 158-pounder who was voted the "most perfect physical specimen" on campus, came to Cal as a prolific scorer, once tallying 198 points in a single season at San Diego High. He didn't disappoint at Berkeley. In the 1918 Big Game, Sprott scored seven of the 10 touchdowns in Cal's 67-0 romp. It does not stand as a

Carlton "Dummy" Wells was Andy Smith's first backfield star.

school record because that game was played during the war and, therefore, is regarded as semiofficial.

Pesky scored three TDs in the 1920 Big Game and added two more against Ohio State in the Rose Bowl, finishing with 15 touchdowns and 90 points that season. But he wasn't even the team scoring-leader. Those honors went to the powerful Morrison, who totaled 17 touchdowns and 104 points in 1920 and topped the nation with 131 points (18 TDs, 22 PATs and a field goal) in 1922. During his Cal career, Morrison scored 42 touchdowns — a school record. His biggest binges produced five touchdowns against St. Mary's in 1920 (127-0) and a like number against Washington in 1921 (72-3).

Irving "Crip" Toomey also had the ability to score points in those days. He doubled as a halfback and a place-kicker, once booting 10 of 11 conversions against St. Mary's. A talented

Cort Majors earned third-team All-American honors as a guard in 1920.

Tackle Stan Barnes was among the greatest of the Wonder Team stars. He came to Cal from San Diego High, which also spawned Golden Bears Brick Muller, Cort Majors and Pesky Sprott.

runner, Toomey scored on TD gallops of 70 and 30 yards in the 1921 opener against the Gaels and accounted for both of the Bears touchdowns in a 14-0 victory over Washington State that season.

When the early Wonder Team stars departed, there were capable replacements and Cal kept winning. Bill Blewett played only the 1923 season, but it was a memorable one for him. His three field goals downed Olympic Club, 16-0, in the opener, and his touchdown pass to Don Nichols on a fake kick produced a 13-7 victory over USC.

Nichols, who succeeded Sprott as the star halfback in 1921, had an outstanding career with the Wonder Teams. His touchdown and TD pass to Muller defeated Olympic Club, 14-0, in the 1921 opener, and he enjoyed two spectacular games one year later. Against Washington at Seattle, Nichols returned a punt 65 yards for a touchdown and had three other TD dashes of more than 50 yards in a 45-7 romp. In the Big Game, he fired two scoring strikes and scored a TD in a 28-0 drubbing.

Talma "Tut" Imlay was a star back at the end of the Wonder Team era, one which also included a record, 54-yard field goal by Archie Nisbet against Washington State in 1922. It also was during this era that Edwin "Babe" Horrell became a first-team All-American center.

Horrell was the ace lineman of his day, gaining fame by blocking an Ernie Nevers kick and recovering for a touchdown in the 9-0 Big Game blanking of Stanford in 1923. He was named All-American in 1924.

The passing of Smith created a change in Cal's football fortunes, but win or lose, the Bears continued to produce their share of talented athletes.

Edwin "Babe" Horrell was among the second wave of Wonder Team standouts. He earned All-American honors at center in 1924.

Irv Phillips was the captain of the 1928 squad, which played Georgia Tech in the Rose Bowl. He earned All-America end honors in the process.

Ted Beckett, a crack guard, made All-American squads, along with Roy Riegels, in 1929-30.

Roy Riegels was among the nation's outstanding centers in the late twenties, but he unfortunately gained notoriety for his wrong-way run in the 1929 Rose Bowl.

LOM AND WILLIAMS
UNHERALDED EXCELLENCE

The time between the Wonder Teams and the Thunder Teams was a period of sporadic success for Cal football. The Bears, thanks to Smith, were regarded as a perennial West Coast power, so the All-American selectors took notice and were generous. End Irv Phillips was a near-unanimous All-American choice in 1928, linemen Bert Schwarz, Roy Riegels and Ted Beckett were honored on first teams the next two years and halfback Ralston "Rusty" Gill made two All-American squads in 1931.

But the two Cal men who were most prominent on sports pages in the late twenties and early thirties were halfbacks Benny Lom and Arleigh Williams. Each triggered several victories with his running, passing and kicking, and each made an impact on the Golden Bears and their fans for three seasons.

Lom, presently a Bay Area businessman and an avid supporter of the Bears, began playing for Cal as a 5-foot-11-inch, 175-pound sophomore in 1927, and he helped his team compile a 20-6-3 record over the next three years. As a

sophomore, his interception and 20-yard TD run edged Olympic Club, 6-5, and he also uncorked a 42-yard touchdown pass in the 27-13 victory over Penn on the day that the Andy Smith Bench was dedicated.

One year later, his 33-yard TD pass topped St. Mary's, 7-0; his 21-yard TD run and 30-yard TD pass burned Oregon, 13-0; his 38-yard TD pass helped to tie Stanford in the Big Game; and his 10-yard TD pass averted a shutout in the 1929 Rose Bowl game with Georgia Tech, a game in which he produced 113 yards. As a senior in 1929, Lom returned a kickoff 54 yards and fired a 25-yard TD pass in a 12-7 victory over Penn; bolted 85 yards on a fake punt for a 15-7 victory over USC; and hurled a 38-yard TD pass for a 7-0 win over Washington. He made three second-team All-American squads that year.

In between Lom and Williams, 5-foot-6½-inch, 160-pound Hank Schaldach created quite a stir. But whenever it seemed Hank might cross the threshold to greatness, he was struck down by injuries. As a sophomore in 1930, Schaldach fired a 4-yard TD pass and kicked the PAT for a 7-6 victory over St. Mary's. One year later, his TD plunge and a key interception thwarted

Benny Lom, carrying the ball against USC at the L.A. Coliseum, was the Bears best all-purpose back of the late twenties. He passed, ran and kicked Cal to great success, triggering several outstanding victories.

Three Stanford defenders struggle to bring down Hank Schaldach in the 1931 Big Game. It proved to be a difficult task for the Indians all afternoon as Schaldach rushed for 134 yards before leaving in the fourth quarter with an injury. He tallied the lone touchdown and came up with a key interception to lead Cal to a 6-0 victory. In his finest hour, however, Hard Luck Hank scored all three West touchdowns and was the MVP in a 21-13 victory in the 1933 Shrine Game.

Sophomore Arleigh Williams, shown rushing against USC at the L.A. Coliseum in 1932, was the Bears best all-purpose back of the early 1930s. Williams, later a dean at Cal, topped the squad in rushing each season in his three years with the Bears.

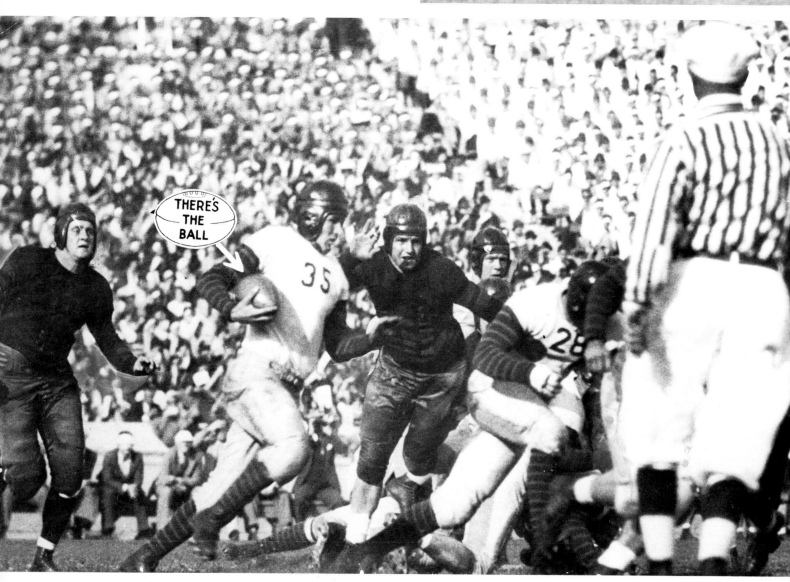

Stanford, 6-0. In an opening double-header in 1932, Hank tossed a 40-yard TD pass and scored on a 50-yard run against the Cal Aggies before throwing an 11-yard TD pass and kicking a PAT against West Coast Navy in the Bears 20-6 and 13-0 sweep. He was injured the following week and wasn't much of a factor the rest of his senior year.

That's where the 5-foot-9-inch, 160-pound Williams comes in. Getting a chance to play because of Schaldach's ailments, Arleigh sparkled as a sophomore in 1932. His 5-yard scoring run helped Cal tie the Gaels, and his 47-yard burst and converion kick edged Washington, 7-6. A few weeks later, Schaldach again was injured, this time after scoring against Idaho, and Williams again went in. Arleigh rushed for 153 yards in 27 carries to power a 21-6 victory, and he finished the season as the squad rushing (508 yards) and scoring (39 points) leader.

In 1933, Arleigh scored a touchdown to erase a 0-13 deficit in a 14-13 victory over St. Mary's, and his touchdown tied the Washington State game at 6-6. Again, he was the team's rushing (434 yards) and scoring (44 points) leader. But the best was yet to come.

Williams earned All-American first-team honors in 1934. As a senior, his 15-yard field goal beat UCLA, 3-0; his 30-yard TD and PAT nipped USC, 7-2; and his TD and kick accounted for all the Cal points in a 7-9 Big Game loss. Williams, who set a punting record with a 72-yarder against USC in 1933, later became dean of students at Cal before retiring.

BOTTARI AND HERWIG CREAM OF THE THUNDER TEAM

An influx of new talent and a coaching change contributed to a 9-1 season in 1935, and the newcomers that year formed the nucleus for the unbeaten 1937 squad that ranked No. 1 in the nation. Sophomores on the 1935 squad included center-linebacker Bob Herwig, quarterback Johnny Meek, halfback Sam Chapman, guard Vard Stockton, end Perry Schwartz (a transfer from Sacramento City College), and fullback Ken Cotton. Best of the veterans on that squad was All-American tackle Larry Lutz.

Herwig, a 6-foot-4-inch, 210-pound giant who played under the aforementioned Nesbit at Pomona High, was to Stub Allison what Muller was to Smith: a pillar of strength capable of any achievement on a football field. An ironman, Herwig played 483 of 600 minutes as a sophomore. As a junior in 1936, he played 494 out of 600 minutes, and he ran 23 yards for a TD with a lateral to down USC, 13-7. In the 1938 Rose Bowl, he made an interception on the

Cal 6 to maintain a shutout against Alabama.

An All-American for two years, Herwig was married to Cal coed Kathleen Winsor during his junior year. Mrs. Herwig went on to write the award-winning novel, "Forever Amber."

When the 1937 Thunder Team went unbeaten, Herwig was joined on first-team All-American squads by teammates Schwartz, Stockton, Meek and Chapman — an unprecedented feat in Cal history.

Chapman, who played for Riegels at Tamalpais High, was a 6-foot-1-inch, 190-pound all-purpose back who made a splash with a 25-yard TD catch in a 21-7 victory over USC in 1935. As a junior, Sam again burned the Trojans, catching a 31-yard scoring strike in a 13-7 victory. He also boomed a punt 57 yards and threw an 18-yard TD pass in a 14-0 decision over Pacific. Chapman crowned his Cal career with an 8-yard TD run and a PAT in a 13-0 Big Game victory in 1937, and he later rushed for 49 yards in 12 carries against Alabama in the Rose Bowl. Ty

Larry Lutz, an All-American tackle in 1935, was the best lineman on the 9-1 squad which launched Stub Allison's Cal coaching career.

Tenacious Bob Herwig, a two-year All-American at center and linebacker, was a workhorse who was regarded as the finest all-around player on the Thunder Team.

Perry Schwartz (99) and an unidentified Cal teammate prepare to pounce on UCLA fullback Fred Funk following Funk's fumble in 1936 action. One year later, Schwartz was an All-American end on the top-ranked Thunder Team.

Cobb recommended the gifted athlete to Connie Mack, who signed him for the Philadelphia Athletics.

The 1936 Bears were struggling with a 3-4 record before a 5-foot-9-inch, 184-pound halfback from the Ramblers (junior varsity) provided the impetus that was to make Cal a national champion one year later. His name was Vic Bottari. He had won 10 letters at Vallejo High and was the national prep record-holder with a 232-foot football throw. The diminutive sophomore was lost in the shuffle at Cal until the eighth game.

Cal was trailing USC, 7-6, in the second half when Bottari came in and rifled a 31-yard touchdown pass for a 13-7 victory. The next week, he unleashed a 42-yard TD pass and also scored in a 28-0 rout of Oregon. The Big Game found him hurling a 35-yard TD pass in a 20-0

victory. In only three games, the Bears unveiled a new star — one who spurred three straight victories and a winning season.

By 1937, Bottari no longer was taking people by surprise. Chapman, then a senior, was the All-American back on that championship squad, but Bottari and junior fullback Dave Anderson were more successful. Vallejo Vic scored twice in a 24-6 romp over Oregon State; fired a 31-yard TD pass and scored twice in a 27-0 whipping of Washington State; tallied twice in a 20-6 win over USC; repeated the two-TD trick in a 27-14 decision over UCLA; and scored in the 13-0 Big Game victory.

Saving his best for last, Bottari gained national attention with a spectacular Rose Bowl performance against Alabama. The Bears won, 13-0, and Vic scored both touchdowns on 4-yard runs. He carried 32 times for 130 yards in a

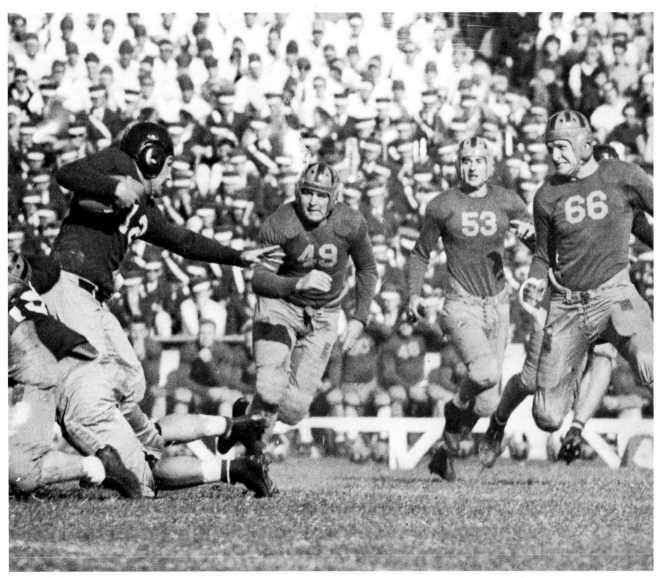

Santa Clara's Don DeRosa is about to encounter Cal's Don Meek (49), Jack Brittingham (53) and Bob Herwig (66) during the Bears 6-0 victory in 1935.

An unheralded aspect of the Bears Thunder Team success was the bruising blocking of fullback Dave Anderson (foreground) and quarterback Johnny Meek (right), shown performing their specialty against Bob Williams of UCLA in Cal's 27-14 triumph at Los Angeles.

Sam Chapman was an excellent all-around back who capped his football career with the 1937 Thunder Team before becoming a major league baseball star.

Vic Bottari (with ball), with blocking by fullback Dave Anderson (56), bursts into the UCLA end zone. Bottari scored twice in Cal's 20-7 victory in 1938. Bruins star Kenny Washington (left) comes up too late to prevent the touchdown.

game in which no other back netted more than 59 yards. For the season, Bottari rushed for 770 yards and a 4.8 average, shattering the school rushing record. He also scored 12 touchdowns, fourth best in the nation. Anderson added 520 yards and a 5.1 average.

Bottari finally attained All-American honors in 1938, powering a 10-1 team. He was a key factor in 26 Cal games, of which the Bears won 23 and tied one. Highlights of his senior season included: a 45-yard TD pass and a 32-yard scoring run in a 27-3 blitz of WSC; two TD runs and a scoring pass while rushing for 148 yards in the first half of a 39-0 rout of Pacific; two TDs in a 20-7 victory over UCLA; a TD plunge in a 14-7 squeaker over Washington; a 6-yard TD in a 13-7 win over OSC; and a brilliant Big Game that featured three tackles on a goal-line stand and a winning, 22-yard touchdown pass to Angelo Reginato for a 6-0 victory.

Vallejo Vic concluded his senior season with 579 yards and a 3.6 average. Anderson was right behind at 510 and 4.0. Bottari's three-year rushing total of 1,536 was the Cal record until Jackie Jensen came along. In fact, the Bears had little to cheer about offensively for almost 10 years after Bottari and Anderson departed following the 1938 season.

Tackle Lee Artoe transferred from Santa Clara and anchored the Cal line in 1939. That season found 6-foot-3-inch, 220-pound Bob Reinhard making his varsity debut at tackle. Reinhard, a two-time All-American in 1940-41, also was a standout punter, setting a school single-game record with a 47.7 average on 12 kicks against Washington in 1940. Versatile, he scored on a 41-yard TD catch against the Huskies in 1941 and also scored after blocking Frankie Albert's punt in the Big Game. "Bob Reinhard is the best offensive and defensive tackle I have ever seen," Allison declared.

JACKIE JENSEN
THE GOLDEN BOY

"The Golden Boy," a nickname that says it all. Jackie Jensen was a 5-foot-11-inch, 190-pound hunk of muscle and grace who made the coeds swoon. A former Oakland prep, Jensen had good looks and wavy blond hair. An Adonis of

Vic Bottari (92) was better known for his offensive prowess during an All-American campaign in 1938, but the Cal superstar also was adept on the other side of the line. Here, he makes a sensational one-handed stop of USC's Grenville Landsdell at the 6-inch line to prevent a touchdown in action at the L.A. Coliseum.

Cal tackle Lee Artoe (airborne) dives to bring down Washington's Ernie Steele in 1939 Memorial Stadium action. Artoe, a transfer from Santa Clara, was an All-American in 1939, and teammate Bob Reinhard (45) earned similar distinction in 1940-41.

148

an athlete, he excelled in football and baseball, eventually signing a contract with the Oakland Oaks and reaching stardom with the Boston Red Sox. Jackie had a stormy stint as Cal's baseball coach in the mid-seventies, but that doesn't diminish the fact that he is the University of California's finest all-around athlete ever.

Jensen was a big-play performer, electrifying fans with his flair for the dramatic. As a freshman in 1946, he returned a punt 56 yards for a touchdown and the only score in a 28-7 loss to Wisconsin. One week later, he fired a 47-yard touchdown pass in a 14-13 loss to Oregon. His 29-yard TD catch accounted for the only points in a 13-6 loss to UCLA. He added a 58-yard TD catch in a 20-6 loss to Washington and scored on a 56-yard run against WSC. Jackie was so impressive as a freshman that he was selected to the West squad for the Shrine Game.

The following spring, he pitched Cal to the first NCAA baseball championship. In a key tournament game, he out-hurled Texas star Bobby Layne, snapping his 24-game win string. Jensen also hammered the longest homer in Cal history, a 535-footer. In the fall, he was equally spectacular for rookie coach Pappy Waldorf's Golden Bear gridders, rushing for 434 yards and a 5.1 average and passing for 271 yards and two touchdowns.

The second game of the 1947 season attracted a record 83,000 fans to Memorial Stadium for the game with Navy. Jensen put on a show, rushing for 113 yards in only 13 carries, including a 64-yard TD, and intercepting a pass in a 14-7 triumph. Wisconsin was singed by his 23-yard TD pass and a 22-yard scoring run, and his 80-yard scoring pass play to Paul Keckley pulled out a 21-18 Big Game victory.

There was concern in 1948, however, because grade problems made "The Golden Boy" ineligible for spring football. He made it, though, and began his All-American campaign with a school-record, 192-yard rushing performance in

All-American Jackie Jensen starts his final season at Cal with a bang, bolting for a 62-yard touchdown in the 1948 opener against Santa Clara. Jensen rushed for a school-record 192 yards on only 12 carries, scoring twice in the Bears 41-19 rout.

the opening, 41-19 demolition of Santa Clara. Jensen scored on runs of 61 and 62 yards and piled up the yardage on only a dozen carries, averaging a remarkable 16 yards per attempt.

In a crucial, 13-7 victory over USC, Jackie virtually was a one-man gang. He scored on runs of 8 and 2 yards and complied 132 yards in 27 carries, proving he could be a workhorse if necessary. In a 7-6 Big Game thriller, Jensen booted a record, 67-yard punt and managed a 32-yard run to daylight in a fourth-and-31 situation while rushing for 170 yards. He broke loose for a 67-yard TD against Northwestern in the Rose Bowl, an appropriate finish to his big-play Cal career, before going to the sidelines with an injury.

Jensen concluded his junior year with a single-season rushing mark of 1,080 yards, and he became the career leader with 1,703 yards and a nifty 6.0 average. He also shared the single-season interception record with seven in 1947. "The Golden Boy" was so gifted that he cast a large shadow over other outstanding Cal backs

of that era, notably Jack Swaner, a 5-foot-11-inch, 200-pound bull from Coalinga.

"Jensen was as good a back as I've ever coached," Waldorf said, "but I remember Swaner for his determination and resourcefulness. If there was a hole, he'd find it; if not, he'd make one." Swaner, 10th on the Cal career rushing charts with 1,335 yards and also 10th on the single-season list with 784 yards in 1948, complemented Jensen beautifully, creating headaches for defenses.

Swaner scooted 65 yards for a touchdown against USC in 1947, and he enjoyed his finest season as a junior in 1948. Jensen had five plus-100 games that season, and Swaner was right behind with four in what became the best one-two punch at Cal (1,864 yards) until Chuck Muncie and Tom Newton totaled 2,004 yards in 1975. Swaner rushed for 107 yards against Santa Clara, 106 against Oregon State, 119 against Washington and 131 against WSC.

His finest performance came against the Huskies, when he scored all three touchdowns in

Jackie Jensen, straining for more yardage, virtually was a one-man offense as the Golden Boy powered the Golden Bears to a 13-7 victory over Southern Cal at the L. A. Coliseum in 1948. Jensen scored twice and rushed for 132 yards against the Trojans.

Jack Swaner, who played in Jackie Jensen's shadow, pokes his head through the Washington line for a touchdown. Swaner scored all three Cal touchdowns in a 21-0 victory at Berkeley in 1949.

Jim Monachino (35) was among a stable of outstanding running backs under Pappy Waldorf. Here, he scoots for 24 yards against Oregon State in 1950, a season in which he rushed for 754 yards and earned All-American honors. Blocking for Monachino are Charles Harris (54), Bob Karpe (72) and Don Curran (71).

a 21-0 victory. Swaner, who had a team-leading 12 TDs in 1948, sizzled down the stretch, scoring twice against both UCLA and WSC, then accounting for the only Cal TD on a 6-yard run in the 7-6 Big Game victory.

With Jensen turning pro and Swaner hobbled with injuries, Jim Monachino was the big gun in 1949, rushing for 781 yards. He established a Big Game record with 190 yards in 20 carries, including an 84-yard run in a 33-14 breeze.

ROD FRANZ
CAL'S ONLY THREE-TIME ALL-AMERICAN

Bespectacled Rod Franz, a 6-foot-1-inch, 205-pound guard, resembled Clark Kent in more ways than one. Mild-mannered off the field, the sturdy San Franciscan didn't bother using telephone booths to change clothes. He used Cal's dressing quarters and turned into a ferocious creature whenever he donned a football uniform. A first-team All-American in 1947-49, he became the only Bear to attain that distinction three years.

"Franz is the hardest-hitting guard I've seen in my 24 years of coaching," Waldorf said. Jensen, for whom Franz opened numerous holes, was more descriptive. "During a game, you can't get Rod to smile," Jackie recalled at the time. "He gets a kind of glare and talks in a growl. Even in practice, he scares you."

While Bear backs like Jensen, Swaner, Monachino, Pete Schabarum, Charley Sarver, Frank Brunk, Billy Main and Staten Webster were running wild in the late forties, Franz certainly wasn't the only accomplished lineman. Tackle Jim Turner earned All-American distinction in 1948-49, and guard Forrest Klein was honored in 1949. Another guard, Jim "Truck" Cullom, was better known for his toe, kicking 103 extra points in 1947-49 and setting a PCC record with 39 in 1949.

JOHNNY OLSZEWSKI
OH, JOHNNY O!

Cal fans were spoiled in Waldorf's heyday, seemingly always being entertained by great running backs. No sooner had Jensen and Swaner departed than Monachino was there to fill the void. He was an All-American in 1950, totaling 754 yards and a 4.9 average, while fellow halfback Schabarum — now a Los Angeles politician — added 647 yards, a 4.6 average and a team-leading 11 touchdowns. But neither halfback was the Bears top rusher.

That distinction went to Johnny Olszewski, a 5-foot-11-inch, 195-pound sophomore strongboy from Long Beach who doubled as a lifeguard during the summer months. Johnny O had a shaky debut as Cal's fullback in the 1950 opener

against Santa Clara. He was tackled in the end zone for a safety while the Broncos built a 9-0 lead in the second quarter. But Olszewski bounced back with a 55-yard TD run and finished with 111 yards in eight carries — a dazzling 13.9 average.

Two weeks later, he rambled 43 yards for a touchdown and totaled 134 yards in 16 carries against Penn. Against Washington, Olszewski rushed for 119 yards, and then bowled over five tacklers on a 73-yard run while gaining 144 against UCLA. Concluding his sophomore season with 58 yards against Michigan in the Rose Bowl, Johnny O finished with 1,008 yards and a 6.0 average, and the superlatives started flying.

"I've never seen anyone his age hit harder," remarked Rams coach Joe Stydahar. "The guy is half Grange, half Nagurski." Olszewski was being groomed for All-American honors as a junior in 1951. The catchy "Johnny O" nickname caught fire on campus. "Johnny O Juice" could be purchased at Memorial Stadium, and Larry Blake's served a "Johnny O Sundae." The fever intensified when Olszewski rushed for a record-breaking 269 yards and a 13.5 average,

Tackle Jim Turner was a two-time All-American, yet he was relatively unheralded at tackle because he played alongside three-time All-American Rod Franz.

Forrest Klein was the third Cal lineman honored as an All-American in 1949.

Rod Franz (67), the only three-time All-American in Cal history, is about to plow into Stanford's Bob White during the 1949 Big Game. Franz was all business on the field offensively and defensively at guard in 1946-49.

scoring twice on runs of 80 and 28 yards in a 42-35 donnybrook with WSC.

That gave the bruising Bear a remarkable 549 yards in four games entering the Memorial Stadium contest with USC. The Trojans, beaten by Cal three straight years, were fired up for this one, and there were reports that Johnny O was a marked man. When linebacker Pat Cannamela twisted Olszewski's knee and put him out of the game, Cal partisans didn't feel it was an accident, and emotions ran high while USC was posting a 21-14 victory.

Johnny O missed the next three games and obviously wasn't himself while rushing for only 63 yards in the final three games of the season. Sufficiently mended, however, Olszewski geared up for a stellar senior year in 1952, rushing for 122 yards and two TDs in an opening, 34-13 victory over Pacific. A few weeks later, he gained 172 yards in only 17 carries at Oregon. When he capped his Cal career with 122 yards

in the Big Game, he had a total of 2,504 yards — breaking Hugh McElhenny's PCC mark of 2,499.

Johnny O, who took ballet lessons to improve his balance, was a first-round draft choice by the NFL's Cardinals, but thanks partially to Cannamela, he never reached the greatness he promised as a college sophomore.

RICHTER AND HAZELTINE LAST OF A BREED

Les Richter and Matt Hazeltine had a lot in common while they ruled the roost as the Bears finest defenders of the fifties. Each made All-American twice, each was a first-round draft pick by the pros and each excelled on offense and defense. They were the last of the great two-way linemen in Bear history. Richter was a guard-linebacker and Hazeltine was a center-linebacker, each gaining all-pro status because of his defensive abilities.

Richter, who was part of one of the largest

Fullback Johnny Olszewski (36) darts through hole during Cal's record rampage against Minnesota on October 6, 1951, at Memorial Stadium. Johnny O bulled for 135 yards in 17 carries and scored once in the Bears 55-14 runaway. Cal established records for total offense — 638 yards — and rushing — 490 yards — which still stand.

Matt Hazeltine, equally adept at handling center and linebacking chores, was a two-time All-American for the Golden Bears in 1953-54.

Les Richter makes an interception during the Bears 35-14 victory over Oregon State in 1951. He gained All-American distinction in 1950-51 not only for his linebacking, but also because of his place-kicking and offensive guard play.

ONE-DAY WONDERS CARVE NICHE IN CAL HISTORY

It was November 13, 1954, a cool, dry day at Memorial Stadium, and 25,000 showed up to watch the Bears take on Oregon State. All-American end Jim Hanifan caught a pair of TD passes as Cal forged an 18-0 lead early in the third quarter. Al Carmichael intercepted a pass and returned it 57 yards for a TD, and the Bears led, 25-0, midway through the period. Nothing really spectacular — merely a routine rout.

What happened the remainder of that game,

however, will be stamped indelibly on the minds of those who witnessed an incredible performance by Jerry Drew, a 195-pound junior reserve fullback. Drew scored on runs of 67, 59 and 55 yards to complete a 46-7 runaway. On his last two carries, he totaled 36 yards to set a school record of 283 yards — erasing Johnny Olszewski's 269. Drew did it in only 11 carries, setting a PCC single-game record of 25.7 yards per carry.

Drew suggested he was more than a flash in the pan by scoring on a 27-yard run the following week against Stanford. But he suffered a broken arm that kept him out of the 1955 campaign, and he totaled only 109 yards in 42 carries as a senior in 1956. Drew had a mediocre Cal career, but for a few fleeting moments in 1954, he was the best. Some people never have that opportunity, but he made the best of it.

Drew has a lot of company, though, when it comes to one-shot stardom for the Golden Bears. As early as 1902, star halfback Locomotive Smith was declared ineligible for the Big Game. Bobby Sherman took his place and powered a 16-0 victory with a 105-yard punt return. That was a Cal record until Don Guest, another one-game wonder, returned a missed field goal attempt 108 yards against WSU in 1966.

Along the same vein, Jim Jurkovich returned an interception 100 yards against Southern Cal, but he did little to distinguish himself thereafter. Ditto halfback John Wilson, who like Drew was a reserve in 1954. Against San Jose State, Wilson bolted 96 yards for a TD — the second longest run from scrimmage in Cal history — but totaled only 49 more yards the rest of the season.

Two quarterbacks from the Mike White era also experienced brief flirts with fame before fading out of the picture. Jay Cruze, on September 30, 1972, at Missouri accumulated 354 passing yards to shatter Dave Penhall's school record of 321 yards. Cruze's mark was topped by Joe Roth, but on October 15, 1977, Charlie Young passed for a record 375 yards against Oregon State. That was broken by Rich Campbell, but Young's total offense mark of 399 yards still stands as a consolation to a man who lost his first-string status a few weeks later.

Fullback Jerry Drew didn't enjoy a spectacular Cal career, but for one day, he was as good as any Bear who ever carried the ball. Against Oregon State in 1954, the reserve back came to life in the second half, rambling for three touchdowns and a school-record 283 yards to cap a 46-7 rout.

trades in NFL history, came to Cal as a 205-pound fullback-linebacker out of Fresno. Richter fullbacked on the 1948 frosh squad, but he was shifted to center by Waldorf in 1949. He also showed signs of developing into an outstanding linebacker as a sophomore, but an injury retarded his progress. Nonetheless, the Dallas Texans drafted him in 1949 following his sophomore campaign.

Growing to 230 pounds, Les became a guard in 1950 and earned All-American honors that season along with Monachino and defensive back Carl Van Heuit. Richter was an All-American again in 1951, a season in which he also established a PCC record with 40 conversion kicks. Succeeding Cullom as the Bears kicking specialist, Richter converted 64 of 75 attempts in two years. But he gained most attention with his catlike quickness and hard-hitting ability at linebacker.

Hazeltine, a 6-foot-1-inch, 200-pounder from Marin County, was among two Bears to make the varsity as freshmen in 1951. By the time he was a sophomore, Matt was a starter, rising to All-American distinction in 1953-54 before achieving stardom with the 49ers. His father, Matt Sr., was a standout rugby player for the Blue & Gold prior to World War I.

Jim Hanifan, now the coach of the St. Louis Cardinals, set a school record with 44 receptions in 1954, but the Bears were without a non-quarterback All-American for 14 years before Ed "Porker" White earned honors at nose guard in 1968. Because of the single-platoon system, White only played defense. But he later became an all-pro offensive lineman with the Vikings and the Chargers, so he surely was of the Richter-Hazeltine caliber.

Ed, a 6-foot-3-inch, 240-pound mound of muscle, was a key figure in coach Ray Willsey's defensive emphasis. Willsey believed in placing his best athletes on defense, and in 1968 he was

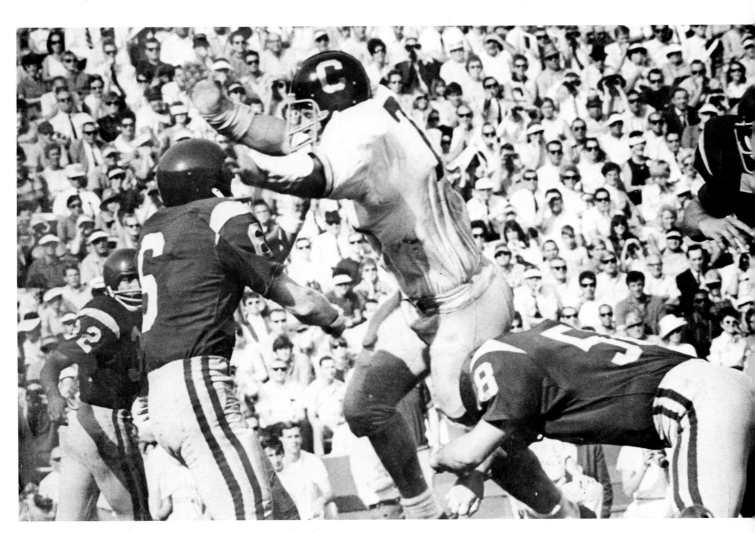

Ed White, Cal's finest lineman of the sixties, breaks through the USC line to smother quarterback Steve Sogge while O. J. Simpson (left) looks on. Though White starred on defense for the Bears, he became an All-Pro on offense with the Vikings and the Chargers.

157

blessed with White, linebackers Irby Augustine and Mike McCaffrey and safety Ken Wiedemann. Three years later, 6-foot-5-inch, 250-pound Sherman White nailed down All-American honors at defensive tackle and was a first-round draft pick of the Bills.

Offensively, the sixties produced few standouts, with the exception of Craig Morton. Wide receiver Jerry Bradley and tailback Paul Williams were good enough to become star defensive backs in the CFL, and Wayne Stewart became an NFL tight end after starring for the Bears as a sophomore safety and as a wide receiver his final two years.

Among the linemen, defensive tackle Stan Dzura was destined for greatness before a knee injury ended his career following the 1964 season, John Garamendi, a California gubernatorial candidate in 1982, was an excellent offensive guard in 1965, and offensive tackle Bob Richards was all-conference in 1969-70. Dan Goich showed promise as a lineman in 1965-66 and later played in the NFL.

The Bears best running back of the sixties was Gary Fowler, a methodically effective athlete who totaled 1,585 yards and a 4.1 average in three seasons — a figure topped only by Olszewski and Jensen until Chuck Muncie and Paul Jones came along in the seventies. Fowler rushed for 741 yards in 1969, fifth on the all-time list at the time. And in a season-ending game in 1968, he gained 206 yards in a Hawaii quagmire, fifth on the all-time single-game list.

CHUCK MUNCIE
KING OF THE HIGH-SCORING SEVENTIES

Not since the days of Jensen had the Bears been blessed with an all-purpose back of Chuck Muncie's quality. The perfect man for Mike White's multifaceted offense, the 6-foot-3-inch, 228-pound Muncie flourished for three seasons — 1973-75 — while rewriting the school rushing records. Like Franz, Muncie was deceptive. Wearing thick, horn-rimmed glasses, he was docile off the field — a black Clark Kent, if you will. Born in Uniontown, Pennsylvania,

Sherman White, an All-American tackle in 1971, is about to sack UCLA quarterback Dennis Dummit during a controversial, 24-21 loss to the Bruins at Memorial Stadium in 1970.

Gary Fowler (left) takes a handoff and sloshes through the mud for some big yardage in Cal's 1968 game at Hawaii. Fowler plowed for 206 yards to lift the Bears to a 17-12 victory during a tropical rainstorm at Honolulu.

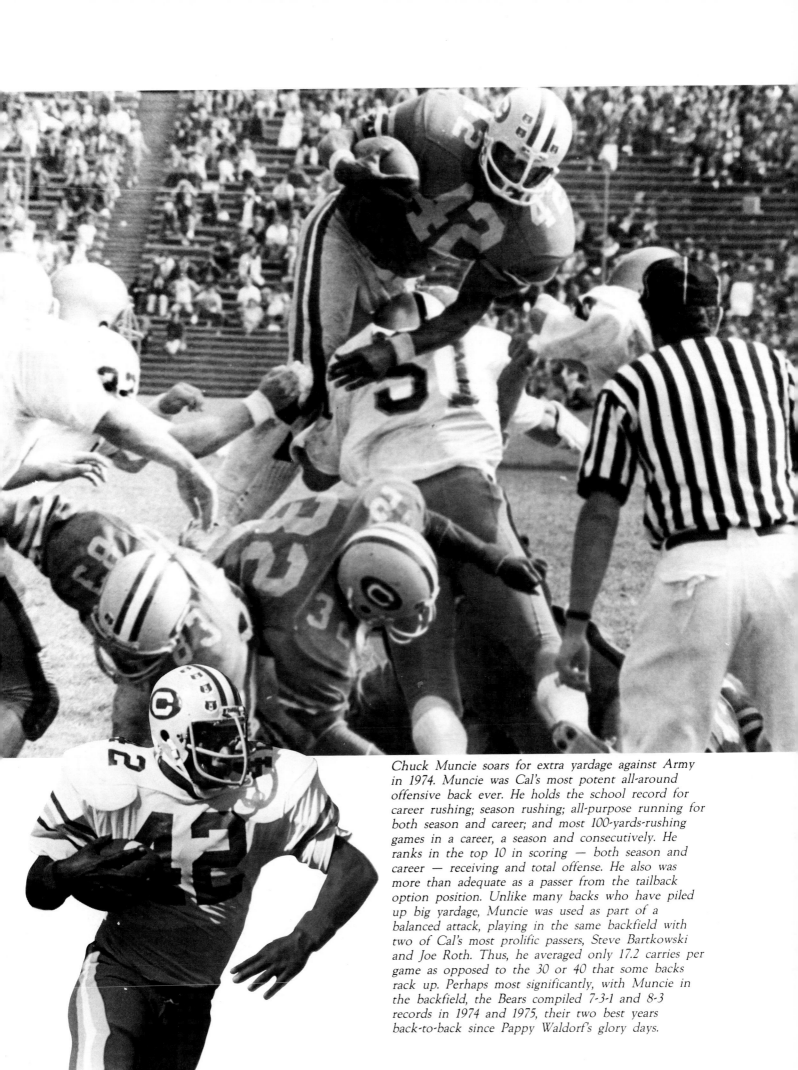

Chuck Muncie soars for extra yardage against Army in 1974. Muncie was Cal's most potent all-around offensive back ever. He holds the school record for career rushing; season rushing; all-purpose running for both season and career; and most 100-yards-rushing games in a career, a season and consecutively. He ranks in the top 10 in scoring — both season and career — receiving and total offense. He also was more than adequate as a passer from the tailback option position. Unlike many backs who have piled up big yardage, Muncie was used as part of a balanced attack, playing in the same backfield with two of Cal's most prolific passers, Steve Bartkowski and Joe Roth. Thus, he averaged only 17.2 carries per game as opposed to the 30 or 40 that some backs rack up. Perhaps most significantly, with Muncie in the backfield, the Bears compiled 7-3-1 and 8-3 records in 1974 and 1975, their two best years back-to-back since Pappy Waldorf's glory days.

Muncie came to Berkeley via Arizona Western Junior College and left a mammoth imprint on the Bears and their followers.

Muncie had the rare combination of size and speed and was capable of breaking tackles like a powerful fullback or eluding them with moves. As a sophomore in 1973, he rushed for 801 yards, a figure topped only by Jensen and Olszewski. He rushed four times for more than 100 yards, and he caught eight passes against WSU. Injury limited him to nine games as a junior, but he still managed 791 yards.

By the time he was a senior, Muncie was virtually unstoppable while becoming an All-American, a Heisman Trophy candidate and a first-round NFL draft pick. Quite simply, it was the finest season ever enjoyed by a Cal back — the incomparable Jensen included. In 11 games during the 8-3 campaign of 1975, Muncie never rushed for less than 87 yards. He was above 100 nine times, with a high of 207 against Oregon.

He was "held" to 95 yards by San Jose State, but his last-ditch reception in a fourth-and-long

situation spurred a 27-24 victory. Against Oregon State, Muncie scored three times and fired a 47-yard TD pass in a 51-24 romp. He was a one-man show in the title-clinching 48-15 Big Game explosion, scoring on runs of 16, 1 and 3 yards, catching a 7-yard TD pass and throwing a 46-yard scoring strike.

His total of 166 yards rushing in that Big Game gave Muncie a school single-season rushing record of 1,460 yards — 380 more than Jensen's 1,080 in 1948 — and his career total was 3,052 — 548 more than Johnny O's 2,504. But the amazing thing is that Muncie didn't carry 30 times a game like many workhorse backs, averaging 17.2 carries for his 32 games at Cal. Muncie's 1,871 all-purpose running yards in 1975 erased Isaac Curtis' school-record 1,449, and his 4,194 career all-purpose yards also is the Bear standard.

Muncie had 97 career receptions for 1,085 yards, an 11.2 average. His 15 touchdowns for 90 points in 1975 tied Monachino's modern single-season record, and his 37 career touchdowns were surpassed only by Morrison's 42.

Steve Sweeney, No. 2 on Cal's all-time receiving list, catches a pass in the end zone against UCLA in 1972.

The Bears had a perfect offense in 1975, topping the NCAA with an equal number of yards rushing and passing, and Muncie definitely was the perfect back. Continuing his success with the Saints and the Chargers, Muncie is the most successful ex-Bear runner ever in the NFL.

SWEENEY, RIVERA AND WALKER THE BEST OF THE REST

When Muncie and the quarterbacks weren't dominating headlines in the seventies, an outstanding crop of receivers was — the most notable being Steve Sweeney, Steve Rivera and Wesley Walker. Jack Schraub, Geoff DeLapp, Bradley and Stewart were excellent receivers in the Willsey days, but they paled in comparison to the clutch performances of Sweeney, Rivera and Walker.

Sweeney, a 6-foot-4-inch, 195-pound junior-college transfer from Yakima, Washington, had three great seasons at Cal — 1970-72 — while working with a half-dozen different starting quarterbacks. As a sophomore, he caught seven passes against Texas and USC, and he finished

Acrobatic catches were commonplace for All-American end Steve Rivera (7) during an illustrious Cal career. Rivera, precise in his patterns, grabbed a school-record 138 passes from the likes of Steve Bartkowski, Vince Ferragamo and Joe Roth in 1973-75.

with 43 receptions. One year later, he set a school record with 195 yards and three touchdowns on seven receptions against Oregon State. As a senior in 1972, the glue-fingered Sweeney set Cal marks with 52 receptions, 785 yards and 13 TDs, the last one beating Stanford with no time on the clock.

Sweeney's 132 catches for 2,043 yards and 21 TDs were school records until Rivera and Walker came along a few years later and reaped the benefits from the passing proficiency of Bartkowski and Roth. The 6-foot, 185-pound Rivera and the 6-foot-1-inch, 180-pound Walker played on the same teams for three years —

Wesley Walker (right) scored on this last-ditch touchdown pass from Joe Roth, despite Gerald Small's defensive efforts, to give the Bears a come-from-behind, 27-24 victory over San Jose State in 1975. One year later, Walker set a school record with 289 yards in receptions against SJS and concluded an electrifying Cal career with an NCAA-record, 25.7-yard average on his catches.

1973-75 — and complemented each other impeccably. Rivera was the sure-handed, pattern receiver, whereas Walker was the blurring bomb threat with 9.3 speed.

Rivera, a Florida native who prepped in Los Angeles, started slowly as a sophomore in 1973, but he blossomed during his junior year and set school records with 56 catches for 938 yards. That season included an 8-for-158 performance, two TDs at Illinois and nine catches for a record 205 yards in the Big Game.

As a senior All-American one year later, Riv turned a fantastic stretch drive — 42 catches in five games — to break his own record by totaling 57 receptions, including 10 apiece against UCLA and Washington. He also erased Sweeney's career marks with 138 catches for 2,085 yards.

When Rivera wasn't driving defenses daffy with his crisp routes, Walker was burning them with blazing speed. Walker, a Los Angeles native, was Cal's first four-year, double-sport letter-winner since before World War II. He wasn't as consistent as Rivera, but he was far more spectacular. Wesley did quite a bit of damage in the relatively few times he touched the football. His 86 career receptions, for instance, merely rank 10th on the all-time Bear list, but nobody in the Blue & Gold ever gained more yards (2,206) had a better yards-per-catch average (25.7) or scored more touchdowns through the air (22) than this graceful athlete.

With Rivera gone, Walker was the main man in 1976, and he achieved greatness when he wasn't slowed by injuries. In the opener at Georgia, Wesley was on the receiving end of Roth TD bombs covering 69 and 88 yards, the latter being the longest in Cal history. A few weeks later, Walker stunned San Jose State by grabbing scoring strikes of 75 and 48 yards from Fred Besana and a 57-yarder from Roth. He finished with eight receptions for a school-record 289 yards.

Walker, used almost exclusively as a return specialist while a freshman in 1973, ranks third on Cal's all-purpose running chart with 3,085. Only Muncie and Paul Jones are higher, but they touched the ball 10 times as much as Walker, who made the most of his opportunities. Wesley, the most successful sprinter-gridder in Cal history, wasn't an All-American — probably because of his injuries — but he was drafted high by the Jets and has been a standout NFL receiver ever since.

Other receivers had big years in the seventies, namely Jesse Thompson, George Freitas, Joe Rose and Matt Bouza. The latter was a walk-on athlete and had a dream campaign in 1979. He

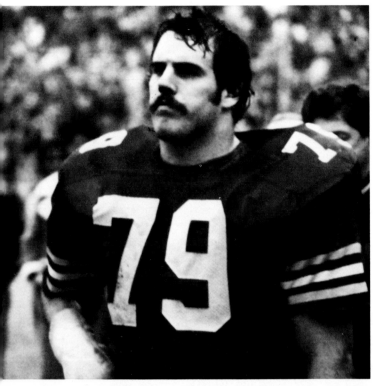

Tackle Ted Albrecht was the offensive line star of the 1975 Cal powerhouse which led the nation in total offense. Albrecht, equally effective on the run or the pass, was an NFL first-round pick.

Fullback Paul Jones (46) plunges for a few of his 81 yards in Cal's upset of Southern Cal in 1977. Although Jones never received the honors of a Muncie or Jensen, his consistent play (4.1 yards per carry) earned top ten rankings in career and season rushing and all-purpose running and career receiving. He is the only Cal back with two 200-yards-rushing games, one coming in 1978 when he was elected the team's offensive MVP.

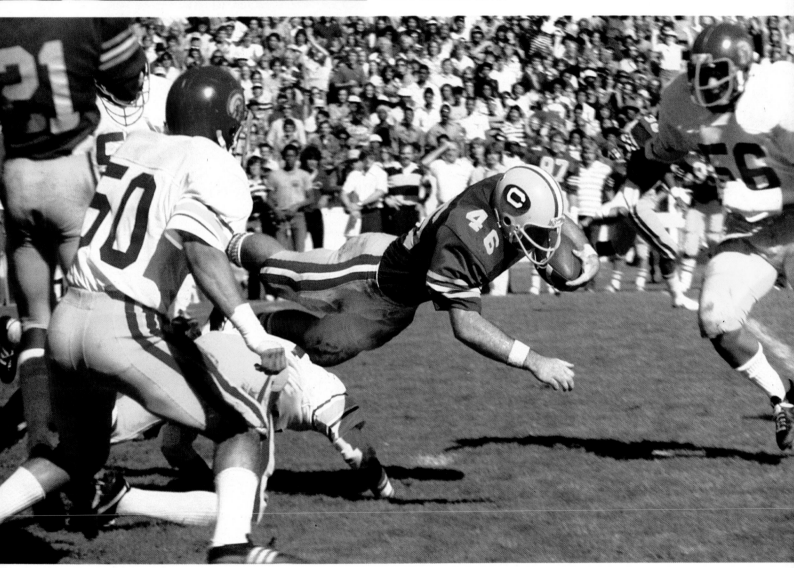

caught 59 passes that year, including 11 apiece against San Jose State and Washington. He is not credited with the school record, however, because seven balls were caught in the Garden State Bowl against Temple.

Some would argue whether Paul Jones was a great fullback — the NFL didn't think so — but he was powerful and persistent enough to rush for 2,930 yards and a 4.1 average in 1975-79. Only Muncie rushed for more yards in his career, only Muncie had more all-purpose yards than Jones' 3,726, and only four Bears caught more passes than Jones' 104. Moreover, with 232 yards against WSU in 1978 and 200 yards against Missouri in 1977, he stands as the only Cal player with a pair of plus-200 performances. Not great, perhaps, but certainly far better than average.

Cal's finest lineman of the seventies was offensive tackle Ted Albrecht, an All-American and a first-round draft choice of the Chicago Bears in 1976. Offensive guard Chris Mackie was an All-American in 1974. The best linebackers of the seventies were Phil Croyle and Loren Toews, though Rob Swenson was converted from the line into an all-pro linebacker with Denver.

Outstanding defensive backs were abundant, including Herman Edwards, Dwayne O'Steen and Anthony Washington, all of whom transferred from Cal before entering pro ball. Of the ones who stayed with the Bears, Ray Youngblood, Anthony Green and Ron Coccimiglio deserve special mention. Of the seventies linemen, Bob Kampa, Chris Mackie, Duane Williams and Ralph DeLoach were all-conference.

Cal also developed some excellent kickers in recent years. Jim Breech stands alone among the place-kickers. With 110 PATs and 50 field goals, he ranks as the school's No. 2 all-time scorer with 260 points. But Randy and Ray Wersching, Ron Miller, Mick Luckhurst, Ron Vander Meer and Joe Cooper had their moments, too.

Luckhurst, who landed with the Atlanta Falcons in 1981, and Vander Meer share the school field-goal record with 54-yarders. Ray Wershing and Breech provided a proud moment for Old Blues in Super Bowl XVI, doing the place-kicking for the 49ers and the Bengals, respectively. Cal's finest punter, however, was Dan Melville, who averaged a record 42.3 yards in 1977 and kicked a record 84-yarder in 1978.

Ray Wersching (5), shown kicking a field goal in 1972, was Cal's premier kicker of the early seventies. He gained notoriety as a pro, however, leading the Super Bowl XVI champion 49ers in scoring in 1981.

Much of the success of Steve Bartkowski and Chuck Muncie in 1974 can be attributed to the All-American line play of offensive guard Chris Mackie.

Place-kicker Jim Breech (3) boots an 18-yard field goal out of Gary Graumann's hold for a 10-7, third-quarter lead over Southern Cal in 1977. The boot placed the Bears ahead to stay, and they posted a 17-14 upset of USC in the first Joe Roth Memorial Game.

CHAPTER
6

100
YEARS
1882
1982

CAL
BLVE
AND
GOLD

Joe Roth was a portrait in courage for Cal during a short, successful and inspirational career in 1975-76. Coming to Berkeley from the junior-college ranks, Roth was a second-stringer before he took control and guided the co-champion 8-3 powerhouse of 1975. One year later, he started swiftly, but he soon was being sapped of strength by the ravages of cancer and succumbed to the virulent disease in February of 1977.

Chapter Six
THE GOLDEN ARMS

Prodigious passing performances and All-American distinction for a Cal quarterback didn't occur until the forties, but Cal football always has been blessed with exemplary field leadership. The men who played quarterback for the Blue & Gold during the first half of the century, however, were not constantly in the spotlight, as has been the case for prolific passers such as Craig Morton, Steve Bartkowski and Rich Campbell.

The game, of course, has changed. More emphasis is placed on statistics, and the T-formation and pro-style offenses have made the quarterback more of a specialist. At Cal, a premium has been placed on passing ability over the last 20 years. In olden days, quarterbacks were not required to be strong-armed. Their value then was in leadership and ballhandling because the single-wing and double-wing formations featured deception and rushing, not throwing the football.

Moreover, specialization and the single-platoon style of play demand that the modern quarterback be less of an all-around athlete and more of a pinpoint passer. Not since the fifties, when Paul Larson and Joe Kapp were equally adept as defensive backs, have the Golden Bears fielded two-way threats at quarterback, though it is assumed great athletes such as Morton and Bartkowski might have been defensive standouts as well.

Before Larson came along in the early fifties, Cal had its share of significant passing performances, but they rarely were the handiwork of the quarterback. Everyone seemed to get into the act, but most of the passing was done by crack halfbacks such as Benny Lom, Arleigh Williams, Sam Chapman and Vic Bottari. It is significant to note that perhaps the two most famous passes in Golden Bear history — Muller-to-Stephens in the 1921 Rose Bowl and Jensen-to-Keckley in the 1947 Big Game — were not thrown by quarterbacks.

The point is that it is totally unfair to compare the early Cal quarterbacks to their pass-happy counterparts of the sixties and seventies simply because the standards were different. Charley Erb of the Wonder Teams and Johnny Meek of the Thunder Teams were regarded as outstanding quarterbacks, but they didn't have to complete a pass to prove it.

Nevertheless, the pass always has been a vital instrument in Cal's gridiron success. When it wasn't fashionable to throw the ball, the Bears did it well anyway — probably because defenses had to concentrate on a great ground game. As early as the 1922 Big Game, Cal completed 8 of 14 passes for 177 yards in a 28-0 romp, but it is not known how many were launched by Erb. In the New Year's Day, 14-0 blanking of Penn in 1925, the Bears connected on 12 of 17 passes for 154 yards — a brilliant performance even by today's standards.

Erb, who stood only 5 feet 8 inches and weighed 160 pounds, couldn't throw a football very far, but he didn't have to pass. He simply made sure the ball got to the right people, and he did that well enough to prevent the Wonder Teams from losing a game. Erb was a gifted defensive back, returning an interception 85 yards for a touchdown against Olympic Club in the 1920 opener.

As was the case with Erb, Lee Eisan didn't get much credit as the quarterback of Nibs Price's squads of the late twenties. Lom was the big star in those days, but as a sophomore quarterback in 1927, Eisan ran 42 yards for a touchdown and returned a punt 60 yards for another in the 27-13 victory over Penn. As a senior, Eisan caught a 38-yard TD pass from Lom for a 7-0 victory over Washington. Eisan was 5 feet 7 inches tall and weighed in at 155 pounds.

Jonnny Meek was a bull-chested, 5-foot-11½-inch, 200-pounder who was listed as Cal's Thunder Team quarterback, but he was better known as the best blocker on the West Coast. Old-timers still speak of his 1936 crunching tackle of UCLA's Bill Spaulding, the Bruin coach's son. Meek could do it all. As a sophomore in 1935, he had a 10-yard TD catch against Washington and returned an interception 50 yards for a score against Pacific.

Meek was a great athlete. He scored one point, rushed for 2 yards and passed sparingly during the unbeaten campaign of 1937, yet landed on the first-team All-American squads selected by *Collier's Magazine* and the *New York Sun.* With stalwarts such as Chapman, Bottari and Dave Anderson in the backfield, Meek undoubtedly was recognized for his defense, yet there were those who felt he would have been an

All-American on offense, too, had he had a chance to carry the ball.

Bob Celeri, at 5 feet 10 inches and 160 pounds, was the first man to place a significant dent on Cal's passing records while guiding Pappy Waldorf's great teams of the late forties. Celeri had an explosive arsenal of talent, and he used it well. His 22-yard touchdown run helped the Bears sink Navy, 14-7, in 1947. The following week, he fired two touchdown passes against St. Mary's.

Two weeks later, Celeri enjoyed the greatest passing performance ever registered by a Cal quarterback. Setting records with eight completions and 154 passing yards, Celeri connected for TDs of 28 and 12 yards to down Washington, 13-7. He finished the season with a record 35 completions for a record 635 yards and six TDs, including a 57-yarder against Wisconsin.

As a junior in 1948, Celeri slipped statistically, but directed the Bears to the Rose Bowl. His best game was against Washington State, one which included a touchdown pass and a recovered fumble for a touchdown.

Celeri enjoyed his most success in 1949, producing another Rose Bowl appearance and a single-season Cal passing record. There were two TD passes in the first half against Oregon State;

Bob Celeri, shown beginning a run against Southern Cal in 1949, was the first Cal quarterback to gain fame as a passer. Though overshadowed by the great runners in Pappy Waldorf's offense, Celeri kept defenses honest with his air strikes. By the time he concluded his senior season in 1949, Celeri had guided the Bears to a pair of Rose Bowl appearances and established school single-game and career passing records. His yardage totals were modest by today's standards, but nobody could question his ability to win.

scoring strikes of 51 and 41 yards against WSC; TD passes covering 8 and 66 yards against Wisconsin; a 49-yard TD run with a bootleg play against Washington; a 39-yard TD pass and a 1-yard run for a score against UCLA; and a 55-yard TD pass in the Big Game.

For the season, he completed an unheard of 48 passes for 1,081 yards and nine touchdowns, was named the squad MVP and earned All-America distinction from *Football Digest* (first team), Associated Press (second team) and the Football Writers (second team). Celeri shattered the Cal career passing records with 110 completions, 2,186 yards and 18 touchdowns.

Celeri, who later had a cup of coffee in pro football after being drafted by the 49ers in 1950, was not a great passer by any stretch of the imagination, but it's all relative. He completed only 38.1 percent of his passes and tossed 37 interceptions in only 289 attempts, but he was the first Cal quarterback to mount a consistent air attack. More than 30 years later, Campbell completed more passes in one game — 43 — than Celeri did in either his sophomore or junior seasons. Like we said, it's not fair to compare apples and oranges.

PAUL LARSON
CAL'S FIRST GREAT PASSER

When Waldorf recruited Paul Larson out of Turlock High, Pappy got more than he bargained for because there was no way of knowing the 5-foot-10½-inch, 180-pound youngster would develop into one of the greatest all-around gridders in the school's history. Before he had completed his eligibility, Larson had led the nation in total offense and passing in two different years — the only two seasons in which he played quarterback.

Larson's latent offensive skills were discovered late because colleges were playing two-platoon football until 1953, his junior season. Prior to that, precocious Paul was more valuable to the squad as a kick-returner, part-time halfback and defensive back. As a freshman in 1951, he gave a hint of what was to come by gaining 100 yards on only eight carries, an average of 12.5 yards per try.

The next season, Larson gained 362 yards in 57 attempts for a fine, 6.4 average. He displayed his versatility by catching four passes for 51 yards and a TD, intercepting three passes for 61 yards, scoring six touchdowns, averaging 10.9 yards on punt returns (eighth in the nation) and returning kickoffs for a 16.7 average. The shifty sophomore had his best day against Minnesota, scoring on runs of 27 and 5 yards.

But it was yet to be determined that he could pass. Entering his junior season, Cal's greatest passer in the school's first 80 years of football had thrown the football only twice! But in the spring of 1953, Waldorf played a hunch and used Larson at quarterback in the final spring scrimmage. His snappy performance rated raves, and the Bears had a new quarterback.

By the third game of the season, the Bears knew they had someone special behind center. Facing mighty Ohio State, Larson set school records with 13 completions in 25 attempts for 170 yards. He rushed for 61 yards, fired a 59-yard TD bomb and scored on an 11-yard run during a 33-19 defeat. The next week, he uncorked a 49-yard TD pass against Penn and followed with a pair of TD tosses against USC.

In Game 8, a 52-25 rout of Washington, Larson established a school-passing-accuracy record. He peppered the Huskies defense for 10 completions in only 12 attempts — a percentage of .833 — for a school-record 240 yards. The season was crowned with a record-tying 13 completions, an 18-yard TD run and three conversion kicks in a 21-21 standoff with Stanford.

As a rookie college quarterback, Larson was good enough to be drafted by the Chicago Cardinals. They were impressed by his nation-leading 1,572 yards of total offense and his versatility. Larson established Cal single-season records with 85 completions and 1,431 yards, but he still found time to intercept six passes and score 50 points. One year later, Larson blossomed into the most accurate passer in college history.

In those days, passers rarely completed more than 50 percent of their attempts. In 1954, Larson clicked on 125 of 195 for a whopping .641 percentage, 1,537 yards and 10 TDs — all school records. Bud Wilkinson and his Oklahoma powerhouse downed the Bears, 27-13, in the season opener, but not before Larson completed 16 of 23 passes for 167 yards and a touchdown. The Sooners had never seen such passing wizardry, and they again marveled at the air show when Joe Roth completed 27 passes at Norman 22 years later.

In the third game of the 1954 season against Ohio State, the Bears were beaten, 21-13, but Larson put on another show by hitting on seven of 11 passes, including a 12-yard TD, and returning a kickoff 68 yards. Then came a 17-yard TD pass, a 2-yard run for a score and a 56-yard punt return for a TD in a 33-27 loss to Oregon. Against WSC, the Cal completion record fell again when he made good on 17 of 31 passes for 235 yards, and his field goal helped edge the Cougars, 17-7.

Larson was tackled for a safety in a 29-27 loss to USC, but he made it close with two TD

Paul Larson came to Cal as a halfback, but he enjoyed tremendous success as a quarterback and defensive back. Until Rich Campbell's short game resulted in numerous completions, Larson was the most accurate passer in Bear history. Pappy Waldorf gambled by making Larson his No. 1 quarterback in 1953, and the talented junior responded by leading the nation in total offense with 1,572 yards. As a senior in 1954, he completed a record 64.1 percent of his passes and topped the nation with 1,537 air yards.

passes, a scoring run and an 84-yard kickoff return. There was another spree against UCLA, Larson brilliantly completing 25 of 38 for 280 yards — all records. Despite an injury, he fired a pair of TDs in the fourth quarter to defeat Washington, and he concluded his Cal career with 14-of-22 passing, a touchdown run, a TD pass and four conversions in a 28-20 Big Game victory.

His sparkling senior season, which included three interceptions on his part for a career total of 12 and a 28.5 average on kickoff returns, resulted in All-America distinction on eight different mythical teams — four firsts and four seconds. He also was the Bears MVP, the Helms Pacific Coast Player of the Year and *Football Digest's* Back of the Year. Other Cal quarterbacks have come along with stronger arms and more impressive career totals than his 210 completions and 2,968 yards, but Larson could do more things well than any quarterback in Golden Bear history.

JOE KAPP
FOUND A WAY TO GET THINGS DONE

Joe Kapp, a rawboned and intense New Mexico native, wouldn't qualify as a picture passer. In fact, he usually was out of focus. But the 6-foot-2-inch, 195-pound Kapp is revered in legendary terms because he was the ultimate underdog, and what he achieved at Cal is a minor miracle. Despite the fact that the Bears record was 11-20 with him at quarterback, an exciting stint which included eight touchdown passes and 29 interceptions, Kapp emerged with the reputation of a winner.

But Kapp, who became Cal's head coach in 1982, cannot be judged by statistics. He, halfback Jack Hart and a bunch of guys named Joe somehow in 1958 carried the school to its last Rose Bowl appearance, a feat which left Kapp indelibly on the minds of Old Blues as an athletic hero. Kapp, you see, had a penchant for making the big play and for rising to the occasion, qualities which characterized his career as a swaggering signal-caller in the CFL and the NFL.

Kapp was a born leader on the football field and on the basketball court, where he played on Pete Newell's championship teams. As a sophomore gridder in 1956, he became the No. 1 quarterback and rambled 56 yards with a fumble recovery for a TD in a 16-7 victory over Washington. In the Big Game, Waldorf's last, he outplayed senior All-American John Brodie of Stanford and rushed for 106 yards in Cal's 20-18 upset.

In 1957, the Bears were 1-9, but Kapp kept them competitive, and six of the losses were by

An exuberant Joe Kapp helps the official signal another touchdown for the Bears. This kind of enthusiasm and his leadership made Kapp a winner at Cal and in his pro career.

a total of 27 points. In a 19-21 loss to Oregon State, Kapp passed for touchdowns covering 33 and 22 yards and also scored from the 1 to account for 18 of the points. He connected with Hank Olguin for an 80-yard TD pass against Washington and fired a 41-yarder in the 12-14 Big Game defeat.

But Kapp was through having tough luck by 1958. In the season opener against Pacific, the senior quarterback scored on touchdown runs of 50 and 4 yards, passed for a two-point conversion and accumulated 216 yards of total offense. His interception of a conversion pass prevented a tie in the 14-12 victory over USC. Then came a 92-yard run on a broken play against Oregon — no Bear has had a longer run from scrimmage since.

Kapp fired a TD pass in a 20-17 victory over UCLA; he set up one touchdown with a 32-yard kickoff return and scored the other on a 1-yard plunge in a 12-7 squeaker over Washington; and he clinched the PCC championship with a trip to the Rose Bowl when his two-point conversion pass edged Stanford, 16-15. He finished his career with 2,022 passing yards and ranked second in total offense (2,988) behind Larson (3,519) until the offensive explosion of sixties and seventies left them both lagging.

Running from pursuing Stanford defenders in the 1957 Big Game, Joe Kapp displays the mobility which made him an exciting, three-year performer for the Golden Bears. Kapp was known for his big-play tactics and leadership, overcoming odds to lead Cal to the Rose Bowl following the 1958 season. The Bears haven't returned to Pasadena since, but Kapp attempted to change that as the school's new head coach, beginning in 1982.

CRAIG MORTON
NOBODY DID IT BETTER

With apologies to the scatter-armed Kapp and Ronnie "Play Me or Trade Me" Knox, the 6-foot-4-inch, 215-pound Craig Morton was the first of the classic, pro-style quarterbacks developed at Cal. As far as the author is concerned, he was the best simply because he was surrounded by inferior material and had gimpy knees, yet kept the Bears competitive virtually every week.

Morton, a three-sport prep superstar from Campbell High in the San Jose Area, wasn't an immediate sensation, playing behind seniors Randy Gold and Larry Balliett as a sophomore in 1962. But the two seniors were injured during a 1-4 start, and Morton was pressed into action during the second quarter against Penn State, which held a 7-0 lead. What transpired the remainder of the game left 30,000 Memorial Stadium spectators gasping in awe. A star was born, and it was to rise over the next two and one-half years in Berkeley, giving light to an otherwise gloomy gridiron situation.

Morton dazzled the Nittany Lions with 20-for-28 passing and a school-record 274 aerial yards. His three touchdown passes just missed a major upset, with Penn State emerging with a

Craig Morton uncorks one of his 20 completions in his spectacular debut against Penn State in 1962. Entering the game in the second quarter, he ignited the crowd with three touchdown passes, falling just short of an upset, 21-23.

23-21 triumph. Craig, then known as "The Hummer," also glittered in his first collegiate start the following week against UCLA, completing 18 of 32 for 236 yards. He had the Bears ahead, 16-13, after three quarters, but the Bruins won, 26-16, behind Kermit Alexander's four TDs.

The sizzling sophomore fired three more TDs at Kansas and had two scoring strikes in the Big Game, concluding with nine touchdown passes in only five games. The fast finish augured well for the future, and Morton certainly didn't disappoint as a junior in 1963, though defensive problems made Cal a 4-5-1 loser.

Morton reached his peak that season against San Jose State, setting a school record with five touchdown passes in a 34-13 victory. It took him only 17 tosses, and he completed 10 for 246

Craig Morton was the Bears first great pro-style quarterback. He wasn't surrounded by a strong supporting cast, but Morton made Cal competitive in virtually every game, springing some upsets along the way, including one his senior year against Navy and future rival Roger Staubach.

yards. By season's end, Morton set a school record of 14 touchdown passes, a stepping stone for his All-American senior season of 1964 under rookie coach Ray Willsey.

Again, the Bears didn't have much material in 1964, but Morton had the good fortune of hooking up with three glue-fingered receivers: longtime pal Jack Schraub, lightning-quick Jerry Bradley and Jerry Mosher. Cal went 3-7 that season, but there were thrills galore as the Bears dropped five games by a total of 26 points. With Morton in control, Cal and its fans never were shortchanged.

Missouri was upset in the opener, 21-14, behind Morton's two TD passes. He completed 24 passes for 251 yards against Illinois, but he was denied another upset when Bradley's foot kicked up some sideline chalk on a potential winning TD. Morton and the Bears beat Roger Staubach and Navy, 27-13, for a 3-2 record, and Cal was on the verge of a major upset at the Los Angeles Coliseum.

Morton, at his finest, hit on 18 of 28 passes for 219 yards and two TDs against mighty Troy, and the Bears held a 21-20 lead and possession of the ball with under two minutes left to play. But a key Cal defender was ejected down the stretch, and USC moved to a game-winning touchdown pass from Craig Fertig to Rod Sherman, stunning the Bears, 26-21.

The mark of a great athlete is how well he performs under pressure. Morton didn't fold after the USC setback. Instead, he bounced back with a school-record, 288-yard passing performance against UCLA. He fired two TDs against the Bruins and duplicated that feat the following week against Washington, giving him a string of 16 consecutive games with at least one touchdown pass and 21 out of 23 since his Penn State debut.

Morton also had 99 straight passes without an interception at one stretch, which was remarkable considering everyone knew he had to pass. He finished his senior season with 185 completions, 308 attempts, 2,121 yards and 13 TDs. All were new school standards, except the TDs which fell one shy of his 1963 mark. New Cal career records included 355 completions, 641 attempts, 4,501 yards and 36 TD passes, the latter being a record which still stands.

Other Cal quarterbacks won more games, of course, but none excelled under handicaps like those Craig endured. The Bears had no running threat whatsoever (Kapp had Hart and Billy Patton), and Morton didn't pad his stats with short stuff. Yet he rewrote the Cal and Pac-8 record books as a passing pioneer, one who was still firing away with success in the NFL 18 years after his senior season.

Craig Morton blitzed Cal's record book, beginning with his spectacular first game against Penn State when he threw for a then-record 274 yards. He still ranks second in career passing and total offense with 4,501 and 4,130 yards respectively. For many, the bottom line is touchdowns, however, and there Morton remains No. 1 with 36 TD passes. He also scored eight himself, thus being responsible for a school-record 44.

STEVE BARTKOWSKI
FROM FLOP TO NO. 1

The 10-year period between Morton's All-American campaign and that enjoyed by Steve Bartkowski in 1974 was like a roller-coaster ride for Cal quarterbacks. All the quarterbacks in that span, including Bartkowski, had their peaks and valleys. Jim Hunt, Morton's successor, beat Penn State with no time left on an end zone grab by Bradley in 1965; Randy Humphries turned in a 7-3-1 record in 1968; and Dave Penhall set a school record with 321 passing yards in the 1969 Big Game before defeating USC and Stanford in 1970.

But bigger and better things were predicted for Bartkowski, a 6-foot-4-inch, 215-pound prep Wunderkind from Santa Clara who was heralded as the second coming of Morton. Bart erased the

Steve Bartkowski, a disappointment as a sophomore and overshadowed as a junior, blossomed into an All-American as a senior in 1974. Bart accumulated a school-record 2,580 yards, powered a 7-3-1 season and was the NFL's first draft pick, a storybook ending that provided countless thrills for Golden Bears fans.

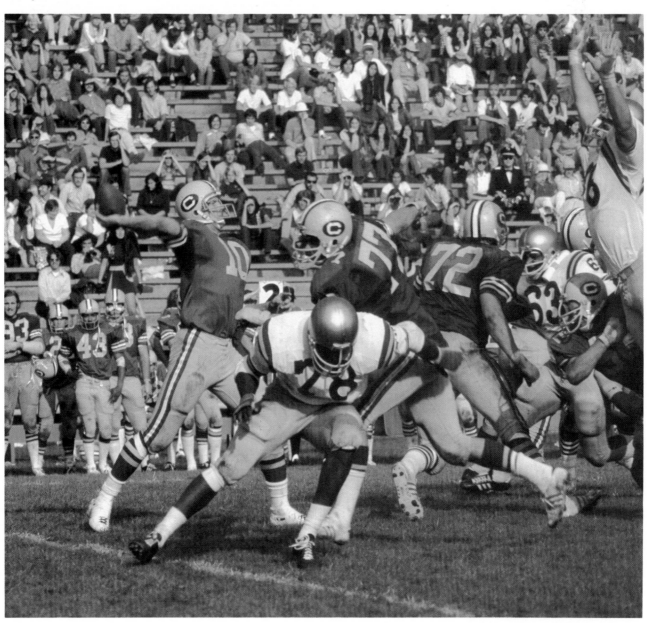

frosh passing records in 1971 and was No. 1 as a sophomore in 1972, a distinction even Morton couldn't claim. All eyes were on Bartkowski in the Bears opener at Colorado, and he responded with a school-record 49 attempts for 260 yards.

There was a hitch, however. Bart could throw the ball through a brick wall, but his lack of touch posed a problem for receivers. By the fourth game of the season, Jay Cruze quarterbacked against Missouri and passed for a school-record 354 yards in a 34-27 loss. But Cruze also faltered and Vince Ferragamo, who was tearing up freshman competition, was promoted to the varsity. In the final three games, Ferragamo defeated Oregon, set a school total offense mark of 300 yards in a loss to Oregon State and became a fans' favorite with a last-ditch pass to Steve Sweeney for a Big Game victory.

When the 1973 season began, Vince was The Prince and Bartkowski was the ugly duckling when it came to football. Fortunately, Bart had an outlet. That year, the powerful Bartkowski used his rifle arm to impress baseball scouts as a catcher. At the plate, he set new Cal home run records and, including semipro ball that summer, bashed 30 homers in about 100 games.

It was speculated he would be a No. 1 draft choice in baseball, so there was solace when Ferragamo was named the starter at quarterback. But Vince couldn't handle a 4-7 season and, as he did in pro ball a few years later, switched teams and went from Cal to Nebraska. As luck would have it, Bartkowski slumped during the baseball season of 1974 and was not drafted as high as he expected. Instead, he turned his thoughts to football, which was a break for him and the Bears.

Entering the 1974 season, no Cal quarterback had more than one 300-plus passing game in his career, and even the great Morton had none. Bart turned the trick four times. Following a 21-17, opening loss to Florida, Bart mounted a five-game winning streak which included 14-for-18 passing, 244 yards and two TDs on a windy day at Illinois. The string was snapped by UCLA, but Bart set a school record with 26 completions and passed for 300 yards.

Pro scouts drooled over his performances and predicted greatness. In a brilliant stretch drive, Bartkowski sealed All-American honors and a 7-3-1 season by passing 316 yards against Washington, 304 against WSU and 318 against Stanford. He had only one full season as the Bears cannon, but it was a beaut: 182 completions, 12 TDs, only seven interceptions and a school-record 2,580 yards. He was the NFL's top pick and has been throwing strikes for the Atlanta Falcons ever since.

Steve Bartkowski scrambles from the grasp of a Stanford defender during the 1974 Big Game. Although Stanford prevailed, 22-20, Bart's 318 yards passing was the top performance of his career.

JOE ROTH
STRENGTH IN THE SHADOW OF DEATH

When Bartkowski departed for the pros, the Bears hardly noticed. Such was the sophistication of Mike White's offense, it seemed any youngster with above-average talent could make the Bears go. But Joe Roth, a 6-foot-4-inch, 205-pound junior-college transfer from San Diego, turned out to be much more. In fact, his courage probably has been unmatched in Golden Bear grid history.

White didn't want to rush Roth, so Fred Besana started the first two games, losses to Colorado and West Virginia. Roth played a little in the second game, but he again was on the bench for the Pac-8 opener with WSU. Besana started and did well, but Roth took over in the second half and ignited a 33-21 triumph with 13-for-23 passing, 182 yards and one TD.

The job was his and Roth responded with seven victories in his eight starts, catching fire following a 28-14 loss to UCLA in the seventh game. Against USC on national television the next week, he connected on 19 of 31 attempts for 244 yards and two TDs in a 28-14 upset. His confidence boosted, Roth was even better one week later against Washington, going 24 for 37 for a school-record 380 yards and four TDs.

By now, the nation had taken notice, and Cal quarterback coach Paul Hackett compared Joe favorably with Bartkowski, mentioning that Roth was more advanced as a junior. Victories over Air Force and Stanford enabled the Bears to tie for the conference championship, and Joe finished with a record-tying 14 TD passes. As a result, Roth was on all the pre-season All-American lists in 1976.

In recognition of his inspirational qualities, Joe Roth's jersey is retired posthumously in ceremonies prior to the Joe Roth Memorial Game against USC in 1977. Cal athletic director Dave Maggard is flanked by Roth's brothers John (left) and Tom. In 100 years of football at Cal, Roth's is the only jersey to be retired.

Joe Roth uncorks one of his 14 completions in the 48-15 romp over Stanford in 1975. Roth engineered the perfect offense that season as Cal gained 2,522 yards rushing and passing for an NCAA-leading 5,044 yards in total offense.

He opened with a flourish, clicking on 21 of 36 for 379 yards and two TDs at Georgia. Then came a school-record 27 completions for 284 yards at Oklahoma, a performance which left the Sooners raving. But it soon was apparent that Roth wasn't right. The passing statistics dwindled and so did his strength. Joe's life was being drained by a virulent form of cancer, a suspicion that was confirmed following the season.

Roth handled the situation with dignity. He gave strength to those around him as he attempted to lead a normal life while undergoing treatments. He was selected to the East-West Shrine Game but could not play because of a related back problem. Joe did appear in the Hula and Japan Bowls in January. One month later, on February 19, 1977, Joe Roth was dead, the victim of a malignant melanoma.

RICH CAMPBELL
A RECORD RAMPAGE

When Roger Theder, expert on the passing game, took over for White in 1978, he had one thing going for him: the luxury of having Rich Campbell starting at quarterback for three years. Campbell, a 6-foot-5-inch, 210-pound sophomore from San Jose, came to Cal with a reputation similar to those Morton and Bartkowski brought out of the Santa Clara Valley. Without great breakaway running talent, Theder designed the Bears offense to maximize Campbell's effectiveness.

What ensued was a 15-16 record (including a forfeit) in the games Campbell started, a long-awaited bowl appearance and 13 school passing marks. Since the Bears have indicated

they will be more balanced under Kapp's coaching, it would be safe to assume Campbell's records will last awhile, especially in the career categories. Rich, for instance, has 244 more completions, 288 more attempts and 2,673 more passing yards than any other Cal quarterback.

Campbell's assault on the record books began immediately. In his first game as a sophomore, the rangy right-hander completed 16 passes for 271 yards and two TDs at Nebraska in 1978. Rich fired a pair of TD tosses in each of his first four games, amassing 992 yards in an auspicious beginning. But when top wide-receiving threat Floyd Eddings was injured, the quarterback was hindered the rest of the season.

Still, he managed a three-TD performance and 347 yards against Arizona State, leaving Frank

Kush shaking his head in disbelief. Campbell finished his sophomore season with 56 percent accuracy and 14 touchdown passes, equaling the mark of Morton and Roth. But the others didn't stand a chance in 1979 when the gifted junior compiled the most prolific passing totals, with the help of a 12th game, in Cal annals.

He dropped a hint by only misfiring on four of 26 attempts against Arizona, the .846 percentage topping Larson's .833. The next week, he tied Roth's record of 27 completions by burning San Jose State for 316 yards. When the smoke had cleared, Campbell stood alone with 241 completions, 360 attempts, 2,859 yards, a .669 percentage and 15 touchdown passes, including two in the Garden State Bowl.

Campbell was being touted as an All-American in 1980, and he made an immediate splash with an NCAA-record 43

No quarterback at Cal was more prolific in piling up yardage than Rich Campbell. He erased all school passing records except for Morton's TD mark and established an NCAA single-season accuracy standard, .707, in 1980. If Campbell, a prototype passer, had not been restricted because of the Bears lack of a breakaway running threat and injuries to receivers, his win total and his passing statistics might have been even more imposing.

completions in 53 attempts for 421 yards in a 41-13 loss at Florida. That game more or less symbolized the entire 3-8 season: lots of yardage and little to show for it. There were 30 completions for 350 yards against Arizona, for instance, but the Bears were beaten, 31-24, because they didn't have the components to complement his passing skill.

When Campbell's college career was terminated by a knee injury suffered against USC, he went out with an NCAA single-season accuracy record of .707 percent (193-273). His career marks include 599 completions in 929 attempts for 7,174 yards and a .645 percentage. He fell short only in touchdown passes, trailing the imcomparable Morton, 36-35. Campbell never realized his All-American dream, but he was the first quarterback selected in the 1981 NFL draft, going to Green Bay in the first round.

Rich Campbell hurls one of his school-record-tying 27 completions against San Jose State in 1979. Campbell completely shattered the record the following year with 43 completions against Florida.

CHAPTER
7

Chapter Seven
FOR THE RECORD

California Football Results 1882-1981 (Rugby 1906-14)

1882-83 (2-1-1)
Coach: No Coach
Captain: W. E. Connor
4	Phoenix Club	7
0	Allies	0
7	Phoenix Club	6
13	Allies	0

1884 (2-0)
Coach: No Coach
Captain: Charles O. Bosse
| 18 | Merions | 0 |
| 9 | Wanderers | 0 |

1885 (4-0-1)
Coach: No Coach
Captain: John G. Sutton
13	Merions*	0
4	Merions*	0
4	Merions*	0
0	Wasps*	0
2	Wasps*	0

1886 (6-2-1)
Coach: Oscar S. Howard
Captain: Frederick C. Turner
20	Wasps*	2
10	Orions	12
1	Hastings Law College**	0
12	Reliance*	12
10	Reliance*	0
29	Orions*	2
4	Reliance*	7
1	Wasps**	0
1	Hastings Law College**	0

1887 (4-0)
Coach: No Coach
Captain: Frederick C. Turner
26	San Francisco Club*	0
14	Volunteers*	0
14	Reliance*	6
12	Reliance*	6

1888 (6-1)
Coach: No Coach
Captain: Charles W. Reed
26	San Francisco Club*	0
6	Volunteers*	10
20	San Francisco Club*	0
14	Posens*	0
1	Wasps**	0
1	Wasps**	0
36	San Francisco Club	0

1889
All scheduled games were cancelled due to excessive rains

1890 (4-0)
Coach: No Coach
Captain: Fred W. McNear
6	Posens*	4
16	Posens*	0
11	Posens*	0
12	Posens*	0

1891 (0-1)
Coach: No Coach
Captain: John H. White
| 0 | San Francisco Club* | 36 |

1892 Spring (4-2)
Coach: No Coach
Captain: George H. Foulks
12	S. F. Boys HS*	0
14	S. F. Boys HS*	0
16	Hopkins Academy*	4
30	Berkeley Gymnasium*	0
0	Olympic Club*	6
10	Stanford	14

*Cal home game

1892 Fall (2-1-1)
Coach: Thomas McClung
Captain: Loren E. Hunt
10	Olympic Club	20
16	Olympic Club	0
8	Olympic Club	4
10	Stanford	10

1893 (5-1-1)
Coach: W. W. Heffelfinger
Captain: H. Percy Benson
30	Reliance Club*	0
14	S. F. All-Stars	12
22	Olympic Club	10
12	Olympic Club	6
22	Reliance Club	10
4	Reliance Club	16
6	Stanford	6

1894 (0-1-2)
Coach: Charles O. Gill
Captain: H. Percy Benson
12	Reliance Club	12
0	Reliance Club	0
0	Stanford	6

1895 (3-1-1)
Coach: Frank Butterworth
Captain: Eddie Sherman
0	Reliance Club*	4
12	Reliance Club*	0
8	Reliance Club*	0
20	Olympic Club	0
6	Stanford	6

1896 (6-2-2)
Coach: Frank Butterworth
Captain: A. W. (Wolf) Ransome
2	Reliance Club	12
0	Olympic Club	0
0	Reliance Club	0
24	Olympic Club	8
16	Reliance Club	10
0	Stanford	20
14	Los Angeles A. C.	0
32	Redlands HS	0
52	San Diego HS	0
10	Whittier School	6

1897 (0-3-2)
Coach: Charles P. Nott
Captain: Percy W. Hall
0	Reliance*	12
0	Reliance*	10
4	Reliance*	4
4	Reliance*	4
0	Stanford	28

1898 (8-0-2)
Coach: Garrett Cochran
Captain: Percy W. Hall
17	Olympic Club	0
4	Washington Volunteers*	0
44	Washington Volunteers*	0
18	Olympic Club	0
33	Kansas Volunteers*	0
0	Iowa Volunteers*	0
51	St. Mary's*	0
5	Olympic Club	5
22	Stanford	0
27	Multnomah A. C.	0

1899 (7-1-1)
Coach: Garrett Cochran
Captain: James R. Whipple
6	Olympic Club*	0
0	Olympic Club	0
11	League of the Cross*	0
15	Olympic Club	0
24	Nevada*	0
12	Oregon*	0
44	State Normal*	0
30	Stanford	0
0	Carlisle Indian School	2

1900 (4-2-1)
Coach: Addison W. (King) Kelly
Captain: Charles A. Pringle
0	Reliance*	0
5	Reliance*	0
11	Reliance*	0
32	Nevada*	0
0	Oregon*	2
5	San Jose Normal*	0
0	Stanford	5

1901 (9-0-1)
Coach: Frank Simpson
Captain: Lloyd A. Womble
0	Reliance*	0
5	Olympic Club*	0
6	Olympic Club*	0
6	Reliance*	0
6	Olympic Club	5
12	Nevada*	0
16	Mare Island Marines*	0
2	Stanford	0
38	So. Calif. All-Stars	0
15	Perris Indians	10

1902 (8-0)
Coach: James Whipple
Captain: William B. Albertson
12	Alumni Club*	0
16	Reliance*	0
44	Alumni Club*	0
17	Reliance*	0
5	'98-'99 Alumni*	0
29	Nevada*	0
16	Stanford	0
29	Perris Indians	12

1903 (6-1-2)
Coach: James Whipple
Captain: Orval F. Overall
0	Reliance*	0
51	Naval Academy*	0
7	Reliance*	0
5	Reliance*	0
40	Chemawa Indians*	0
6	Alumni*	0
11	Multnomah A. C.*	0
2	Nevada*	6
6	Stanford	6

1904 (6-1-1)
Coach: James Hopper
Captain: Benjamin K. Stroud
6	Sherman Indians*	0
10	Olympic Club*	0
20	Multnomah A. C.*	0
12	Oregon*	0
5	Pomona*	0
16	Nevada*	0
0	Stanford*	18
6	Washington	6

1905 (4-1-2)
Coach: J. W. Knibbs
Captain: James A. Force
23	St. Vincent's*	0
0	Willamette*	0
0	Oregon*	0
21	Sherman Indians*	0
10	Oregon Aggies*	0
16	Nevada*	0
5	Stanford	12

1906 (2-4)
Coach: Oscar Taylor
Captain: Calvin W. Haffey
5	S. F. All-Stars*	8
6	Pomona	0
5	Vancouver*	0
0	Vancouver*	3
0	Nevada*	3
3	Stanford*	6

* Forfeit

1907 (4-3)
Coach: Oscar Taylor
Captain: Walter Fuller
0	Barbarians*	6
9	Barbarians*	0
6	Barbarians*	0
25	Nevada*	0
16	Vancouver*	12
0	Vancouver*	3
11	Stanford	21

1908 (7-3-1)
Coach: Oscar Taylor
Captain: Ralph H. Butler
14	Olympic Club*	0
3	Barbarians*	0
14	Olympic Club*	3
0	Barbarians*	11
32	St. Mary's*	0
17	Barbarians*	6
3	Vancouver*	3
0	Vancouver*	3
17	Olympic Club*	8
11	Nevada*	0
3	Stanford*	12

1909 (12-3-1)
Coach: James Schaeffer
Captain: Cedric (Skook) Cerf
39	Reliance*	0
6	Barbarians*	3
30	Reliance*	0
16	Olympic Club*	0
3	Barbarians*	6
10	Castaways	10
19	So. Calif. All-Stars	3
6	Barbarians*	0
19	Olympic Club*	0
24	Vancouver*	3
39	Vancouver*	0
24	Nevada*	8
19	Stanford	13
0	Vancouver	3
0	Vancouver	5
14	Vancouver	3

1910 (12-0-2)
Coach: James Schaeffer
Captain: Jay Dwiggins, Jr.
9	Barbarians*	0
32	Barbarians*	5
17	Olympic Club*	3
26	Barbarians*	0
16	Olympic Club*	0
22	Barbarians*	0
40	Olympic Club*	10
6	St. Mary's*	0
18	Olympic Club*	0
62	Nevada*	0
25	Stanford*	6
0	Victoria All-Stars	0
3	Victoria All-Stars	0
3	Victoria All-Stars	3

1911 (11-2-1)
Coach: James Schaeffer
Captain: Amos W. Elliott
11	Barbarians*	0
8	Olympic Club*	0
31	Barbarians*	3
16	Olympic Club*	8
29	Nevada	0
14	Barbarians*	3
18	Olympic Club*	3
21	British Col. All-Stars*	0
24	British Col. All-Stars	0
60	Olympic Club*	0
21	Stanford	3
3	Victoria All-Stars	6
0	Victoria All-Stars	8

1912 (10-2-1)
Coach: James Schaeffer
Captain: John A. Stroud, Jr.

8	Barbarians*	3
5	Olympic Club*	3
16	Barbarians*	0
9	Olympic Club*	0
34	Nevada*	0
21	St. Mary's*	0
5	Olympic Club*	0
16	Barbarians*	3
0	Australian Waratahs*	18
6	Australian Waratahs*	5
3	Australian Waratahs*	23
3	Stanford*	3
18	USC	0

1913 (6-3-3)
Coach: James Schaeffer
Captain: Sterling B. Peart

6	Titans*	6
0	Barbarians*	0
4	Titans*	3
21	Barbarians*	0
18	UC Alumni Club*	0
0	New Zealand All-Blacks*	31
6	Santa Clara*	3
13	UC Alumni Club*	3
3	New Zealand All-Blacks*	38
8	Stanford	13
23	Barbarians	10
3	USC	3

1914 (14-1)
Coach: James Schaeffer
Captain: Joseph L. McKim

8	Olympic Club*	3
8	Titans*	3
12	Barbarians*	5
17	UC Alumni*	5
13	Olympic Club*	3
17	Titans*	3
22	UC Alumni*	3
11	Barbarians*	0
28	St. Mary's*	0
18	Titans*	0
24	St. Mary's*	3
25	Santa Clara*	0
27	UC Alumni*	3
8	Stanford*	26
38	Nevada	3

1915 (8-5)
Coach: James Schaeffer
Captain: Clifford G. Canfield

17	Olympic Club*	0
0	Commercial Club*	10
18	Olympic Club*	2
19	Olympic Club*	9
7	Originals*	0
44	Sherman Indians*	7
6	St. Mary's*	7
10	Southern California*	28
10	St. Mary's*	9
0	Washington*	72
7	Washington	13
81	Nevada	6
23	Southern California	21

1916 (6-4-1)
Coach: Andy Smith
Captain: Brud Montgomery

23	Olympic Club*	0
23	Originals*	0
0	Olympic Club*	0
13	Originals*	0
21	Whittier*	17
14	Oregon*	39
13	Occidental*	14
27	Southern California*	0
48	St. Mary's*	6
3	Washington*	13
7	Washington	14

1917 (5-5-1)
Coach: Andy Smith
Captains: D. P. Foster, Fred Brooks

0	Mare Island Marines*	27
2	Olympic Club*	6
0	Mare Island Marines*	26
40	Olympic Club*	0
33	Navy Hospital Corps*	7
20	Occidental*	0
14	Oregon Aggies*	3
27	Washington*	0
13	St. Mary's*	14
0	Oregon	21
0	Southern California	0

1918 (7-2, PCC Champions)
Coach: Andy Smith
Captain: Carlton G. Wells

7	Fort MacDowell*	21
13	S. F. Presidio*	21
1	Fort Scott**	0
40	St. Mary's*	14
0	Mather Field*	13
6	Oregon*	0
67	Stanford*†	0
20	San Pedro Navy*	0
33	Southern California	7

1919 (6-2-1)
Coach: Andy Smith
Captain: Fred T. Brooks

12	Olympic Club*	0
6	Olympic Club*	6
19	St. Mary's*	0
61	Occidental*	0
0	Washington State*	14
21	Oregon Aggies*	14
14	Southern California	13
14	Stanford	10
0	Washington	7

1920 (9-0, PCC Champions)
Coach: Andy Smith
Captain: Olin C. Majors

21	Olympic Club*	0
88	Mare Island Marines*	0
127	St. Mary's*	0
79	Nevada*	7
63	Utah*	0
17	Oregon Aggies	7
49	Washington State*	0
38	Stanford*	0
28	Ohio State (Rose Bowl)	0

1921 (9-0-1, PCC Champions)
Coach: Andy Smith
Captain: George H. Latham

21	St. Mary's*	0
14	Olympic Club*	0
51	Nevada*	6
21	Pacific Fleet*	10
39	Oregon*	0
14	Washington State	0
38	Southern California*	7
72	Washington*	3
42	Stanford	7
0	Washington & Jefferson (Rose Bowl)	0

1922 (9-0, PCC Champions)
Coach: Andy Smith
Captain: Charles F. Erb., Jr.

45	Santa Clara*	14
80	Mare Island Marines*	0
41	St. Mary's*	0
25	Olympic Club*	0
12	Southern California	0
61	Washington State*	0
45	Washington	7
61	Nevada*	13
28	Stanford*	0

1923 (9-0-1, PCC Champions)
Coach: Andy Smith
Captain: Donald P. Nichols

3	Alumni All-Stars*	0
49	St. Mary's†	0
48	Santa Clara*	0
16	Olympic Club*	0
26	Oregon Aggies*	0
9	Washington State	0
0	Nevada*	0
13	Southern California	7
9	Washington*	0
9	Stanford*	0

1924 (8-0-2)
Coach: Andy Smith
Captain: Edwin C. Horrell

13	Santa Clara*	7
17	St. Mary's*	7
28	Pomona*	0
9	Olympic Club*	3
20	Washington State*	7
7	Southern California*	0
7	Washington	7
27	Nevada*	0
20	Stanford*	20
14	Pennsylvania*	0

1925 (6-3)
Coach: Andy Smith
Captain: Talma W. Imlay

28	Santa Clara*	0
54	Nevada*	0
0	Olympic Club*	15
6	St. Mary's*	0
28	Oregon	0
27	Pomona	0
35	Washington State*	0
0	Washington*	7
14	Stanford	27

1926 (3-6)
Coach: Clarence M. Price
Captain: Bert Griffin

13	Santa Clara*	6
32	Olympic Club*	0
7	St. Mary's*	26
7	Oregon Aggies*	27
0	Southern California*	27
13	Oregon*	21
7	Washington	13
20	Nevada*	6
6	Stanford*	41

1927 (7-3)
Coach: Clarence M. Price
Captain: Fritz Coltrin

14	Santa Clara*	6
54	Nevada*	0
13	St. Mary's*	0
16	Oregon	0
6	Olympic Club*	5
0	Southern California	13
33	Montana*	13
0	Washington*	6
6	Stanford	13
27	Pennsylvania*	13

1928 (6-2-2)
Coach: Clarence M. Price
Captain: Irvine Phillips

22	Santa Clara*	0
7	St. Mary's*	0
13	Washington State*	3
0	Southern California*	0
0	Olympic Club*	12
13	Oregon*	0
6	Washington	0
60	Nevada*	0
13	Stanford	13
7	Georgia Tech (Rose Bowl)	8

1929 (7-1-1)
Coach: Clarence M. Price
Captain: Roy Riegels

27	Santa Clara*	6
0	St. Mary's*	0
14	Washington State*	0
12	Pennsylvania	7
21	Olympic Club*	19
15	Southern California	0
53	Montana*	18
7	Washington*	0
6	Stanford	21

1930 (4-5)
Coach: Clarence M. Price
Captain: Carl Handy

19	Santa Clara*	7
0	Washington State*	16
7	St. Mary's*	6
7	Olympic Club*	13
0	Washington	13
46	Montana*	0
0	Southern California	74
8	Nevada*	0
0	Stanford*	41

1931 (8-2)
Coach: William A. Ingram
Captain: Edward C. Griffiths

6	Santa Clara*	2
0	St. Mary's*	14
6	Olympic Club*	0
13	Washington State	7
0	Southern California*	6
25	Nevada*	6
13	Washington*	6
18	Idaho*	0
6	Stanford	0
19	Georgia Tech	6

1932 (7-3-2)
Coach: William A. Ingram
Captain: Richard C. Tozer

20	California*	6
13	West Coast Navy*	0
0	Santa Clara*	12
22	Olympic Club*	6
12	St. Mary's*	12
2	Washington State*	7
7	Washington	6
38	Nevada*	0
7	Southern California	27
21	Idaho*	6
0	Stanford*	0
27	Georgia Tech*	7

1933 (6-3-2)
Coach: William A. Ingram
Captain: John Ransome

0	Santa Clara*	7
39	California Aggies*	0
34	Nevada*	0
14	St. Mary's*	13
23	Olympic Club*	0
6	Washington State	6
3	Southern California*	6
0	UCLA	0
33	Washington*	0
6	Idaho*	0
3	Stanford	7

1934 (6-6)
Coach: William A. Ingram
Captain: Arleigh Williams

54	California Aggies*	0
33	Nevada*	0
0	St. Mary's*	7
7	College of the Pacific*	6
3	UCLA*	0
7	Washington	13
0	Santa Clara*	20
7	Southern California	2
45	Idaho*	13
7	Stanford*	9
13	Honolulu Town Team	26
0	University of Hawaii	14

1935 (9-1, PCC Co-Champions)
Coach: Leonard B. Allison
Captain: Larry Lutz

47	California Aggies*	0
6	Whittier*	0
10	St. Mary's*	0
6	Oregon	0
6	Santa Clara*	0
21	Southern California*	7
14	UCLA	2
14	Washington*	0
39	College of the Pacific*	0
0	Stanford	13

1936 (6-5)
Coach: Leonard B. Allison
Captain: Ray Nordstrom

14	College of the Pacific*	0
39	California Aggies*	0
0	St. Mary's*	10
7	Oregon State	0
6	UCLA*	17
0	Washington	13
13	Washington State*	14
13	Southern California	7
28	Oregon*	0
20	Stanford*	0
7	Georgia Tech	13

1937 (10-0-1, PCC Champions)
Coach: Leonard B. Allison
Captain: John Meek

30	St. Mary's*	7
24	Oregon State*	6
27	Washington State*	0
14	California Aggies*	0
20	College of Pacific*	0
20	Southern California*	6
27	UCLA	14
0	Washington*	0
26	Oregon	0
13	Stanford	0
13	Alabama (Rose Bowl)	0

1938 (10-1, PCC Co-Champions)
Coach: Leonard B. Allison
Captain: Vic Bottari

12	St. Mary's*	7
27	Washington State	3
48	California Aggies*	0
39	College of the Pacific*	0
20	UCLA*	7
14	Washington	7
13	Oregon State*	7
7	Southern California	13
20	Oregon*	0
6	Stanford*	0
13	Georgia Tech*	0

*Cal home game

• Forfeit

† SATC Game

1939 (3-7)
Coach: Leonard B. Allison
Captain: Game Captains

32	California Aggies*	14
0	College of Pacific*	6
3	St. Mary's*	7
0	Oregon*	6
13	Washington State*	7
0	Southern California*	26
7	UCLA	20
6	Washington*	13
0	Oregon State	21
32	Stanford	14

1940 (4-6)
Coach: Leonard B. Allison
Captain: Game Captains

0	Michigan*	41
9	St. Mary's*	6
6	Washington State*	9
9	UCLA*	7
6	Washington	7
13	Oregon State*	19
20	Southern California	7
14	Oregon*	6
7	Stanford*	13
0	Georgia Tech	13

1941 (4-5)
Coach: Leonard B. Allison
Captain: Game Captains

31	St. Mary's*	0
6	Washington State	13
0	Santa Clara*	13
7	Oregon	19
14	Southern California*	0
27	UCLA	7
6	Washington*	13
0	Oregon State*	6
16	Stanford	0

1942 (5-5)
Coach: Leonard B. Allison
Captain: Game Captains

6	St. Mary's*	0
8	Oregon State	13
6	Santa Clara*	7
0	UCLA*	21
19	Washington	6
20	Oregon*	7
7	Southern California	21
13	Montana*	0
7	Stanford*	26
12	Navy Pre-Flight*	6

1943 (4-6)
Coach: Leonard B. Allison
Captain: Game Captains

27	St. Mary's*	12
0	Southern California*	7
6	College of the Pacific*	12
13	UCLA	0
0	St. Mary's Pre-Flight*	39
0	Southern California	13
32	University of San Francisco*	0
13	UCLA*	6
0	Alameda Coast Guard*	7
8	Del Monte Pre-Flight*	47

1944 (3-6-1)
Coach: Leonard B. Allison
Captain: Game Captains

31	St. Mary's*	7
6	UCLA*	0
6	Southern California	6
14	College of the Pacific*	0
2	Fleet City*	19
7	Washington*	33
6	Coast Guard*	12
0	UCLA	7
0	Southern California*	32
6	St. Mary's Pre-Flight*	33

1945 (4-5-1)
Coach: Lawrence T. Shaw
Captain: Game Captains

13	St. Mary's*	20
2	Southern California*	13
27	Washington*	14
0	UCLA	13
19	Nevada*	6
7	Washington State*	7
0	Southern California	14
13	Oregon*	20
6	UCLA*	0
6	St. Mary's Pre-Flight*	0

1946 (2-7)
Coach: Frank Wickhorst
Captain: Game Captains

7	Wisconsin*	28
13	Oregon*	14
20	St. Mary's*	13
6	UCLA*	13
6	Washington	20
47	Washington State*	14
0	Southern California	14
7	Oregon State*	28
6	Stanford*	25

1947 (9-1)
Coach: Lynn O. Waldorf
Captains: John Graves, Harry Agler

33	Santa Clara*	7
14	Navy*	7
45	St. Mary's*	6
48	Wisconsin	7
21	Washington State*	6
14	Southern California*	39
6	UCLA	0
13	Washington*	7
`60	Montana*	14
21	Stanford	18

1948 (10-1, PCC Co-Champions)
Coach: Lynn O. Waldorf
Captain: Gene Frassetto

41	Santa Clara*	19
21	Navy	7
20	St. Mary's*	0
40	Wisconsin*	14
42	Oregon State*	0
21	Washington	0
13	Southern California	7
28	UCLA*	13
44	Washington State*	14
7	Stanford*	6
14	Northwestern	20
(Rose Bowl)		

1949 (10-1, PCC Champions)
Coach: Lynn O. Waldorf
Captains: Rod Franz, Jim Turner

21	Santa Clara*	7
29	St. Mary's*	7
41	Oregon State	0
35	Wisconsin	20
16	Southern California*	10
21	Washington*	7
35	UCLA	21
33	Washington State*	14
41	Oregon*	14
33	Stanford	14
14	Ohio State	17
(Rose Bowl)		

1950 (9-1-1, PCC Champions)
Coach: Lynn O. Waldorf
Captains: Pete Schabarum, Jim Monachino

27	Santa Clara*	9
28	Oregon	7
14	Pennsylvania*	7
13	Southern California	7
27	Oregon State*	0
40	St. Mary's*	25
14	Washington	7
35	UCLA*	0
13	San Francisco*	7
7	Stanford*	7
6	Michigan	14
(Rose Bowl)		

1951 (8-2)
Coach: Lynn O. Waldorf
Captains: Les Richter, Charlie Harris

34	Santa Clara*	0
35	Pennsylvania	0
55	Minnesota*	14
42	Washington State	35
14	Southern California*	21
35	Oregon State*	14
7	UCLA	21
37	Washington*	28
28	Oregon*	26
20	Stanford	7

1952 (7-3)
Coach: Lynn O. Waldorf
Captains: John Olszewski, Bill Mais

34	College of the Pacific*	13
28	Missouri*	14
49	Minnesota	13
41	Oregon	7
27	Santa Clara*	7
0	Southern California	10
7	UCLA*	28
7	Washington	22
28	Washington State*	13
26	Stanford*	0

*Cal home game

Dr. Jerry Patmont, team physician, and Bob Orr, head athletic trainer, help Chuck Muncie off the field. Patmont and Orr are recognized leaders in their fields and have served at Cal since 1962 and 1970, respectively.

1953 (4-4-2)
Coach: Lynn O. Waldorf
Captains: Tom Dutton, Lloyd Talley

0	Baylor*	25
26	Oregon State	0
19	Ohio State*	33
40	Pennsylvania	0
34	San Jose State*	14
20	Southern California*	32
7	UCLA	20
52	Washington*	25
0	Oregon*	0
21	Stanford	21

1954 (5-5)
Coach: Lynn O. Waldorf
Captains: Paul Larson, Jim Hanifan,
Matt Hazeltine

13	Oklahoma*	27
45	San Jose State*	0
13	Ohio State	21
27	Oregon*	33
17	Washington State*	7
27	Southern California	29
6	UCLA*	27
27	Washington	6
46	Oregon State*	7
28	Stanford*	20

1955 (2-7-1)
Coach: Lynn O. Waldorf
Captain: Jim Carmichael

7	Pittsburgh	27
13	Illinois*	20
27	Pennsylvania*	7
20	Washington State*	20
0	Oregon	21
6	USC*	33
0	UCLA	47
20	Washington*	6
14	Oregon State*	16
0	Stanford	19

1956 (3-7)
Coach: Lynn O. Waldorf
Captains: Don Gilkey, Herb Jackson

6	Baylor*	7
20	Illinois	32
14	Pittsburgh*	0
13	Oregon State	21
20	UCLA*	34
16	Washington	7
6	Oregon*	28
7	Southern California	20
13	Washington State*	14
20	Stanford*	18

1957 (1-9)
Coach: Pete Elliott
Captains: Mike White, Bob Currie,
Art Forbes

6	Southern Methodist*	13
7	Washington State	13
0	Michigan State*	19
6	Navy*	21
12	Southern California*	0
6	Oregon	24
14	UCLA	16
19	Oregon State*	21
27	Washington*	35
12	Stanford	14

1958 (7-4, PCC Champions)
Coach: Pete Elliott
Captains: Joe Kapp, Jack Hart

20	College of the Pacific*	24
12	Michigan State	32
34	Washington State*	14
36	Utah*	21
14	Southern California	12
23	Oregon*	6
8	Oregon State	14
20	UCLA*	17
12	Washington	7
16	Stanford*	15
12	Iowa	38
	(Rose Bowl)	

1959 (2-8)
Coach: Pete Elliott
Captains: Pat Newell, Pete Domoto

20	Washington State	6
12	Iowa*	42
0	Texas	33
6	Notre Dame*	28
12	UCLA	19
20	Oregon State*	24
7	Southern California*	14
18	Oregon	20
0	Washington*	20
20	Stanford	17

1960 (2-7-1)
Coach: Mark Levy
Captains: Steve Bates, Bill Patton

3	Tulane*	7
7	Notre Dame	21
10	Army*	28
21	Washington State*	21
10	Southern California	27
0	Oregon*	20
14	Oregon State	6
0	UCLA*	28
7	Washington	27
21	Stanford*	10

*Cal home game

*Forfeit

1961 (1-8-1)
Coach: Marv Levy
Captain: Jim Burress

3	Texas*	28
7	Iowa	28
14	Missouri	14
21	Washington*	14
14	Southern California*	28
16	Penn State	33
15	UCLA	35
14	Air Force*	15
7	Kansas*	53
7	Stanford	20

1962 (1-9)
Coach: Marv Levy
Captain: Larry Balliett

10	Missouri*	21
25	San Jose State*	8
24	Pittsburgh*	26
7	Duke	21
6	Southern California	32
21	Penn State*	23
16	UCLA*	26
0	Washington	27
21	Kansas	33
13	Stanford*	30

1963 (4-5-1)
Coach: Marv Levy
Captain: Jim Anderson

15	Iowa State*	8
0	Illinois	10
15	Pittsburgh	35
22	Duke*	22
34	San Jose State*	13
6	Southern California*	36
25	UCLA	0
26	Washington*	39
36	Utah	22
17	Stanford	28

1964 (3-7)
Coach: Ray Willsey
Captains: Craig Morton, Ron Calegari

21	Missouri*	14
14	Illinois*	20
20	Minnesota*	26
9	Miami	7
27	Navy*	13
21	Southern California	26
21	UCLA*	25
16	Washington	21
0	Utah*	14
3	Stanford*	21

1965 (5-5)
Coach: Ray Willsey
Captains: Jim Phillips, San Dzura

6	Notre Dame*	48
7	Michigan*	10
17	Kansas*	0
24	Air Force*	7
16	Washington*	12
3	UCLA	56
21	Penn State*	17
0	Southern California*	35
24	Oregon	0
7	Stanford	9

1966 (3-7)
Coach: Ray Willsey
Captains: John Beasley, Dan Goich

21	Washington State	6
7	Michigan*	17
30	Pittsburgh*	15
0	San Jose State*	24
24	Washington	20
15	UCLA*	28
15	Penn State	33
9	Southern Cal	35
3	Army*	6
7	Stanford*	13

1967 (5-5)
Coach: Ray Willsey
Captains: Bob Crittenden,
George Gearhart

21	Oregon*	13
8	Notre Dame	41
10	Michigan*	9
14	Air Force*	12
14	UCLA	37
14	Syracuse	20
6	Washington*	23
12	Southern Cal*	31
30	San Jose State*	6
26	Stanford	3

1968 (7-3-1)
Coach: Ray Willsey
Captains: John McGaffie,
Mike McCaffrey

21	Michigan*	7
10	Colorado*	0
46	San Jose State*	0
7	Army	10
39	UCLA*	15
43	Syracuse*	0
7	Washington	7
17	Southern Cal.	35
36	Oregon*	8
0	Stanford*	20
17	Hawaii	12

1969 (5-5)
Coach: Ray Willsey
Captains: Irby Augustine, Jim Calkins

0	Texas*	17
17	Indiana	14
31	Rice*	21
44	Washington*	13
0	UCLA	32
17	Washington State	0
9	Southern Cal*	14
3	Oregon State*	35
31	San Jose State*	7
28	Stanford	29

1970 (6-5)
Coach: Ray Willsey
Captains: Bob Richards, Phil Croyle

24	Oregon	31
15	Texas	56
56	Indiana*	14
0	Rice	28
31	Washington	28
21	UCLA*	24
45	Washington State*	0
13	Southern Cal	10
10	Oregon State	16
35	San Jose State*	28
22	Stanford*	14

1971 (6-5)
Coach: Ray Willsey
Captains: Sherman White,
Ray Youngblood

20	Arkansas	51
20	West Virginia*	10
34	San Jose State*	10
3	Ohio State	35
30	Oregon State*	27
24	Washington State	23
31	UCLA	24
0	Southern Cal*	28
7	Washington*	30
17	Oregon	10
0	Stanford	14

1972 (3-8)
Coach: Mike White
Captains: Steve Sweeney,
Bob Kampa

10	Colorado	20
37	Washington State*	23
10	San Jose State*	17
27	Missouri	34
18	Ohio State*	35
14	Southern Cal	42
13	UCLA*	49
21	Washington	35
31	Oregon*	12
23	Oregon State	26
24	Stanford*	21

1973 (4-7)
Coach: Mike White
Captains: Kevin O'Dorisio and
Fred Weber

0	Alabama	66
7	Illinois*	27
51	Army	6
54	Washington*	49
10	Oregon	41
24	Oregon State*	14
21	UCLA	61
14	USC*	50
19	San Jose State*	9
28	Washington State	31
17	Stanford	26

1974 (7-3-1)
Coach: Mike White
Captains: Steve Bartkowski and
Rob Swenson

17	Florida	21
17	San Jose State*	16
27	Army*	14
31	Illinois	14
40	Oregon*	10
17	Oregon State	14
3	UCLA*	28
15	USC	15
52	Washington	26
37	Washington State*	33
20	Stanford*	22

1975 (8-3, Pac-8 Co-Champions)
Coach: Mike White
Captains: Chuck Muncie and
Paul Von der Mehden

27	Colorado	34
10	West Virginia*	28
33	Washington State	21
27	San Jose State*	24
34	Oregon	7
51	Oregon State*	24
19	UCLA*	21
17	USC*	14
27	Washington*	24
31	Air Force	14
48	Stanford	15

1976 (5-6)
Coach: Mike White
Captains: Joe Roth and Phil Heck

24	Georgia	36
17	Oklahoma	28
31	Arizona State	22
43	San Jose State*	16
27	Oregon*	10
9	Oregon State	10
19	UCLA*	35
6	USC	20
2	Washington	0
23	Washington State*	22
24	Stanford*	27

1977 (8-3)
Coach: Mike White
Captains: George Freitas and
Burl Toler

27	Tennessee	17
24	Air Force*	14
28	Missouri	21
52	San Jose State*	3
10	Washington State	17
41	Oregon State*	17
19	UCLA*	21
17	USC*	14
31	Washington*	50
48	Oregon	16
3	Stanford	21

1978 (6-5)
Coach: Roger Theder
Captains: Duke Leffler and
Ralph DeLoach

26	Nebraska	36
34	Georgia Tech	22
24	Pacific*	6
28	West Virginia	21
21	Oregon*	18
33	Arizona	20
0	UCLA*	45
17	USC	42
31	Arizona State	35
22	Washington State*	14
10	Stanford*	30

1979 (7-5)
Coach: Roger Theder
Captains: Paul Jones and Ron Hill

17	Arizona State	9
10	Arizona	7
13	San Jose State*	10
10	Michigan*	14
14	Oregon*	19
45	Oregon State*	0
27	UCLA	28
14	Southern Cal*	24
24	Washington*	28
45	Washington State	13
21	Stanford	14
17	Temple	28
	(Garden St. Bowl)	

1980 (3-8)
Coach: Roger Theder
Captains: Rich Campbell,
Ron Coccimiglio and
Kirk Karacozoff

13	Florida	41
19	Army	26
24	Arizona*	31
13	Michigan	38
31	Oregon*	6
27	Oregon State*	6
9	UCLA*	32
7	Southern Cal	60
6	Arizona State	34
17	Washington State*	31
28	Stanford*	23

1981 (2-9)
Coach: Roger Theder
Captains: Harvey Salem
and Ron Rivera

28	Texas A&M*	29
13	Georgia	27
14	Arizona	13
24	San Jose State*	27
26	Washington*	27
17	Arizona State	45
6	UCLA	34
45	Oregon State*	3
3	USC*	21
0	Washington State	19
21	Stanford	42

Outstanding Performers

TOP TEN CAREER SCORERS

	TD	PAT	FG	PTS
Duke Morrison (1920-22)	42	22	1	277
Jim Breech (1974-77)	0	110	50	260
Chuck Muncie (1973-75)	37	1	0	224
Pesky Sprott (1918-20)	28	0	0	168
Vic Bottari (1936-38)	22	13	0	145
Archie Nisbet (1920-22)	20	18	2	144
Paul Jones (1975-79)	24	0	0	144
Wesley Walker (1973-76)	23	0	0	138
Crip Toomey (1920-21)	13	46	4	136
Fred Brooks (1915-16)	21	5	1	134

TOP TEN SINGLE SEASON SCORING PERFORMANCES

	YEAR	TD	PAT	FG	PTS
Duke Morrison	1922	18	20	1	131
Duke Morrison	1920	17	2	0	104
Pesky Sprott	1920	15	0	0	90
Crip Toomey	1920	7	39	3	90
Jim Monachino	1949	15	0	0	90
Chuck Muncie	1975	15	0	0	90
Jim Breech	1977	0	34	16	82
Fred Brooks	1915	12	5	1	80
Pesky Sprott	1918	13	0	0	78
Steve Sweeney	1972	13	0	0	78

TOP TEN SINGLE SEASON TOTAL OFFENSE LEADERS

	YEAR	PLAYS	RUSH	PASS	TOTAL
Rich Campbell	1979	391	-195	2618	2423
Steve Bartkowski	1974	398	-193	2580	2387
Rich Campbell	1978	386	-80	2287	2207
Rich Campbell	1980	308	-80	2026	1946
J. Torchio	1981	435	-176	2112	1936
Craig Morton	1964	354	-238	2121	1883
Charlie Young	1977	297	1	1875	1876
Joe Roth	1975	271	-65	1880	1815
Dave Penhall	1970	310	-57	1785	1728
Joe Roth	1976	331	-157	1789	1632

TOP TEN CAREER TOTAL OFFENSE LEADERS

	PLAYS	RUSH	PASS	TOTAL	TDR
Rich Campbell (1977-80)	1134	-375	7174	6799	43
Craig Morton (1962-64)	797	-371	4501	4130	44
Steve Bartkowski (1972-74)	785	-496	4434	3938	22
Paul Larson (1951-54)	610	551	2968	3519	31
Joe Roth (1975-76)	602	-222	3669	3447	25
Chuck Muncie (1973-75)	555	3052	153	3205	40
Joe Kapp (1956-58)	587	965	2023	2988	16
Dave Penhall (1969-70)	545	-85	2751	2666	22
John Olszewski (1950-52)	418	2504	30	2534	16
J. Torchio (1980-)	537	-230	2756	2526	16

TOP TEN SINGLE GAME TOTAL OFFENSE LEADERS

	YARDS
Charlie Young vs. Oregon State, Oct. 15, 1977	399
Rich Campbell vs. Florida, Sept. 13, 1980	377
Joe Roth vs. Washington, Nov. 8, 1975	375
Joe Roth vs. Georgia, Sept. 11, 1976	372
Rich Campbell vs. Arizona, Sept. 27, 1980	329
Charlie Young vs. UCLA, Oct. 22, 1977	318
Steve Bartkowski vs. Washington, Nov. 9, 1974	309
Rich Campbell vs. Washington, Nov. 3, 1979	309
Rich Campbell vs. Stanford, Nov. 17, 1979	307
J. Torchio vs. Stanford, Nov. 21, 1981	307

TOP SEASON INTERCEPTION PERFORMANCES

	YEAR	NO	YDS	AVE	TD
Jack Jensen	1947	7	114	16.3	0
Ken Wiedemann	1968	7	69	9.9	0
Jim Hunt	1964	7	65	9.3	0
Paul Keckley	1948	7	54	7.7	0
Joe Stuart	1944	7	NA	NA	1
Anthony Washington	1978	6	224	37.3	2

TOP TEN CAREER INTERCEPTORS

	NO	YDS	AVE	TD
Ken Wiedemann (1967-69)	16	184	11.5	2
Paul Larson (1951-54)	12	163	13.6	0
Paul Keckley (1946-48)	12	158	13.2	1
Ray Youngblood (1969-71)	12	84	7.0	0
Ron Coccimiglio (1978-80)	11	227	20.6	0
Anthony Green (1975-77)	10	176	17.6	0
Matt Hazeltine (1951-54)	10	90	9.0	0
Ken Moulton (1963-65)	10	27	2.7	0
Bob Smith (1965-67)	9	232	25.8	0
Darrell Roberts (1956-57)	9	117	13.0	0
Carl Van Heuit (1948-50)	9	107	11.8	0

TOP TEN CAREER RUSHERS

	TCB	YG	YL	NYG	AVE
Chuck Muncie (1973-75)	549	3153	101	3052	5.6
Paul Jones (1975-79)	715	3016	86	2930	4.1
John Olszewski (1950-52)	416	2603	99	2504	6.0
Jack Jensen (1946-48)	285	1906	203	1703	6.0
Gary Fowler (1967-69)	389	1672	87	1585	4.1
Jim Monachino (1948-50)	302	1634	64	1570	5.2
Vic Bottari (1936-38)	388	1689	153	1536	4.0
Arleigh Williams (1932-34)	526	1612	218	1404	2.8
Howard Strickland (1973-74)	262	1468	103	1365	5.2
Jack Swaner (1946-49)	236	1382	47	1335	5.7

TOP TEN SEASON RUSHING PERFORMANCES

	YEAR	TCB	YG	YL	NYG	AVE	TD
Chuck Muncie	1975	228	1477	17	1460	6.4	13
Jack Jensen	1948	148	1183	103	1080	7.3	7
John Olszewski	1950	168	1047	39	1008	6.0	4
Paul Jones	1979	214	913	25	888	4.1	6
John Olszewski	1952	160	883	38	845	5.3	7
Paul Jones	1977	189	824	19	805	4.3	6
Paul Jones	1978	212	831	30	801	3.8	7
Chuck Muncie	1973	157	844	43	801	5.1	11
Chuck Muncie	1974	164	832	41	791	4.8	8
Jack Swaner	1948	137	811	27	784	5.7	12

TOP TEN SINGLE GAME RUSHING PERFORMANCES

	YDS	TCB
Jerry Drew vs. Oregon State, Nov. 15, 1954	283	(11)
John Olszewski vs. Washington St., Oct. 13, 1951	269	(20)
Paul Jones vs. Washington St., Nov. 11, 1978	232	(46)
Chuck Muncie vs. Oregon, Oct. 11, 1975	207	(26)
Gary Fowler vs. Hawaii, Nov. 30, 1968	206	(27)
Paul Jones vs. Missouri, Sept. 24, 1977	200	(35)
Jack Jensen vs. Santa Clara, Sept. 18, 1948	192	(12)
Jim Monachino vs. Stanford, Nov. 19, 1949	189	(20)
John Graves vs. St. Mary's, Oct. 4, 1947	184	(12)
John Olszewski vs. Oregon, Oct. 11, 1952	172	(17)

Steve Rivera cradles a pass against USC. Rivera's 138 career receptions is the Cal record, and his 57 receptions in 1975 and 56 in 1974 rank as the top two single-season performances.

TOP TEN CAREER ALL-PURPOSE RUNNERS

	RUSH	REC	RET	TOTAL
Chuck Muncie (1973-75)	3052	1085	57	4194
Paul Jones (1975-79)	2930	733	63	3726
Wesley Walker (1973-76)	158	2206	721	3085
John Olszewski (1950-52)	2504	207	32	2743
Tom Blanchfield (1962-64)	968	685	1067	2720
Gary Fowler (1967-69)	1585	409	443	2437
Jack Jensen (1946-48)	1703	120	601	2424
Jerry Bradley (1964-66)	3	1139	1249	2391
Jack Hart (1956-58)	1088	751	496	2355
John Tuggle (1979-)	1275	762	124	2161

TOP TEN SINGLE SEASON
ALL-PURPOSE RUNNING PERFORMANCES

	YEAR	RUSH	REC	RET	TOTAL
Chuck Muncie	1975	1460	392	19	1871
Isaac Curtis	1971	475	175	799	1449
Jack Jensen	1948	1080	23	209	1312
Chuck Muncie	1974	791	410	0	1201
Paul Jones	1979	888	300	0	1188
Bob Darby	1969	532	89	556	1177
John Olszewski	1950	1008	109	30	1147
Chuck Muncie	1973	801	283	38	1122
Steve Rivera	1974	0	938	183	1121
Howard Strickland	1974	724	73	318	1115

TOP TEN SEASON PUNTING PERFORMANCES

	YEAR	NO	YDS	AVE
Dan Melville	1977	44	1863	42.3
Bill Armstrong	1972	64	2676	41.8
Dan Melville	1978	57	2370	41.6
Mike Ahr	1981	77	3188	41.4
Dan Berry	1965	43	1771	41.2
Gary Fowler	1969	67	2758	41.2
Joe Hibbs	1953	12	489	40.8
Steve Maehl	1976	69	2702	39.2
Ken Floyd	1965	22	562	39.2
Bob Reinhard	1940	NA	NA	39.1

TOP TEN CAREER PUNT RETURNERS

	NO	YDS	AVE	TD
Paul Keckley (1946-48)	35	453	12.9	0
Jerry Bradley (1964-66)	53	662	12.5	2
Carl Van Heuit (1949-50)	38	422	11.1	0
Bill Main (1946-48)	26	285	11.0	0
Paul Larson (1952-54)	42	450	10.7	1
Joe Stuart (1943-45)	58	594	10.2	0
Scott Stringer (1971-72)	60	545	9.1	0
Ken Wiedemann (1967-69)	41	425	7.9	0
Don Robison (1949-51)	25	188	7.5	0
Stan Murphy (1969-70)	22	164	7.5	0

TOP TEN SEASON PUNT RETURN PERFORMANCES

	YEAR	NO	YDS	AVE	TD
Paul Keckley	1948	16	245	15.3	0
Jerry Bradley	1966	23	296	12.9	2
Carl Van Heuit	1949	18	228	12.7	0
Jerry Bradley	1965	18	220	12.2	0
Jerry Bradley	1964	12	146	12.2	0
Joe Stuart	1945	19	222	11.7	0
Scott Stringer	1972	34	375	11.0	0
Vic Bottari	1938	21	231	11.0	0
Paul Larson	1952	24	261	10.9	0
Vern Smith	1975	14	123	8.8	0

TOP TEN SEASON KICKOFF RETURN PERFORMANCES

	YEAR	NO	YDS	AVE	TD
Frank Brunk	1949	10	295	29.5	1
Tom Blanchfield	1963	16	470	29.4	0
Paul Larson	1954	10	285	28.5	0
Frank Porto	1942	14	398	28.4	0
Jim Blakeney	1963	14	397	28.4	1
Isaac Curtis	1971	30	799	26.6	0
Don Johnson	1952	10	260	26.0	1
Jim Blakeney	1962	18	456	25.3	0
Jerry Bradley	1966	11	275	25.0	0
Bob Darby	1969	23	556	24.2	0

TOP TEN CAREER KICKOFF RETURNERS

	NO	YDS	AVE	TD
Isaac Curtis (1970-71)	41	1036	25.3	0
Jim Blakeney (1962-64)	44	1081	24.2	1
Tom Blanchfield (1962-64)	37	879	23.8	0
Jerry Bradley (1964-66)	25	585	23.4	0
Bob Darby (1968-70)	36	795	22.1	0
Howard Strickland (1974-75)	31	654	21.1	0
Wesley Walker (1973-76)	31	635	20.5	0
Mark Funderburk (1980-)	30	609	20.3	0
Paul Larson (1952-54)	32	645	20.2	0
Floyd Eddings (1977-81)	25	496	19.8	0

TOP TEN SEASON RECEIVING PERFORMANCES

	YEAR	NO	YDS	AVE	TD
Steve Rivera	1975	57	790	13.9	4
Steve Rivera	1974	56	938	16.8	4
Steve Sweeney	1972	52	785	15.1	13
*Matt Bouza	1979	52	717	13.8	4
Jack Schraub	1964	52	633	12.2	2
Jesse Thompson	1977	51	797	15.6	5
Wayne Stewart	1968	50	679	13.6	4
George Freitas	1977	50	673	13.5	4
Geoff DeLapp	1971	48	464	9.7	1
Mariet Ford	1981	45	600	13.3	2

*Bouza's seven catches for 114 yards in the Garden State Bowl are counted for career, but not season totals.

TOP SINGLE GAME RECEIVING PERFORMANCES

	REC	YDS
Jack Schraub vs. Illinois, Sept. 28, 1964	13	132
Wayne Stewart vs. Colorado, Sept, 28, 1968	12	144
Geoff DeLapp vs. Stanford, Nov. 22, 1969	12	115
Dave Palmer vs. Florida, Sept. 13, 1980	12	79
Matt Bouza vs. Washington, Nov. 3, 1979	11	175
Matt Bouza vs. San Jose State, Sept. 22, 1979	11	135
Geoff DeLapp vs. USC, Oct. 30, 1971	11	116
Many players tied with 10 receptions. Last performed by:		
Steve Rivera vs. Washington, Nov. 8, 1975	10	183

TOP TEN CAREER RECEIVERS

	NO	YDS	AVE	TD
Steve Rivera (1973-75)	138	2085	15.1	9
Steve Sweeney (1970-72)	132	2043	15.5	21
Matt Bouza (1978-80)	111	1628	14.7	10
George Freitas (1974-77)	110	1271	11.6	5
Paul Jones (1975-79)	104	970	9.3	2
Geoff DeLapp (1969-71)	100	1176	11.8	5
Chuck Muncie (1973-75)	97	1085	11.2	6
Wayne Stewart (1967-68)	95	1182	12.4	6
Jesse Thompson (1975-77)	93	1276	13.7	7
Wesley Walker (1973-76)	86	2206	25.7	22

TOP TEN CAREER PUNTERS

	NO	YDS	AVE
Dan Melville (1977-78)	101	1863	41.9
Bill Armstrong (1972)	64	2676	41.8
Mike Ahr (1979-)	158	6278	39.7
Dan Berry (1965-66)	103	4075	39.6
Steve Maehl (1976)	69	2702	39.2
Gary Fowler (1967-69)	214	8359	39.1
Steve Curtis (1970)	71	2725	38.4
Tom Keough (1953-54)	59	2174	36.8
Don Gilkey (1955-57)	82	3003	36.6
Jack Jensen (1946-48)	99	3616	36.5

TOP TEN CAREER PASSERS

	PA	PC	PCT	YDS	HI	TD
Rich Campbell (1977-80)	929	599	64.5	7174	42	35
Craig Morton (1962-64)	641	355	55.4	4501	31	36
Steve Bartkowski (1972-74)	619	313	50.6	4434	27	20
Joe Roth (1975-76)	521	280	53.7	3669	25	21
Paul Larson (1951-54)	368	210	57.1	2968	24	16
J. Torchio (1980-)	438	198	45.2	2756	15	11
Dave Penhall (1968-70)	396	203	51.3	2751	23	13
Bob Celeri (1947-49)	289	110	38.1	2186	37	18
Jay Cruze (1971-72)	351	186	53.0	2113	26	14
Joe Kapp (1956-58)	303	154	50.8	2022	29	8

TOP TEN SEASON PASSING PERFORMANCES

	YEAR	PA	PC	PCT	YDS	HI	TD
Rich Campbell	1979	322	216	67.1	2618	12	13
Steve Bartkowski	1974	325	182	57.0	2580	7	12
Rich Campbell	1978	293	164	56.0	2287	19	14
Craig Morton	1964	308	185	60.1	2121	9	13
J. Torchio	1981	363	155	42.7	2112	12	9
Rich Campbell	1980	273	193	70.7	2026	11	6
Joe Roth	1975	226	126	55.8	1880	7	14
Charlie Young	1977	249	135	54.2	1875	13	12
Joe Roth	1976	295	154	52.2	1789	18	7
Dave Penhall	1970	227	118	52.0	1785	13	10

TOP TEN SINGLE GAME PASSING PERFORMANCES

	YARDS
Rich Campbell vs. Florida, Sept. 13, 1980	421
Joe Roth vs. Washington, Nov. 8, 1975	380
Joe Roth vs. Georgia, Sept. 11, 1976	379
Charlie Young vs. Oregon State, Oct. 15, 1977	375
Jay Cruze vs. Missouri, Sept. 30, 1972	354
Rich Campbell vs. Arizona, Sept. 27, 1980	350
Rich Campbell vs. Arizona State, Nov. 4, 1978	347
Rich Campbell vs. Washington, Nov. 3, 1979	322
Dave Penhall vs. Stanford, Nov. 22, 1969	321
J. Torchio vs. Stanford, Nov. 21, 1981	321

All-Time Longest Plays

ALL-TIME LONGEST RUNS FROM SCRIMMAGE

98 Bill Powell vs. Oregon State, Oct. 27, 1951 (td)
96 John Wilson vs. San Jose State, Sept. 25, 1954 (td)
92 Joe Kapp vs. Oregon, Oct. 25, 1958 (td)
91 Jerry Drew vs. Pennsylvania, Oct. 10, 1953 (td)
90 Heine Heitmuller vs. Perris Indians, Nov. 28, 1902 (td)
87 Joe Stuart vs. Coast Guard, Nov. 4, 1944 (td)
85 Benny Lom vs. USC, Nov. 22, 1929 (td)
     Perry Thomas vs. St. Mary's, Sept. 25, 1937 (td)
84 Jim Monachino vs. Stanford, Nov. 19, 1949
     Don Johnson vs. Minnesota, Oct. 4, 1952 (td)

ALL-TIME LONGEST PASS PLAYS

88 Joe Roth to Wesley Walker vs. Georgia, Sept. 11, 1976 (td)
85 Charlie Young to Oliver Hillmon vs. Oregon State, Oct. 15, 1977 (td)
83 Bob Powell to Bob Edmonston vs. St. Mary's, Sept. 22, 1945 (td)
     Charlie Young to Floyd Eddings vs. Oregon State, Oct. 15, 1977 (td)
80 Jack Jensen to Paul Keckley vs. Stanford, Nov. 22, 1947 (td)
     Rich Campbell to Holden Smith vs. Arizona, Oct. 14, 1978 (td)
     Joe Kapp to Hank Olguin vs. Washington, Nov. 16, 1957 (td)
77 Randy Humphries to John McGaffie vs. Michigan, Sept. 30, 1967 (td)
75 Steve Bartkowski to Mike Shaughnessy vs. Washington, Oct. 6, 1973 (td)
     Fred Besana to Wesley Walker vs. San Jose St., Oct. 2, 1976 (td)

ALL-TIME LONGEST PUNTS

84 Dan Melville vs. Nebraska, Sept. 9, 1978
72 Arleigh Williams vs. USC, Oct. 28, 1933
71 Dan Berry vs. Penn State, Oct. 29, 1966
70 Bill Armstrong vs. Washington, Oct. 28, 1972
68 Tom Keough vs. Santa Clara, Oct. 18, 1952
67 Roger Stull vs. UCLA, Nov. 5, 1960
     Jack Jensen vs. Stanford, Nov. 20, 1948
66 Jerry Scattini vs. Washington, Nov. 14, 1959
     Jerry Walter vs. Washington, Nov. 7, 1964
65 Dan Berry vs. Michigan, Sept. 25, 1965

ALL-TIME LONGEST FIELD GOALS

54 Mick Luckhurst vs. Oregon State, Oct. 18, 1980
     Ron Vander Meer vs. Illinois, Oct. 5, 1974
52 Joe Cooper vs. Georgia Tech, Sept. 16, 1978
51 Jim Breech vs. Air Force, Nov. 15, 1975
     Jim Breech vs. Stanford, Nov. 20, 1976
50 Ron Miller vs. Oregon, Nov. 16, 1968
     Ron Miller vs. Syracuse, Oct. 26, 1968
     Jim Breech vs. Washington State, Sept. 27, 1975
49 Ron Miller vs. USC, Nov. 4, 1967
     Jim Breech vs. Oregon State, Oct. 19, 1974
     Jim Breech vs. Missouri, Sept. 24, 1977
     Mick Luckhurst vs. Washington, Nov. 3, 1979
     Joe Cooper vs. Washington, Oct. 10, 1981

ALL-TIME LONGEST KICKOFF RETURNS

102 Ed Solinsky vs. Cal Aggies, Oct. 16, 1937 (td)
      Frank Brunk vs. USC, Oct. 15, 1949 (td)
98   Don Johnson vs. UCLA, Nov. 1, 1952 (td)
92   Tom Blanchfield vs. San Jose State, Oct. 19, 1963
85   Jim Blakeney vs. Pittsburgh, Oct. 5, 1963 (td)
84   Paul Larson vs. USC, Oct. 23, 1954

ALL-TIME LONGEST PUNT RETURNS

108 Don Guest vs. Washington State, Sept. 17, 1966 (td) (Missed FG attempt)
105 Bobby Sherman vs. Stanford, Nov. 8, 1902 (td)
92   Grover Garvin vs. Washington State, Sept. 19, 1959 (td)
76   Jerry Bradley vs. Pittsburgh, Oct. 1, 1966 (td)
73   Jerry Bradley vs. Washington State, Sept. 17, 1966 (td)
69   Tom Blanchfield vs. Stanford, Nov. 23, 1963 (td)

ALL-TIME LONGEST INTERCEPTION RETURNS

100 Jim Jurkovich vs. USC, Nov. 9, 1940 (td)
90   Bobby Smith vs. Oregon, Nov. 13, 1965
85   Perry Thomas vs. St. Mary's, Sept. 25, 1937 (td)
      Will Lotter vs. UCLA, Nov. 6, 1948 (td)
82   John Cunningham vs. Washington State, Oct. 4, 1941
80   Harry West vs. St. Mary's, Oct. 28, 1950
79   Anthony Washington vs. Georgia Tech., Sept. 16, 1978
78   Rich Dixon vs. Washington State, Nov. 10, 1979 (td)
75   Steve Bancroft vs. Stanford, Nov. 24, 1928 (td)
      Bob Norton vs. Santa Clara, Sept. 29, 1928 (td)

California Lettermen 1896-1981

A

Abrams, Charles J., 1911, 13
Abreu, Dennis, 1962, 63, 64
Acker, Joseph, 1969, 70, 71
Acree, Dennis, 1969, 70
Adams, Kenneth, 1969, 70
Agler, Harry, 1942, 47
Agness, Neil, 1970, 71
Agnew, William, 1945
Agorastos, Manny, 1956
Ahr, Mike, 1979, 80, 81
Alaman, Don, 1976, 77
Albertson, William B., 1900, 01, 02
Albrecht, Ted, 1974, 75, 76
Alford, Ray M., 1917
Alexander, Don, 1971
Allen, Chester A., 1909, 10, 11, 12
Amling, Raymond, 1939, 40
Amling, Wallace, 1946
Andersen, Lance, 1972
Anderson, Ahmad, 1979, 80, 81
Anderson, Andy, 1970
Anderson, Arthur, 1940
Anderson, David A., 1934, 35
Anderson, David L., 1936, 37, 38
Anderson, Don, 1964, 65, 66
Anderson, Edwin M., 1944
Anderson, Eric, 1977, 78, 79
Anderson, Frank M., 1896
Anderson, Fred, 1937, 38
Anderson, Jim, 1961, 62, 63
Anderson, Ned, 1967
Anderson, Rick, 1978
Andrew, Paul, 1950, 51, 52
Archer, William 1934, 35, 36
Arkley, William, 1896
Armendariz, Gus, 1946
Armstrong, Bill, 1971, 72
Arner, Brock, 1966
Arnold, Walt, 1958, 59, 60
Arrillaga, Gabe, 1957
Artoe, Lee, 1939
Aschenbrenner, Rick, 1966
Ashley, Harold H., 1909, 10
Athearn, Fred W., 1898, 99
Augustine, Irby, 1967, 68, 69
Avery, H.S., 1896
Avery, Lewis, 1943
Avery, Russell, 1928, 29, 30

B

Bachman, Forrest, 1946
Backstrom, Bill, 1971
Baggett, Matthew A., Jr., 1962
Bagley, Bob, 1950, 51
Baham, Robert L., 1951
Bailey, Brian, 1977, 78, 79, 80
Bailey, Jack, 1945
Bailey, Mark, 1973, 74
Bailey, Rick, 1974
Bailey, Tim, 1979, 80, 81
Baker, Jon, 1944, 46, 47, 48
Baldwin, Maurice, 1931, 32
Baldwin, Paul, 1949
Balliett, Larry, 1960, 61
Bancroft, Steven G., 1926, 27, 28
Barnes, Jeff, 1975, 76
Barnes, John W., 1897
Barnes, Stanley N., 1918, 19, 20, 21
Barnes, Theodore L., 1898
Barnett, Edward, 1943, 44
Barnicott, John W., 1907, 08
Barr, Stanley L., 1927, 28, 29
Barsochini, Robert 1943
Barsotti, Gael, 1959, 60
Bartkowski, Steve, 1972, 73, 74
Bartlett, Ed, 1949, 50, 51
Bartlett, Robert, 1929
Bateman, Dave, 1972, 73, 74
Bates, Henry, 1917
Bates, Steve, 1958, 59, 60
Bates, Tom, 1958, 59, 60
Baxter, Jim, 1953
Baze, Ross B., 1926
Beagle, Gregg, 1979, 80, 81
Beal, Bob, 1950, 51, 52
Beam, Stewart N., 1922, 23
Beard, Wendell, 1945
Beasley, John, 1964, 65, 66
Bebelaar, John, 1960
Becker, Norm, 1955, 56
Beckett, Theodore, 1928, 29, 30
Beedy, J. Crosby, 1934
Begovich, Dan, 1949
Bell, Albert, 1906, 07
Bell, Charles R., 1916

Bell, William M., 1922
Bender, Allan, 1951, 52
Bender, Ralph W., 1899
Bender, William L., 1915
Bennett, Harlo, 1936
Bennett, Rick 1966
Berkey, Robert A., 1920, 21, 22
Berry, Dan, 1965, 66
Bertoli, Charles, 1934
Besana, Fred, 1975, 76
Best, Arthur LeRoy, 1923
Best, Sam, 1975, 76
Bican, Nickolas L., 1930
Biedermann, Leo, 1975, 76, 77
Binggeli, Ernie, 1976, 77
Binkley, Jack, 1953
Bridsall, Ernest S., 1896
Blackmon, Allen, 1977, 78, 79
Blakeney, Jim, 1962, 63, 64
Blanchfield, Tom, 1962, 63, 64
Blewett, Richard E., 1925, 26
Blewett, William F., 1923
Blower, Floyd, 1933, 34, 35, 36
Bock, Lauren, 1960, 61
Boensch, Fred, 1943
Bogardus, Darrell J., 1913, 14
Bohlke, Russ, 1948
Boone, William 1932, 33, 34
Booth, Rick, 1974
Boothe, D. Power, 1904
Bordonaro, Sebastian, 1954
Borghi, Henry, 1944, 46, 47, 48
Borgia, Gerald, 1967, 68, 69
Bornstein, Jeff, 1975
Bottari, Vic, 1936, 37, 38
Boucher, David, 1919
Bouza, Matt, 1978, 79, 80
Boynton, William H., 1904
Bracelin, Greg, 1976, 77, 79
Bradley, Jerry, 1964, 65, 66
Brady, Jim, 1968, 69, 70
Brady, Michael, 1980, 81
Brady, Patrick, 1980, 81
Braley, Harold H., 1900
Brandt, Ed., 1953, 54, 55
Brandt, Fred, 1943
Brant, David O., 1911, 13
Brazil, Jim 1976, 77
Brazill, Nat, 1955, 56
Breakenridge, Harold R., 1926, 28
Breech, Jim, 1974, 75, 76, 77
Breeden, Jack, 1937, 38
Breidenthal, John, 1978, 79, 80
Brittingham, Jack, 1933, 34, 35
Brittingham, Robert, 1933, 34, 35
Bronk, Barry, 1966, 67
Brooks, Bob, 1952
Brooks, Fred T., 1914, 15, 16, 19
Brooks, Gerald I., 1954
Brown, Donald, 1944
Brown, Mike, 1965, 66
Brown, Myron M., 1924, 25
Brown, Robert L., 1917
Brown, Tom, 1962, 63, 65
Brumsey, Larry, 1971
Brunk, Frank, 1947, 48, 49
Buchman, Brad, 1980
Budelman, Herman D., 1906, 07, 08
Buestad, Bud, 1945
Bugbee, Dennis, 1967
Buggs, Michael, 1978, 79, 80
Burke, Tom, 1961
Burns, Samuel, 1972
Burress, Jim, 1959, 60, 61
Burrows, Bruce, 1968
Bush, Franklin W., Jr., 1905
Butler, James B., 1906, 08
Butler, Ralph H., 1909
Byrd, Emerson, 1958
Bystrom, Gary, 1963

C

Cacciari, Steve, 1980, 81
Cadenasso, John, 1951
Cahill, Mark, 1974
Cahn, Albert, 1929, 30
Calender, Clayton, 1943
Calkins, Jim, 1967, 69
Calkins, Russell, 1933, 34
Calegari, Ron, 1962, 64
Callaghan, Judson, 1935, 37
Callan, Howard, 1944
Camp, Reggie, 1979, 80, 81
Campbell, Rich, 1978, 79, 80
Canfield, Clifford G., 1913, 14, 15
Cantlon, John E., 1964, 65

Carabello, Hector, 1945
Carey, H. Dana, 1923, 24, 25
Carlsen, Dick, 1960
Carlson, Arthur, 1931, 32, 33
Carlson, Glenn E., 1924, 25
Carlton, Robert, 1932, 35
Carmichael, Jim, 1953, 54, 55
Carnell, Mike, 1978
Carpenter, Kenneth L., 1909
Carr, S.D., 1896
Carter, David, 1981
Carter, Jerome, 1970, 71
Carvajal, Rudy, 1961, 62, 63
Casey, Mike, 1953
Cass, Harold P., 1919
Castelhun, Paul, 1900
Castle, James S., 1935
Castro, Augustus, 1930, 31
Celeri, Robert, 1944, 47, 48, 49
Cerf, Cedric S., 1906, 07, 08
Cezario, Michael A., 1962
Chambers, Roland, 1945, 46
Champion, Jerome, 1967, 68, 69
Chapman, Darnell, 1977, 78, 79
Chapman, Samuel, 1935, 36, 37
Cherry, Jim, 1955, 56
Chiappone, Bob, 1957
Christensen, Brunel, 1941, 42
Christie, Howard, 1932, 33
Clark, Jack, 1976, 77
Clark, Webster V., 1920, 21, 22
Clay, John A., 1900
Cline, James J., 1918, 19
Clymer, John F., 1924
Clymer, Paul S., 1926
Coccimiglio, Ron, 1978, 79, 80
Cock, Howard B., 1926
Cockburn, James D., 1927, 28
Coffeen, J.M., 1917
Cohen, Douglas B., 1914
Coleman, Jim, 1967
Collier, John H., 1899
Collier, Leonard, 1936
Collins, Greg, 1974, 75
Collins, Robert H., 1900
Coltrin, Frederic C., 1925, 26, 27
Conley, John, 1970
Contestabile, Joe, 1956
Coombs, Malcolm, 1931
Cooper, Bill, 1958
Cooper, Joe, 1978, 81
Cornell, George, 1936, 38
Cornish, Henry L., 1898, 99
Cotton, Charles, 1933, 34, 35
Cotton, Kenneth, 1935, 36, 37
Couper, Frank C., 1925
Covarrubias, Jesse, 1979, 80
Cox, Donald, 1948
Cox, Howard V., 1926
Cox, James, 1943
Cox, Stanley, 1940, 41
Cox, Stewart, 1941
Craig, John W., 1896, 98
Craig, V.H., 1897
Crane, Markey, 1976, 77
Crane, Percy L., 1913
Cranmer, Lee D., 1919, 20, 21
Crittenden, Bob, 1965, 66, 67
Crosby, Vern, 1943
Crow, Wayne, 1958, 59
Croyle, Phil, 1968, 69, 70
Crumpacker, Karl, 1973, 74
Cruze, Jay, 1971, 72
Cullom, Jim, 1947, 48, 49
Culpepper, John, 1972, 73, 74
Cummings, Bob, 1949, 50
Cummins, Greg, 1974, 75
Cunningham, Bill, 1950
Cunningham, John, 1946, 47, 48
Curran, Don, 1950, 51, 52
Currie, Bob, 1955, 56, 57
Currie, Ron, 1959
Curry, Robert, 1972
Curtis, Dick, 1961
Curtis, Isaac, 1970, 71
Curtis, Steve, 1969, 70

Dal Porto, Robert, 1946, 47, 48
Daniels, Victor, 1933
Dantzler, Alex, 1970
Darby, Robert, 1968, 69, 70
Day, Dick, 1951, 53
Dean, Calvin, J., 1920, 21, 22
DeCoudres, Charles, 1942
Deeds, Karl S., 1918, 19, 20

Degnan, George, 1931
DeJong, Raymond, 1947, 48, 49
De La Cruz, Tino, 1981
DeLapp, Geoff, 1969, 70, 71
DeLoach, Ralph, 1976, 77, 78
De Rosa, Joe, 1974, 75
Del Giorgio, Seldon, 1930
Demeritt, Reno E., 1901, 02, 03
Derian, Alvin, 1940, 41
Derian, Steve, 1973, 74
Desmond, James, 1945
De Varona, David, 1936, 37, 38
Diffenbang, William, 1945, 46
Dill, Forrest, 1972
Dillon, Jim, 1952, 53
Dills, Thomas H., 1910, 12
Dimeff, Steve, 1953, 54, 55
Dinkler, Ted, 1959, 60
DiResta, Louis, 1930, 31
Dixon, James A., 1923, 24
Dixon, John, 1975, 76
Dixon, Rich, 1978, 79, 80
Dodds, John, 1942
Dodds, Robert, 1946, 47, 49
Doerr, Donald, 1942, 43, 46
Dolan, Lawrence J., 1911
Dolman, Sam, 1962
Dolman, Willard, 1936, 37, 38
Domoto, Pete, 1957, 58, 59
Donnelly, Ray, 1954
Donohoe, Charles A., 1939
Doretti, Frank, 1957, 58, 59
Dotur, Steve, 1945
Dougery, James C., 1926, 27
Dougery, Ralph H., 1927
Douglas, James M., 1912, 13, 14
Dozier, Melville, Jr., 1899
Drew, Jerry, 1953, 54, 56
Drnovich, Louis, 1934
Duddleson, William J., 1915
Duden, Ernest, 1900, 01
Dunbar, Palmer H., 1899
Duncan, Douglas, 1946, 47, 48
Duncan, Scott, 1973
Dunn, Raymond, 1939, 40, 41
Dunn, Richard M., 1921, 22, 23
Dunn, Steve, 1981
Duren, Clarence, 1971, 72
Dutriz, Antonio, 1934
Dutton, Bill, 1953
Dutton, Tom, 1951, 52, 53
Dwiggins, Jay, Jr., 1908, 09, 10
Dyer, Ephraim, 1906, 07
Dzura, Stan, 1963, 64

E

East, Raymond, 1930
Easterbrooks, Gerald, 1930, 31
Eaton, Lou, 1934
Eddings, Floyd, 1977, 78, 80, 81
Edmonston, Don, 1950
Edmonston, Robert, 1944, 45
Edwards, Herman, 1972, 74
Eells, Walter H., 1918, 19, 20
Eickmeyer, Herman, 1929, 30
Eisan, Dan, 1976
Eisan, Lee G., 1927, 28, 29
Eisenbrand, Clay, 1981
Elerding, Eugene, 1930
Elliott, Amos W., 1908, 09, 10, 11
Elliott, John, 1944, 46
Elliott, Roy H., 1905
Ellis, Frank F., 1896
Ellis, Hal, 1951, 52
Elmore, William, 1938, 39, 40
Ely, Dwight, 1951
Engerbretson, Karl L., 1918, 19
Epstein, Michael P., 1962
Erb, Charles F., Jr., 1920, 21, 22
Erb, Charles F., III, 1946, 49
Erby, John, 1960, 61
Erickson, Richard, 1946, 47, 48
Evans, Claude, 1936, 37
Evans, Clinton W., 1910, 12
Evans, F. Howard, 1923
Evans, Jack V., 1926, 27
Everett, Whit, 1974, 75

F

Fackrell, Carlos, 1955, 59
Fairbanks, John R., 1907
Farmer, Clarence W., 1917
Farmer, Milton T., 1906
Favro, Dave, 1961
Fay, John, 1967, 68
Fenston, Earl J., 1915

Ken Wiedemann, Cal's career interception leader with 16 in 1967-69, makes a spectacular theft against San Jose State in 1967. Jim Coleman helps out for the Bears against the Spartans Dwight Tucker.

Ferguson, Jim, 1960, 61
Ferguson, John, 1941, 42
Ferragamo, Vince, 1972, 73
Fetherston, Jim, 1965, 66, 67
Fiebiger, Roy, 1974, 75
Field, Drew, 1979
Fike, Harold, 1973, 74, 75
Firpo, Anthony, 1938, 39
Fish, George W., 1912, 13
Fisher, Emerson W., 1919
Fitz, Frank M., 1927
Fitzgerald, Chuck, 1950
Fleming, Howard W., 1911, 12, 13
Fletcher, Harold A., 1912
Fodor, Bob, 1979, 81
Folmer, Richard, 1939, 40
Fong, George, 1946, 47
Forbes, Art, 1955, 56, 57
Force, James A., 1903, 04, 05
Ford, Mariet, 1981
Ford, Orrin, 1981
Foster, Daniel P., 1914, 15, 17
Foster, Robert N., 1904
Foster, Roger, 1963, 64, 65
Fowler, Donald, 1935
Fowler, Gary, 1967, 68, 69
Fox, Charley, 1949
Francis, Robert C., 1926
Franklin, Oran, 1957
Frantz, John, 1965, 66, 67

Franz, Rod, 1946, 47, 48, 49
Fraser, Jim, 1969, 70
Frassetto, Gene, 1942, 47, 48
Freedman, Tony, 1942, 43
Freeman, Edgar A., 1906, 07, 08
Freitas, George, 1974, 75, 76, 77
Frey, Dave, 1972, 73, 74
Frisbee, Bob, 1943
Frisch, John, 1972, 73
Funderburk, Mark, 1980, 81
Furuta, Doug, 1959

G
Galas, Tim, 1979, 80
Galbraith, Huxley, 1945
Gallagher, William G., Jr., 1922
Gammon, Walter, 1900
Garamendi, John, 1963, 64, 65
Garamendi, Sam, 1969, 70, 71
Garlinger, Howard, 1955
Garrity, Clarence, 1928, 29, 30, 31
Garthwaite, Edwin, 1943, 44
Garvin, Grover, 1958, 59
Garzoli, John, 1954
Gay, Thomas E., 1916
Gearhart, George, 1966, 67
Gendotti, Joseph, 1901
Gentner, Ernie, 1942
George, Dave, 1959, 60
Gerner, Kenneth, 1945

Ghilarducci, Harry, 1954
Gianelli, Rudolph L., 1913, 14, 15
Gianulias, Gus, 1955, 56, 58
Gibbert, Vince, 1967
Gibbs, Ronald D., 1915
Giddings, Mike, 1953, 54
Gierlich, James, 1944, 45
Gifford, John V., 1917
Gilbert, Gale, 1980
Gilbert, Robert, 1935, 36
Gilkey, Charles, 1945
Gilkey, Don, 1954, 55, 56
Gill, Carol, 1932, 33, 34
Gill, Frank, 1928
Gill, Harry W., 1927, 28, 29
Gill, Ralston, 1929, 30, 31
Gill, Sam, 1931, 32
Gillespie, George, 1956
Gillies, Ed, 1976
Gillis, Kenneth C., 1907
Gimbal, LeRoy M., 1919
Giroday, Paul, 1971, 72, 73
Glagola, Steve, 1957
Glascock, John R., 1907
Glass, Charles, 1978
Gleason, Dave, 1971, 72
Glenn, Stan, 1976, 77
Glick, Steve, 1951, 52
Godde, Harry A., 1918
Goich, Dan, 1965, 66
Gold, Randy, 1960, 61
Gonzales, Bob, 1958
Gordon, Walter A., 1916, 17, 18
Gordon, Walter A., Jr., 1941, 42
Gosbey, J.S., 1896
Gosling, George, 1953
Gough, Harlan, 1939, 40
Grady, Larry, 1975, 76
Graf, Robert E., 1915
Graff, Edwin C., 1909
Graham, Doug, 1959, 60, 61
Graham, Pat, 1977, 78, 79, 80
Granger, Ted, 1954, 55
Graumann, Gary, 1977, 78
Graves, John, 1941, 42, 47
Gray, Dan, 1974, 75
Gray, David, 1980, 81
Gray, Prentiss N., 1904, 05
Gray, Robert, 1945
Gray, Robert F., 1915
Grealish, Steve, 1973
Green, Anthony, 1975, 76, 77
Green, Edward P., 1927
Green, Jim, 1957, 58, 59
Green, Robert C., 1927
Greisberg, Frederick J., 1896, 97, 98, 99
Gridley, Mike, 1962, 64, 65
Grieb, Tom, 1970
Griffin, Bert F., 1924, 25, 26
Griffiths, Edwin, 1929, 30, 31
Gritsch, Steve, 1973, 74, 75
Groefsema, Kenneth, 1943, 46, 47
Groger, Dick, 1949, 50
Grothus, Joe, 1944
Guest, Don, 1965, 66
Guiberson, Nathaniel G., 1901
Gulvin, Glen, 1950, 51, 52

H
Hachten, Bill, 1943
Haffey, Calvin W., 1904, 05, 06, 09
Hahn, Leighton, 1951, 52
Hailey, Mike, 1972
Hale, Max, 1956, 57
Hale, William M., 1919
Hall, Lowell C., 1920
Hall, Percy W., 1896, 97, 98, 99
Hammes, Bob, 1964
Hampton, Chris, 1980, 81
Handy, Carl, 1929, 30
Hanford, Ray, 1936, 38
Hanford, William, 1936
Hanifan, Jim, 1952, 53, 54
Hansen, George D., 1911
Hansen, J. Owen, 1901
Hansen, Thorvald, 1930
Hanson, Kenneth I., 1917
Hard, Sam, 1964, 65, 66
Harding, Roger, 1943, 44
Hardy, David P., 1909, 10, 11
Harmon, Mike, 1978, 79
Harrell, Tubby, 1975
Harris, Al, 1943
Harris, Charles, 1950, 51
Harris, Don, 1951, 52
Harris, George, 1968
Harris, John, 1977, 78
Harris, Myron W., 1908, 09, 10
Harris, Neal, 1908
Harrison, Jack, 1973, 74, 75
Hart, Jack, 1956, 57, 58
Hartman, Dick, 1955

Haskell, Robert K., 1896, 97
Haskins, William H., 1912
Hatcher, Orville, 1939, 40
Hatfield, Greg, 1966
Hawkins, Tom, 1970, 71
Hawley, Loren, 1961, 63, 64
Hay, Jack, 1935
Hay, Richard, 1935
Hayes, Horace H., 1917
Hayes, Kenneth A., 1914
Hazeltine, Matthew E., 1912, 13, 15
Hazeltine, Matt Jr., 1951, 52, 53, 54
Hazzard, Roy T., 1916
Heck, Dave, 1978, 79
Heck, Phil, 1973, 74, 75, 76
Heitmuller, William F., 1902, 03, 04
Heltne, Bruce, 1951
Henderson, Vic, 1974, 76, 77, 78
Hendren, Greg, 1969, 70
Henry, Leslie A., 1904
Herrero, George, 1940, 41
Herrero, Jack, 1941, 42
Herwig, Robert, 1935, 36, 37
Hewitt, Lloyd E., 1918
Hextrum, Chuck, 1973, 74, 75
Hibbs, Doug, 1956
Hibbs, Joe, 1952, 53
Hickingbotham, Joe, 1929, 30
Hickman, Dallas, 1973, 74
Hicks, George M., 1916
Higgins, John M., 1944
Higson, John W., 1917
Hileman, Robert, 1943, 47, 48
Hill, Harvey C., 1912
Hill, Reuben C., 1899
Hill, Ron, 1977, 78, 79
Hillesland, Brian, 1981
Hillmon, Oliver, 1976, 77
Hischler, David, 1944, 46, 47, 48
Hoberg, Carl, 1939, 40
Hodgins, Mike, 1974
Hoeber, Paul, 1965
Hoenisch, Robert, 1945
Hoffman, Ralph, 1955
Holleman, Jack, 1974, 75
Holloway, Stan, 1978, 79
Holston, Charlie, 1957, 58, 59
Honegger, Arthur, 1942, 43
Hongola, Robert, 1940, 41
Hood, Dave, 1951, 52
Hooper, Burt E., 1897
Hooper, Leon L., 1917, 18
Hopper, James P., 1896, 97, 99
Horrell, Edwin C., 1923, 24
Hoskins, John O., 1912
Houghton, Mark, 1977, 78
Houston, Norman B., 1942
Howard, C. Harry, 1900, 02, 03
Howard, Harry M., 1902, 03, 04
Howard, Jack, 1935, 36
Howard, John C., 1915
Howard, Randolph, 1972
Huber, Gordon, 1924, 25, 26
Huber, Skip, 1958, 59
Hubert, Theodore, 1937, 38, 39
Hudgins, Scott, 1971
Hudson, C. Harry, 1900, 02, 03
Hudson, Don, 1978, 79
Hufford, Guy D., 1924
Hughes, James, 1976, 77
Hulfgren, Mark, 1967, 68, 69
Humpert, Frank, 1949
Humphries, Randy, 1967, 68, 69
Hunt, Archie M., 1913, 14
Hunt, Jim, 1963, 64, 65
Huston, Norman, 1942
Huters, William, 1937, 38, 39, 40

I
Iaukea, Kurt, 1956, 57
Imlay, Talma W., 1924, 25
Ingram, Wilbur, 1937
Ipson, Dan, 1960

J
Jabs, Earl F., 1925, 26
Jack, Raymond, 1934
Jackson, Herb, 1955, 56
Jackson, John, 1973, 74
Jacobs, Proverb, 1957
Jacuzzi, Remo, 1955, 56
James, Don, 1981
James, Paul, 1972, 73, 74
Jamile, Alex, 1959
Jensen, Jack, 1946, 47, 48
Jessen, Jess E., 1933
Johns, Walter R., 1907, 08, 09
Johnson, Charles, 1957, 58
Johnson, Don, 1952
Johnson, Gordon, 1968
Johnson, Raymond, 1943
Johnson, Richard J., 1936

Martin, Tevis, 1952, 53
Martucci, Charles, 1952, 54
Martyr, Paul, 1967, 68, 69
Mason, Jon, 1961
Mason, Tom, 1940, 41, 42
Mathewson, Morley, 1938, 39, 40
Mattarocci, Frank, 1956
Mayer, Mathias, 1897
Mayfield, Duane, 1966, 67
Mazik, Ron, 1962, 63
Mazzucco, Tom, 1981
McArthur, Robert, 1931, 32
McAllister, Ken, 1976, 77
McAteer, Eugene, 1934, 36
McCaffrey, Mike, 1966, 67, 68
McCarthy, Dan, 1942
McCormick, James, 1932, 33
McCoy, Paul J., 1919
McCray, Broderick, 1979
McCulloch, Frank D., 1917
McCutcheon, William, 1930
McDaniels, James, 1937, 38, 39
McDermott, M.C., 1897
McGaffie, John, 1967, 68
McGillis, Mike, 1972
McIntyre, Eric, 1978, 79
McIsaac, Hugh, 1896
McKim, Joseph L., 1912, 13, 14
McLean, Norm, 1959, 60, 61
McLaughlin, Hollis G., Jr., 1944
McMahon, John, 1977
McMahon, Rhett, 1911
McMillan, Dan A., 1920, 21
McNab, John B., 1899
McNutt, William F., Jr., 1896
McQuary, Jack, 1939, 40, 41
Mead, Harry R., 1904, 05
Meade, Ken, 1959
Medanich, Frank, 1929, 30, 31
Medaris, John, 1970
Meek, Dave, 1932, 33, 34
Meek, John, 1935, 36, 37
Meers, Mike, 1967, 68, 69
Mehan, Tim, 1975
Mell, Charles N., 1923, 25
Mell, Lowell W., 1924
Melville, Dan, 1977, 78
Meredith, Bob, 1976, 77
Mering, Pete, 1950, 51
Merlo, Fred, 1971
Merlo, Joe, 1941, 42
Meserve, Keith, 1951, 52, 54
Meshak, Tom, 1961
Messner, Russell, 1941, 42
Meyer, Herb, 1944
Meyers, Walter, 1945
Meyersieck, Jim, 1976, 77
Micco, Pat, 1972, 74, 75
Michael, John, 1956, 57, 58
Michaelsen, Ed, 1952
Miksits, John, 1950, 51
Miller, Don, 1974
Miller, Otis A., 1925, 26
Miller, Rich, 1977, 78
Miller, Robert E., 1912
Miller, Ron, 1966, 67, 68
Miller, Roswell, 1915
Miller, Tim, 1977
Minahen, Bob, 1948, 49, 50
Minahen, Timothy, 1946, 47, 48
Minamide, Ron, 1965
Mini, Elvezio, 1901, 02, 03
Mitchell, Don, 1955
Mixco, Edgardo, 1979, 80
Moeller, Kenneth, 1933, 34
Moen, Kevin, 1979, 80, 81
Moffett, Ron, 1977, 78
Mogni, Dave, 1977, 78
Mohn, Elden, 1945
Momson, Chris M., 1916
Monachino, James, 1948, 49, 50
Monhux, Claude E., 1916
Montague, William, 1947, 48, 49
Montgomery, Carl, 1981
Montgomery, Willis R., 1914, 15, 16
More, John F., 1898, 1901, 02, 03
Morey, Charles, 1934
Morris, Howard, 1932, 33
Morris, Laird M., 1909, 10, 11, 12
Morrison, Jesse B. (Duke), 1920, 21, 22
Morse, Clinton R., 1896
Morton, Craig, 1962, 63, 64
Mosher, Jerry, 1963, 64, 65
Moskowite, George, 1979, 80
Mosley, Dan, 1979, 80
Moye, Jeff, 1975, 76
Moyle, Mike, 1972
Moulton, Ken, 1963, 64, 65
Muehlberger, Roy, 1949
Muga, Dave, 1961
Muir, James, 1944, 46, 47
Muller, Harold P., 1920, 21, 22

Muncie, Chuck, 1973, 74, 75
Munn, Greg, 1973, 74
Munroe, Richard, 1973
Murphy, Stan, 1969, 70

N
Najarian, George, 1952, 53, 54
Najarian, John, 1945, 47, 48
Najarian, Paul, 1979, 80
Nelson, Alan, 1961, 62
Nelson, Gill, 1952
Nelson, Lyle, 1949
Neuhaus, John A., 1915
Neuhaus, Robert, 1930
Newberry, Dave, 1976
Newell, Pat, 1957, 58, 59
Newman, Sterling R., 1927, 28
Newmeyer, Donald, 1923
Newton, Tom 1975, 76
Nichelmann, Will O., 1925
Nicholau, George E., 1942
Nichols, Donald P., 1921, 22, 23
Nicolson, Murdo, 1955
Nisbet, Archie, 1920, 21, 22
Niswander, Roy F., 1926
Niualiku, George, 1981
Nordstrom, Raymond, 1934, 35, 36
Northcraft, James F., 1909
Norris, Hal, 1951, 52, 53, 54
Norton, Robert B., 1927, 28, 29
Norwood, Jim, 1963
Nourse, William, 1943

O
O'Brien, Mike, 1976, 77
O'Brien, Walter M., 1922
O'Dorisio, Kevin, 1972, 73
Ogden, Brenton R., 1951
O'Hare, Dean, 1951
Olguin, Hank, 1958
Oliver, Bob, 1953, 54, 55
Oliver, Steve, 1972, 73, 74
Olivia, Joe, 1954, 56
Olson, Pete, 1961
Olszewski, John, 1950, 51, 52
Orlich, Jeff, 1973, 74
Ortlieb, Craig, 1943
O'Steen, Dwayne, 1973, 74
O'Toole, Lawrence S., 1905
Overall, Orval F., 1900, 01, 02, 03
Overton, Scott, 1973

P
Palamountain, Greg, 1963, 65
Palmer, David, 1978, 79, 80, 81
Palmer, Jeff, 1963, 64, 65
Papais, Louis, 1947, 48
Papini, John, 1960
Pappa, John, 1949, 50, 51
Parkinson, Stan, 1960, 61
Parks, Ted, 1965
Parque, Larry, 1958, 59
Partee, Ben, 1974
Pascoe, Robert, 1930, 31, 32
Patterson, Craig, 1981
Patton, Billy, 1958, 59, 60
Pauley, Charles W., 1908, 10, 11
Pavlow, Fred, 1944
Paxton, Marshall W., 1917
Pearce, Gerald G., 1924
Peart, Stirling B., 1909, 10, 11, 12, 13
Pelonis, George, 1951
Penaflor, Manuel, 1960, 61
Penhall, Dave, 1969, 70
Perrin, Paul V., 1925
Perrin, Toni, 1958
Perry, Cliff, 1939
Perry, Donald C., 1923
Perry, Gerald, 1952
Peters, Greg, 1974, 75, 76
Peterson, Howard, 1944, 45
Peterson, John, 1951
Phillips, Don, 1953
Phillips, Irvine L., 1926, 27, 28
Phillips, Jim, 1962, 63, 65
Phillips, John, 1968, 69
Phleger, Carl A., 1908, 10, 11
Phleger, Herman H., 1910, 11
Pickett, Gene, 1940, 41, 42
Pieper, Harry, 1942, 46, 47
Pierovich, George, 1959, 60, 61
Piestrup, Don, 1956, 58, 59
Piestrup, Mel, 1961
Piller, Lloyd, 1932
Pinson, Jim, 1962, 63, 64
Pitta, Dennis, 1967, 68
Pitto, Louis, 1928, 29
Pittore, Jess, 1961
Plasch, William, 1937, 38, 39
Pleis, Matt, 1977
Plummer, Gary, 1981
Plunkett, W.T., 1896
Poddig, Herbert, 1946, 47, 48

Poe, Keith, 1981
Pollack, Milton, 1936, 37
Pollock, Morris, 1936, 37
Poppin, Nick, 1954, 55
Portee, Tyrone, 1979, 80, 81
Porto, Frank, 1942
Potter, Sheldon, 1930
Powell, Robert, 1944, 45
Powell, William, 1951, 52
Premo, George W., 1901
Pressley, Legro, 1918
Pressley, Norman, 1948, 49
Price, Tyrone, 1962
Prindiville, Terry, 1956
Pringle, Charles A., 1897, 98, 99, 1900
Purnell, Rick, 1976, 77
Purnell, Rob, 1970, 71
Pyle, Bob, 1972, 73

Q
Queen, David, 1938, 40
Quisling, Milo, 1932, 33
Quist, George, 1943

R
Radich, Steve, 1963, 64, 65
Ralston, John, 1950
Ramseier, Roger, 1955, 56, 57
Ransome, Arthur W., 1896
Ransome, Clark, 1961
Ransome, John, 1931, 32, 33
Rasmussen, George, 1943
Rau, Walter F., Jr., 1923, 24, 25
Rawn, Walter, 1941
Ray, Thomas, 1938
Reece, Steve, 1969, 70
Reed, C.W., Jr., 1898
Reed, Chuck, 1967
Reed, Delroy, 1979
Reed, James, 1975, 76
Reedy, Mountford, 1933, 34
Reginato, Angelo, 1938
Reinhard, Robert, 1938, 40, 41
Reinhard, William, 1941, 46
Reis, Larry, 1966, 67, 68
Reist, Lloyd, 1965, 66, 67
Relles, George, 1932, 33
Relles, Tom, 1963, 64, 65
Renouf, Clement A., 1907
Rice, Leland, 1928, 29
Richards, Bob, 1968, 69, 70
Richardson, Darrell H., 1917
Richardson, Stanley M., 1905
Richter, Les, 1949, 50, 51
Ricks, Greg, 1975, 76
Riegels, Roy, 1927, 28, 29
Rigisich, Serge, 1977
Risley, Thomas E., 1905
Rivera, Ron, 1980, 81
Rivera, Steve, 1973, 74, 75
Roberts, Darrell, 1956, 57
Roberts, Frank, 1945
Robison, Don, 1949, 50, 51
Rodger, Tom, 1957
Rodgers, Richard, 1980, 81
Rogers, Bob, 1970, 71
Rojeski, Frank, 1944
Rose, Joe, 1977, 78, 79
Rosso, Ray, 1938, 39
Roth, Joe, 1975, 76
Rottke, Curtis, 1944
Rowe, Andrew C., 1917, 19
Roycroft, Glen, 1976
Rozier, Bob, 1977, 78
Rusev, John, 1963, 64
Russell, William A., 1913, 14, 15, 16
Ryan, Dan, 1967, 68

S
Sabichi, George C., 1903
Saffold, Terry, 1977
Salem, Harvey, 1979, 80, 81
Salisbury, John, 1965, 67, 68
Sally, Frank, 1957, 58, 59
Sanquinetti, Don, 1979
Sargent, John E., 1924, 25, 26
Sarver, Charles, 1948, 49
Sasaki, Kenji, 1961
Sauer, Ralph, 1937, 38, 39
Saunders, Ward B., 1913, 14, 15
Sawin, Steve, 1968, 69, 70
Scarlett, Richard, 1929
Scattini, Jerry, 1959, 60, 61
Schabarum, Pete, 1948, 49, 50
Schaeffer, James G., 1906, 07
Schaldach, Henry, 1930, 31, 32
Schell, Mike, 1968
Schlichting, Fred, 1929
Schmalenberger, Herb, 1948, 49
Schmidt, Charles, 1928
Schmidt, John, 1964, 65, 66
Schmidt, Randy, 1972, 73

Schraub, Jack, 1963, 64
Schultz, Eric, 1948, 49
Schultz, Steve, 1967, 68, 69
Schurr, Werner A., 1921
Schwartz, Perry, 1935, 36, 37
Schwarz, Bert F., 1926, 27, 28, 29
Schwocho, Kenneth L., 1953
Scott, Dennis, 1938
Scott, Gerald L., 1949
Seaver, Donald, 1942, 46, 47
Segale, Andy, 1958, 59, 61
Seifert, Ted, 1972, 73
Selfridge, James R., 1897
Semmens, Paul, 1937, 39
Senior, Walt, 1955
Seppi, Dave, 1968, 69, 70
Setoga, Setoga, 1973
Sevy, Jeff, 1972, 73
Sewell, Edward G., 1918
Sharp, Leroy B., 1914, 15, 16
Shaughnessy, Mike, 1972, 73
Shaw, Dave C., 1977, 78
Shaw, David S., 1977, 78
Sheeman, Edward J., 1901, 02
Sheridan, Jim, 1966, 68, 69
Sherman, Marc, 1981
Sherman, Robert P., 1901, 02
Shore, Nathan, 1946, 47
Shotwell, Steve, 1980, 81
Shwayder, David, 1945
Simmons, Cliff, 1966
Simpson, Frank W., 1896, 97
Sinclair, Dan, 1965, 66
Sitta, Pete, 1975, 76
Skaugstad, Daryle, 1975, 78, 79
Skinner, Edward A., 1917
Skinner, Horace R., 1913
Slauson, Sal, 1957
Smidt, Joe, 1956
Smiland, Bob, 1976, 77
Smith, Bobby, 1965, 66, 67
Smith, Byron, 1981
Smith, Donn, 1955
Smith, G.V., 1896
Smith, George, 1934
Smith, Holden, 1976, 78, 80
Smith, Jack, 1937, 38, 39
Smith, Jerry D., 1972
Smith, John H., 1914, 15
Smith, Joseph, 1931
Smith, Louis, 1937, 38, 39
Smith, Mortimer, Jr., 1942
Smith, Robert, 1972, 74, 75
Smith, Tim, 1942
Smith, Tim, 1980, 81
Smith, Vern, 1975, 76
Smith, Warren W., 1900
Snedigar, Olie F., 1901, 02, 03, 04
Snow, Jeff, 1958, 60
Sockolov, Ronald, 1946, 47
Solari, Ray, 1949, 50
Solinsky, Edward, 1937
Solvin, Howard, 1957
Sorenson, Bruce, 1979, 80
Sorenson, Robert S., 1907, 08
Souza, Alfred, 1936
Souza, George, 1948, 49
Souza, George, 1955
Sparks, Henry, 1935, 36, 37
Spalding, James E., 1923
Sperry, Willard E., 1904, 05
Spitz, Jeff, 1976, 77
Sprague, Don, 1979, 80
Sprott, Albert B., 1918, 19, 20
Stachowski, Rich, 1979, 80, 81
Staffler, Theodore, 1938, 39, 40
Stafford, Pete, 1981
Stafford, Roger A., 1946
Stanek, Stan, 1972
Stanton, Forrest Q., 1906
Starr, Claude D., 1901
Staskus, Kim, 1973, 74
Stassi, Sam, 1961
Stathakis, George, 1949
Stephens, Howard W. (Brodie), 1920, 21
Stephens, Paul, 1904
Stern, Lewis E., 1903, 04, 05
Stewart, Charles, 1932, 33
Stewart, Jimmy, 1979, 80, 81
Stewart, John, 1955, 56, 57
Stewart, John A., 1918
Stewart, Wayne, 1966, 67, 68
Stockton, Vard, 1935, 36, 37
Stroll, William, 1936, 37, 38
Stone, Bud, 1946
Stone, James, 1937, 38
Stone, Mike, 1966
Stone, Ralph, 1930, 31
Story, Ron, 1981
Stow, Edgar W., 1905, 06, 07
Stow, S.M., 1900, 01, 02, 03
Stowers, Bill, 1971

California Hall of Famers

National Football Foundation
Stan Barnes, C,G,T, — 1954
Vic Bottari, HB — 1981
Ron Franz, G — 1977
Walter Gordon, T — 1975
Bob Herwig, C — 1964
Babe Horrell, C — 1969
Dan McMillan, T — 1971
Brick Muller, E — 1951
Les Richter, G,C,LB — 1982
Andy Smith, Coach — 1951
Pappy Waldorf, Coach — 1966

(indicates position and year selected)

California football superstars spanning three decades assemble during an Albany Boosters dinner in 1949. The illustrious group of seven All-Americans includes: (left to right) Jackie Jensen, Rod Franz, Sam Chapman, Brick Muller, Ted Beckett, Vic Bottari and Perry Schwartz.

California All-Americans*

1921	Harold P. (Brick) Muller, End (W. C.)
1922	Harold P. (Brick) Muller, End (W. C.)
1924	Edwin C. (Babe) Horrell, Center (W. C.)
1928	Irvine L. Phillips, End (UPI, NSY, NANA, A-A B)
1929	Bert F. Schwarz, Guard (AP, NYS)
	Roy M. Riegels, Center (CP, AP)
1930	Theodore T. (Ted) Beckett, Guard (A-A B, GR, SF Chron)
1931	Ralston W. (Rusty) Gill, Halfback (AFP, NYJ)
1934	Arleigh Williams, Halfback (INS)
1935	Lawrence Lutz, Tackle (AP, A-AB, NANA)
1936	Robert Herwig, Center (UPI, UN, FC)
1937	Samuel Chapman, Halfback (AP, NYS, UPI, INS,A-AB, GR)
	Perry Schwartz, End (A-A B)
	John Meek, Quarterback (Colliers, NYS)
	Vard Stockton, Guard (UPI, INS)
	Bob Herwig, Center (Colliers)
1938	Victor Bottari, Halfback (INS, A-AB, CP, CR, ISWA, NW, HW)
1940	Robert Reinhard, Tackle (GR)
1941	Robert Reinhard, Tackle (GR)
1947	Rod Franz, Guard (A-AB, FC, GR)
1948	Rod Franz, Guard (AP, NYS)
	Jackie Jensen, Fullback (A-AB, INS, GR, NYDN, NEA)
	Jim Turner, Tackle (INS)

1949	Rod Franz, Guard (Look, AP, UPI, INS, NYS)
	Jim Turner, Tackle (INS)
	Forest Klein, Guard (NEA)
	Bob Celeri, Quarterback, (FD)
1950	Les Richter, Guard (AP, UPI, INS, NEA, Look, SN)
	Jim Monachino, Running Back (Look)
	Carl Van Heuit, Defensive Back (Look)
1951	Les Richter, Guard (AP, UPI, INS, SN, Look)
1952	John Olszewski, Halfback (INS, NEA, FC)
1953	Matt Hazeltine, Center (INS, NBC, Look)
1954	Matt Hazeltine, Center (INS)
	Paul Larson, Quarterback (FW, FN)
	Sam Williams, Quarterback (Acad A-A)
1958	Joe Kapp, Quarterback (FW, Time)
1964	Craig Morton, Quarterback (FW, FC, FN, SN, NEA)
1968	Ed White, Nose Guard (AP, FW, Kodak, FC)
1971	Sherman White, Def. Tackle (AP, UPI, SN, NEA, FW)
1974	Steve Bartkowski, Quarterback (Consensus)
	Chris Mackie, Guard (FW)
1975	Chuck Muncie, Halfback (Consensus)
	Steve Rivera, Wide Receiver (Consensus)
1976	Ted Albrecht, Tackle (AP)
	Joe Roth, Quarterback (SN)

LEGEND

A-A B	All-American Board	FN	Football News	Look	Look Magazine	NW	Newsweek Magazine		
AP	Associated Press	FW	Football Writers	NANA	N. Am. Nwspr. Alliance	SN	Sporting News		
AFP	American Football Players	GR	Grantland Rice	NBC	Natl. Brdcst. Co.	T	Time Magazine		
CP	Central Press	HW	Hearst Writers	NEA	Nwspr. Ent. Assoc.	WC	Walter Camp		
FC	Football Coaches (Kodak)	INS	International News Service	NYDN	New York Daily News				
FD	Football Digest	ISWA	Intercollegiate Sports Writers Association	NYS	New York Sun				

*These are first team All-American selections only

California Athletic Personnel

Athletic Director*

1900-01	Reno Hutchinson
1901-06	Ezra Decoto
1906-08	O. F. Snedigar
1910-12	Ralph P. Merritt
1912-14	Milton T. Farmer
1914-17	J. A. Stroud, Jr.
1917-18	F. G. Booth
1918-19	R. B. Watson
1919-26	Luther A. Nichols
1926-35	Bill Monahan
1936-42	Kenneth Priestley
1943-46	Clint Evans
1947-55	Brutus Hamilton
1956-59	Greg Englehard
1960-67	Pete Newell
1968-71	Paul Brechler
1972-	Dave Maggard

* Also known as Graduate Manager prior to 1960

Business Manager

-62	Harry Davis
1963-72	Pat Farran
1973-74	Jane Kirksey
1975-	Lauren Moore

Publicist

	Charles Raymond
	Lewis Reynolds
-35	Kenneth Priestley
1936-41	Walter Frederick
1942-45	Dick Kelly
1946-50	Norrie West
1951-57	Bob Rubin
1958-59	Paul Christopolos
1960-62	Wiles Hallock
1963-73	Bob Steiner
1974	Buck McCleneghan
1975-	John McCasey

Ticket Manager

-46	Harry Davis
1947-49	George Briggs
1950-51	Joan Hauser
1952	George Briggs
1953-59	Harry Davis
1960-81	Joan Hauser
1982-	Melva Wilder

Head Trainer

1898-31	Charlie Volz

1932-41	Bert Jones
1942-69	Jack Williamson
1970-	Bob Orr

Team Physician

-37	William Donald, Sr.
1938-61	James Harkness
1962-	Jerome Patmont

California Assistant Coaches

Allen, Pokey, 1982-
Allison, Stub, 1931-34
Anderson, Dave, 1939
Andrews, Frank, 1930
Andros, Dee, 1957-59

Banascek, Cas, 1979-80
Beckett, Ted, 1931
Boles, Albert, 1925-27
Boles, Alfred, 1928-29
Bottari, Vic, 1939, 46
Breakenridge, H., 1929

Capers, Dom, 1978-79
Carlton, Bob, 1936
Carvajal, Rudy, 1967-71
Carzo, Rocco, 1960-65
Cerf, Cedric, 1910-14
Chaney, Zeb, 1946-55
Church, Mike, 1979-80
Coltrin, Fritz, 1928-29
Cooper, Bill, 1982-
Corrick, Dick, 1966-71
Cotton, Ken, 1938
Criner, Jim, 1970-71
Cullen, Lou, 1960-62
Cullom, Jim, 1964-71
Cunningham, Gunther, 1977-80

Davis, Les, 1972-73
Davis, Mouse, 1981
Dickey, Bill, 1972-73
Dutton, Bill, 1964-71

Elliott, H.R., 1906
Elliott, Pat, 1916
Erber, Lew, 1974
Erby, John, 1968-71
Erkenbeck, Jim, 1972-76
Evans, Claude, 1938
Evans, Clint, 1925-42
Evans, John, 1928

Ferrigno, Dan, 1981
Franz, Rod, 1956-57
Frease, Don, 1979-81
Fry, Wes, 1947-56

Ghilotti, Bob, 1964-69
Gigantino, Artie, 1975-78
Gill, Sam, 1933
Gordon, Walter, 1919, 21-24, 37-39, 41-43
Grant, Harold, 1948-55
Griffin, Dr., 1905
Gruneisen, Sam, 1982-

Hackett, Paul, 1974-75
Hall, Percy, 1903
Haluchak, Mike, 1981
Hanifan, Jim, 1970-71
Harris, Walt, 1974-77
Hart, Jack, 1960-63
Herndon, Bobby, 1958-59
Herwig, Bob, 1938-39, 41-42
Hole, James, 1931-35
Howe, William, 1909
Hudson, Ron, 1972-76

Jackson, Milt, 1975-76
Johnson, Corey, 1979-81
Johnson, Johnny, 1972-74
Johnson, Walter, 1917

Kelly, Addison (King), 1899
Kuharich, Lary, 1982-

Lambert, Ed, 1982-
Laprotti, Stan, 1947
Latham, George, 1929-30
Laveroni, Bill, 1978
Lawson, Jim, 1956
Leahy, Bob, 1978
Lutz, Larry, 1936-37, 39, 46
Lynn, Ron, 1980-

Mahan, Eddie, 1916
Malone, Fred, 1977
Manske, Edgar, 1947-52
Marvin, Joe, 1966-69
McCartney, Max, 1972-76
McMillan, Dan, 1925, 27-30
McPhail, Buck, 1957-59
Medanich, Frank, 1932, 37
Meek, Dave, 1935
Meister, Herm, 1951-56
Meyers, Bill, 1977-78
Mitchell, Brick, 1927, 29-30
Moore, Myrel, 1964-71

Mudd, Howard, 1972-73
Muller, Brick, 1923-25, 27-29

Neumann, John, 1960-62
Nikcevich, John, 1963
Nott, Charles, 1896

Peay, Francis, 1978-80
Phillips, Irvine, 1932-37
Phillips, Wayne, 1963
Price, Nibs, 1918-25, 40-53

Ralston, John, 1956-58
Reidy, Monte, 1935
ReRosa, Don, 1945
Riegels, Roy, 1930
Rosenthal, Boles, 1920-24, 26
Ruffo, Al, 1945

Saunders, Al, 1976-81
Schaeffer, James, 1908
Sherman, Ray, 1981
Smith, Andrew W., 1915
Smith, Carnie, 1947
Smith, Doug, 1977-80
Smith, Joe, 1932-33
Sprott, Pesky, 1923
Stanfel, Dick, 1963
Stauber, Gene, 1957-59
Stockton, Vard, 1938
Stone, Perke, 1939
Stress, Skip, 1978-81
Stroud, John, 1917-19
Sutherland, Jim, 1953-54

Taylor, Bill, 1957-59
Tessier, Bob, 1947-50
Theder, Roger, 1972-77
Thomas, Perry, 1938
Thorell, Al, 1936

Uteritz, Irwin, 1935-46

Van Deren, Bud, 1964-65
Van Heuit, Carl, 1955-56

Walsh, Bill, 1960-62
Wells, Dummy, 1920
West, Charlie, 1982-
White, Howard, 1964-66
White, Mike, 1959-63
Wickhorst, Frank, 1931-42
Wright, Nate, 1979
Womble, Lloyd (Wrec), 1902

Ziegler, Gus, 1916

ACKNOWLEDGEMENTS

John McCasey, Cal's sports information director, and Nick Peters first discussed the idea of a book on the history of football at Cal more than five years ago. John believed that Cal fans would want, and should have, a lasting commemorative of Cal football's 100th anniversary. He brought publisher and author together, and his intense enthusiasm for the project has made *100 Years of Blue & Gold* a reality. The book, of course, would not have been possible without the support of athletic director Dave Maggard nor the tireless efforts of public relations assistants Mike Matthews and Kevin Reneau and centennial coordinator Laura Elliott.

This is a pictorial history, so it could not have been done without the cooperation of many people. In addition to the photo credits, we especially want to thank Louise Waldorf, widow of the legendary Pappy Waldorf, for opening her personal collection to us; Jim Kantor and his staff at the University Archives; the *Oakland Tribune*; the San Francisco *Examiner*; the San Francisco *Chronicle*; and Mrs. Charles Bradfield, who provided several photos from the collection of her uncle, the late Elbert Willard Davies, of action from before the turn of the century. Perhaps most importantly, the University as well as the publishers owe a debt of gratitude to Ed Kirwan, who through his company, Kirwan Graphics, has maintained and preserved thousands of photos of Cal football, dating back to the Wonder Team of 1920.

Finally, the author acknowledges his own debt to two previous chroniclers of Cal football, Clinton "Brick" Morse and S. Dan Brodie. Morse's *California Football History*, written in 1923 and updated in 1937, and Brodie's *Sixty-Six Years on the California Gridiron* (1882-1948), proved invaluable as reference sources.

Photography Credits

Photos courtesy of University of California Sports Information
Pages 2-3, 6-7, 8-9, 12-13, 14-15, 29, 32, 33 top, 38 bottom, 42 top, 51, 52, 53 top, 54, 55, 57, 58 bottom, 60, 61 bottom, 84-85, 88, 97, 110, 113 top, 119 top, 120 top, 125, 126, 127, 129, 139, 142 top, 155 bottom, 159, 160, 161, 162, 163, 165, 168, 174, 175, 177, 178, 180, 182 left, 186, 190-191, 193, 195, 197, 198, 202.

Photo donated by Kirby P. West to California Sports Information
Pages 107-110.

Photo by Ellen Fitzgerald courtesy of University of California Sports Information
Page 59.

Photos by David K. Madison Photography courtesy of University of California Sports Information
Pages 53 bottom, 128, 179, 180-181, 194.

Photo by George Olson courtesy of University of California Sports Information
Page 182 right.

Photo by John Reed courtesy of University of California Sports Information
Page 183.

Photo by Andy Whipple courtesy of University of California Sports Information
Pages 10-11.

Photo by Bill Young courtesy of University of California Sports Information
Page 164.

Reproduced by permission University Archivist, The Bancroft Library, University of California
Pages 4-5, 23, 24-25 top, 27, 28, 64, 66, 67, 81, 104 bottom, 105,114 top, 118 top, 136 right, 138 left.

Photos from Ed Kirwan, Kirwan Graphics
Pages 16, 20, 26, 46, 47 top, 76, 93 top, 94, 95, 96, 104 top, 119 bottom, 121, 122, 123, 134, 135, 136 left, 137, 138 right, 140 top right, 143, 153 bottom, 170, 176.

Photos courtesy of the *Oakland Tribune*
Pages 22, 24-25 bottom, 30 top, 30-31 bottom, 33 bottom, 34, 35, 36, 37, 38 top, 39, 40 bottom, 41, 42 bottom, 44, 45, 58 top, 69, 70, 71, 72-73, 74-75, 80, 86-87, 87 right, 89, 90, 91, 92-93, 103 bottom, 111, 112-113, 114-115, 116, 117, 120 bottom, 130, 131, 140 bottom, 142 bottom, 144, 145, 146, 146-47, 148, 149, 150, 151, 152, 153 left and top, 154, 155 top, 156, 200.

Photos courtesy of the San Francisco *Chronicle*
Pages 49, 50 bottom, 173.

From the collection of Nick Peters
47 bottom, 48, 50 top, 61 top, 77, 106, 124, 140 top left, 141, 157, 158, 172, 189.

From the collection of Elbert Willard Davies courtesy of Mrs. Charles Bradfield
Pages 21, 101, 103 top.

From the collection of Mrs. Lynn O. Waldorf
Pages 43, 118.

From the collection of Vic Bottari
Page 73 top.